Theory of Mind and the Triad of Perspectives on Autism and Asperger Syndrome

also by Olga Bogdashina

Communication Issues in Autism and Asperger Syndrome
Do we speak the same language?
ISBN 1 84310 267 6

Sensory Perceptual Issues in Autism and Asperger Syndrome
Different Sensory Experiences – Different Perceptual Worlds
ISBN 1 84310 166 1

of related interest

Asperger's Syndrome
A Guide for Parents and Professionals
Tony Attwood
ISBN 1 85302 577 1

Mental Health Aspects of Autism and Asperger Syndrome
Mohammad Ghaziuddin
ISBN 1 84310 727 9 paperback
ISBN 1 84310 733 3 hardback

Enabling Communication in Children with Autism
Carol Potter and Chris Whittaker
ISBN 1 85302 956 4

The Development of Autism
A Self-Regulatory Perspective
Thomas L. Whitman
ISBN 1 84310 735 X

Understanding and Working with the Spectrum of Autism
An Insider's View
Wendy Lawson
ISBN 1 85302 971 8

Theory of Mind and the Triad of Perspectives on Autism and Asperger Syndrome

A View from the Bridge

Olga Bogdashina

Jessica Kingsley Publishers
London and Philadelphia

Quotation on p.254 from Stanton 2001 is reproduced with permission of the author. Copyright ©
Mike Stanton 2001, all rights reserved. www.mike.stanton.dsl.pipex.com/speech1.html.

First published in 2006
by Jessica Kingsley Publishers
116 Pentonville Road
London N1 9JB, UK
and
400 Market Street, Suite 400
Philadelphia, PA 19106, USA

www.jkp.com

Library of Congress Cataloging in Publication Data
Bogdashina, Olga.
Theory of mind and the triad of perspectives on autism and Asperger
syndrome : a view from the bridge / Olga Bogdashina. -- 1st American
pbk. ed.
    p. cm.
Includes bibliographical references and index.
ISBN-13: 978-1-84310-361-5 (pbk. : alk. paper)
ISBN-10: 1-84310-361-3 (pbk. : alk. paper)
  1. Autism. 2. Autism--Miscellanea. 3. Asperger's syndrome.
4. Mind and body--Health aspects. I. Title.
RC553.A88B64 2005
616.85'882--dc22

                                                              2005020604

British Library Cataloguing in Publication Data
A CIP catalogue record for this book is available from the British Library

ISBN-13: 978 1 84310 361 5
ISBN-10: 1 84310 361 3

Printed and Bound in Great Britain by
Athenaeum Press, Gateshead, Tyne and Wear

To my children, Alyosha and Olesya

Acknowledgements

My special thanks go to Ian Wilson who kindly drew the pictures to illustrate some of my ideas. My warmest thanks to:

- all the autistic individuals who are willing to share their insights in order to help us understand the Theory of Autistic Mind

- the parents who do their best to help their autistic children achieve their potential and live happy lives

- the professionals 'bitten by the bug of autism' who do their best to improve the quality of life of autistic individuals and their families

- my children, Alyosha and Olesya, for their unconditional love, support and understanding

- Jacqui Amber, a senior lecturer in SEN at Bradford College, who (unintentionally) gave me the idea for this book when she invited me to be a speaker at a conference and suggested the topic 'A View from the Bridge' ('Could you talk about autism from two different perspectives – as a professional and as a mother of an autistic boy, please?').

And finally, I would like to acknowledge certain people, whose lack of understanding of autistic children's differences and needs (leading to their mistreatment) motivated me to write this book.

Contents

Prologue

The Triad of Perspectives, Theory of Mind and the Autism Jigsaw

Whenever we talk about autism, the attribute 'mysterious' comes to mind. We may describe autism as a devastating condition or a gift, but it is still mysterious, as we do not understand it. After several decades of intensive research in the field of autism, and dozens of theories attempting to explain the enigma of autism, we are not very much wiser. This book is an attempt to remove a few (out of many) obstacles on the way to understanding autism.

One of the main obstacles is 'one-sidedness'. For example, a very interesting and influential theory attempting to account for autism is weak central coherence theory (Frith 1989) which focuses on an inability of autistic people to integrate pieces of information into coherent wholes. This fragmentation is illustrated in many logos of autistic societies around the world. We are accustomed to the pictures of jigsaws as emblems of autism. However, if we remove 'one-sidedness' from this explanation, the question arises – 'Do we look at autism as a whole or just juggle bits and pieces of this condition?' We often focus on certain pieces of the 'autism jigsaw' and miss an opportunity to see the whole picture. How can we put these pieces together to reveal the meaning of autism? At present, the situation in the field of autism (research, theorizing, treatments) resembles the situation described in the fable 'The Blind Men and the Elephant' (see Box 0.1). And it is no surprise, as our limited knowledge of the condition 'blinds' us and prevents us from seeing the whole. However, we have a bonus: our 'elephant' is not mute! But are we prepared to listen? From the very beginning of the 'official history' of autism (Kanner 1943), the syndrome of autism has been described from the outside, how it looks, rather than how it feels from the inside. Now we can get a unique opportunity to learn what it is like to live with autism. Numerous personal accounts have been published and many autistic individuals are willing to talk at conferences and congresses about their experiences. The

Box 0.1 The Blind Men and the Elephant

John Godfrey Saxe's (1816–1887) version of the famous Indian legend.

It was six men of Indostan
To learning much inclined,
Who went to see the Elephant
(Though all of them were blind),
That each by observation
Might satisfy his mind.

The First approached the Elephant,
And happening to fall
Against his broad and sturdy side,
At once began to bawl:
'God bless me, but the Elephant
Is very like a wall!'

The Second, feeling of the tusk,
Cried, 'Ho! What have we here
So very round and smooth and sharp?
To me 'tis mighty clear
This wonder of an Elephant
Is very like a spear!'

The Third approached the animal,
And happening to take
The squirming trunk within his hands,
Thus boldly up and spake:
'I see,' quoth he, 'the Elephant
Is very like a snake!'

The Fourth reached out an eager hand,
And felt about the knee:
'What most this wondrous beast is like
Is mighty plain,' quoth he;
''Tis clear enough the Elephant
Is very like a tree!'

The Fifth, who chanced to touch the ear,
Said: 'E'en the blindest man
Can tell what this resembles most;
Deny the fact who can
This marvel of an Elephant
Is very like a fan!'

The Sixth no sooner had begun
About the beast to grope,
Than, seizing on the swinging tail
That fell within his scope,
'I see,' quoth he, 'the Elephant
Is very like a rope!'

And so these men of Indostan
Disputed loud and long,
Each in his own opinion
Exceeding stiff and strong,
Though each was partly in the right,
And all were in the wrong!

autistic authors feel they have to give their side of the story as hundreds of books on autism written by professionals and parents often 'get it wrong'. They want to clarify things and their views must be taken seriously. They want us to know what it is like to live with a nervous system that functions differently, what it is like to be different, what it is like to be misunderstood and mistreated.

Another useful metaphor I will refer to throughout is the Iceberg theory of autism (Peeters 1997; Schopler and Mesibov 1995). It indicates the right directions in which to look – the behavioural symptoms of autism are like the tip of an iceberg, whereas the causes and mechanisms producing these symptoms are hidden under the water. To extend the metaphor, I would say that until we discover the biggest part of the iceberg, many 'Titanics' will crash and many people will perish (though, not physically); only the strongest and more able will survive. To explore better the invisible part of the iceberg one should not only accumulate the research findings but also seek explanations in the insight reports of people with autism ('survivors') and those who live or work with them. In 1985, Baron-Cohen, Leslie and Frith put forward the theory that people with autism lack a Theory of Mind (ToM); that is, they lack understanding of what other people are thinking, feeling, intending to do, etc. This theory seemed to explain many 'autistic' behaviours, and it was enthusiastically welcomed by the researchers and developed further. Numerous experiments have been conducted in order to prove that, unlike normally developing children and children with other developmental disabilities, autistic individuals cannot understand and predict actions of others as they fail to look at the world from the perspective of others. New terms have been coined that have spread rapidly in the field – 'mind-blindness' and 'mind-reading'. The proponents of the ToM theory state that the ability to understand one's own and others' minds appears to occur spontaneously in childhood. In autism, however, this lack of ability leads to many developmental abnormalities which are characteristic of the disorder (Howlin, Baron-Cohen and Hadwin 1999). But is the development of ToM always spontaneous, independent from any other variables? What about, for example, feral (non-autistic) children? Do they develop ToM? They certainly do, but their ToM is significantly different from that developed by babies in typical circumstances. Let us consider several scenarios:

> Mother hugs her baby and smiles to show happiness and affection. The baby responds to the hug feeling happy and loved. They share experience and the first 'seed' of ToM is planted. If the same happens to the baby who feels pain when being touched, would the baby learn that the smile means 'affection'?

> Mother is angry with her toddler and punishes him by sending him to his room. The child learns that Mummy is cross because he has misbehaved. Another toddler (who has experienced sensory information overload) suddenly finds himself in the safety of his own bedroom. The lesson has been learned – the 'punishment' (from the mother's point of view) means 'affection' for the child.

In the field of autism, the interpretation of the lack of ToM is often one-sided. It is true that autistic people lack ToM and are 'mind-blind' to the thoughts, feelings and intentions of those around them. Non-autistic people's behaviours become unpredictable and confusing to an individual with autism. However, are non-autistic individuals 'mind-sighted' when they deal with persons with autism? Can they understand and predict the behaviours of those whose experiences are different? If autistic people lack Theory of Mind, then non-autistic individuals are sure to have deficits in the ability to understand the Theory of Autistic Mind (ToAM). If we could remove one-sidedness from our interpretation of 'mind-blindness', we would see how limited we are in our ability to 'mind-read'.

Autistic individuals have to learn about many aspects of neurotypical people (NTs – non-autistic people) theoretically, like, for example, colour-blind people have to learn the vocabulary of colours that is meaningless to them. Let us learn 'autistic vocabulary', even if merely theoretically. Autistic people become aware that they are different but they do not know why. They often find it difficult to take another person's perspective. However, to be logical, NTs are also aware that they are different from autistic people, and they do not know why yet. NTs also find it difficult to take the perspective of a person with autism. So, let us look at the 'autistic interpretation' of autism and let them explain autism to us. They know a great deal more about autism than most non-autistic people. Let us take it on trust that they know what they are talking about. Of course, each individual gives his or her *personal* perspective on autism which may not coincide with each other. Nevertheless, despite the differences, there are many similarities that can be seen in their accounts.

Autism is a spectrum disorder and autistic people have a wide range of social awareness, sensory perceptual differences, communicative skills and cognitive abilities. It is time to get away from the assumption that it is nearly impossible to reach an autistic child, often described as being in a glass ball. Very often it is we who do not notice their attempts to reach us, because we cannot even assume they are trying. Their problem (but not their fault) is that they use different systems to process information, interact and communicate. I remember a wedding reception when a mother of an autistic boy married her partner. After the vows were exchanged, the guests were taken aback by the boy's loud announcement, 'Mummy, now I will be "ours".' This little 'unreachable' person, who did not seem to understand much of what was going on around him, declared his longing to 'belong'. This moving example shows the necessity to find ways to build the bridges between the two worlds – autistic and non-autistic ones. And this process should not be one-sided. We must recognize and respect their attempts to reach us.

A lack of Theory of (Different) Mind does not apply only to autistic and non-autistic perspectives. For example, do professionals working from 9 a.m.

to 5 p.m. five days a week and coming home 'free from autism' for a weekend understand thoughts, feelings and behaviours of parents of an autistic child living with autism 24 hours a day, seven days a week? (I wish they could!) Though it is possible to imagine what it is like theoretically, in practice it is a different matter. They do not share experiences and that is why their Theories of Mind do not coincide. Bearing this in mind, ToM as a theoretical construct may be very useful not only when dealing with autistic and non-autistic populations, but also with different groups of people closely involved personally or professionally.

Using the Theory of (Different) Minds as a framework for the discussion we can look at autism from different perspectives. In this book I try to describe autism through the ToM of three large groups of people, united by shared experiences: autistic people, their parents (or significant others, living with them) and professionals working (directly or indirectly) with autistic individuals and their families. It is natural that individuals within these groups are likely to have different views on certain issues. For example, different parents may have different ideas about treatments for their child because their views are formed by their particular experiences, backgrounds and environment. And it is impossible to expect all the members of the given group to agree on all the issues. What unites them, however, is that the effects of autism, although they may vary in each particular case, tend to have a lot of similar features. Numerous perspectives on autism exist. In this book these perspectives are shown as a reflection of certain shared experiences, similar in each group. Each of these perspectives is often not fully understood by other groups, resulting in, at best, uncomfortable coexistence and, at worst, openly declared war.

Addressing the needs of individuals with autism involves a number of hard choices which are often decided in large part by values held by those 'in charge' (parents and/or professionals). However, even individuals within a given group may hold different passionate views, and it is not reasonable to expect all individuals to agree on all issues and choices. It is, however, reasonable to hope that an explicit discussion of perspectives held by different individuals or groups (*including* people with autism) will help promote a better mutual understanding and better relations between all the parties involved (Perner Undated, b).

I hope that this book will give an opportunity to people from different 'camps' to step into each other's shoes, or at least to try them on. I hope the discussion of perspectives (formed by different experiences, social roles, and background) will encourage all the people involved to learn from each other and bring better understanding between (and within) the groups. Only by combining different perspectives of insights of all the parties concerned can we all become 'mind-sighted'.

How to use this book

The book is divided into four parts with seven chapters and a section of further reading in each. The first part, 'Autism as it is Officially Defined (External View)', creates the framework for the whole book. It briefly outlines the issues of what is known about autism at present, including definitions and classifications, diagnosis, causes, development, theories and treatments. The second, third and fourth parts discuss exactly the same issues from different perspectives – Part 2 from the point of view of autistic individuals themselves; Part 3 contains the perspective of parents and relatives; and Part 4 from that of professionals working with autistic people and their families.

There are three possible ways to read the book – 'vertically', 'horizontally' and 'diagonally'.

'Vertical reading' is a conventional one – from the beginning to the end.

'Horizontal reading' is reading about one and the same issue from different perspectives. It will allow the reader to get a full picture of the 'elephant'. The structure of the book makes the 'horizontal' navigation easy. Start with reading Chapter 1.1, then move to Chapters 2.1 and 3.1, and finally 4.1. Cross-referencing is given throughout the book. (At the end of the book, there is a contents list for 'horizontal reading'.)

'Diagonal reading' is for those who want to use the book for reference, or quick access to certain issues (for example, diagnostic criteria, or treatments).

Part 1

Autism as it is Officially Defined (External View)

Definitions and Classifications

Autism is defined as a lifelong complex developmental disability that typically appears during the first three years of life and affects the way a person communicates and relates to people. Since 1943 when Kanner described 'early infantile autism' and Asperger (1944) identified 'autistic psychopathy', we have learned quite a lot about it but still not enough to truly understand this puzzling condition. Both Kanner and Asperger singled out autism as a unique and markedly different developmental disorder that had not been clinically described before and people suffering from it were unjustifiably considered mentally handicapped. The following decades saw a strong movement towards an understanding of autism and research studies on causes, diagnosis and treatment of autism have been carried out all over the world. A seminal work of Lorna Wing and Judith Gould (1979) has changed the clinical understanding of autism tremendously. After having conducted an intensive epidemiological study, Wing and Gould concluded that autism represents a continuum and has different manifestations that are all part of a 'spectrum' of related disorders. Both 'Classic/Kanner' autism and Asperger syndrome (AS) are seen now as parts of a whole group of conditions commonly known as autistic spectrum disorders (ASDs). As autism is a spectrum disorder, it means that people are affected to a different degree. Some individuals will be severely affected, while for others, their difficulties may appear to be quite subtle. Some people with autism may also have learning difficulties, while others are more able, with average or above average intelligence (Wing 1996). About 15 to 20 per cent of autistic people may develop epilepsy (usually during adolescence). It was estimated that about 50 per cent of autistic individuals remain non-verbal throughout their lives. (However, recent research shows that with early appropriate intervention only about 14 per cent never develop verbal language.) Some people with autism may possess very good language skills but lack the ability to understand and express pragmatic/social functions, both verbal and non-verbal. About 10 per cent of autistic individuals are reported to have unusual islets of ability or savant skills (such as special talents in art, music, calculation).

In Box 1.1 there are two definitions of autism – one by the National Autistic Society (UK) and the other by the Autism Society of America. The criteria for defining and diagnosing autism, probably the most universally accepted now, are based on certain behavioural characteristics which the person exhibits in three main areas: impairments of social interaction, impairments in social communication and impairments in imagination, known

---

Box 1.1 Definitions of autism

The NAS definition

Autism is a disability which affects the way a child communicates and relates to people around them. Although it is a condition with wide-ranging degrees of severity, all those affected have a triad of impairments in:

- social interaction
- social communication
- imagination.

In addition to this triad, repetitive behaviour patterns are a notable feature.

The ASA definition

Autism is a severe lifelong developmental disability that typically appears during the first three years of life. Autism interferes with the normal development of the brain in areas which control:

- verbal and non-verbal communication
- social interaction
- sensory development.

collectively as the Triad of Impairments (Wing 1992) (see Figure 1.1). As autism is a developmental disorder, its behavioural manifestations vary with age and ability. However, its 'triadic' features (impairments in socialization, communication and imagination) are present in different forms at all stages of development.

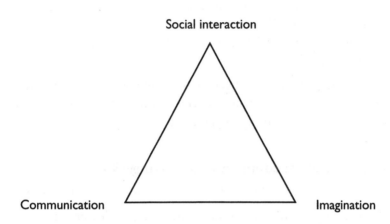

Figure 1.1 The Triad of Impairments (Wing 1992)

As the Triad of Impairments is widely accepted, it is worth considering each of its aspects in more detail.

Impairments in social interaction (Wing 1996)

According to the impairments in social interaction, Wing (1996) has singled out four subgroups of individuals with ASD:

- The *aloof* group does not initiate and react to social interaction. 'Aloof' children seem to be indifferent to other people, especially other children, although some may enjoy certain forms of active physical contact.

- The *passive* group does respond to social interaction, but does not initiate it. They may passively accept social contact, even may show some pleasure in this, but they do not make any spontaneous approaches.

- The *active but odd* group makes contact, but it lacks reciprocity ('one-way interaction'). Children in this group do approach other people spontaneously, but do so in an odd, inappropriate way, paying little or no attention to the way people respond to their approach.

- The *stilted* group initiates and sustains contact, but it is often formal and rigid. These are more able people with autism, who exhibit an inappropriately stilted and formal manner of interaction.

This subgrouping shows a great diversity of manifestations of social impairments and illustrates the spectrum character of the disorder. With development, the person may shift from one group to another.

Impairments in social communication (Wing 1993)

The spectrum of communication impairments in autism is illustrated by:

- lack of appreciation of the social uses and the pleasure of communication; even those who have speech use it to talk 'at' others, not with them

- lack of understanding that language is a tool for communication; they may be able to ask for their own needs but have difficulty in talking about their feelings and thoughts and in understanding feelings, emotions and thoughts of other people

- poor comprehension and lack of use of gestures, facial expressions, body postures, vocal intonation, etc. for communication

- those who have good language exhibiting a pedantic, concrete understanding and use of words; an idiosyncratic choice of words and phrases; and limited content of speech.

The communication/language problems in autism vary significantly from one individual to another. Some may be unable to speak, whereas others may have extensive vocabularies and may be very articulate about their topics of special interest while quite helpless in social conversations.

Verbal autistic individuals often display specific 'autistic' features such as:

- echolalia: the parrot-like repetition of words and phrases either immediately (immediate echolalia) or after some time (delayed echolalia)

- pronoun reversal: difficulty in using pronouns, especially *I/me* and *you*, and other deictic words such as *this – that; here – there*, etc.

- extreme literalness: the understanding and use of language is literal – what the words mean, not what the speaker's intentions are

- metaphorical language: words may have some private meanings different from their common definitions

- neologisms: new words are created and understood only by those who have created them

- affirmation by repetition: the absence of the 'yes' concept; instead the whole phrase is repeated to respond in the affirmative

- repetitive questioning: asking the same question(s) again and again, not for the sake of getting information, but to maintain a predictable reaction

- demanding the same verbal scenario: saying (and demanding in response) exactly the same words that have been used in similar situations

- autistic discourse style: the speech may be overly formal, pedantic in both vocabulary and grammar

- poor control of prosody: peculiar prosodic features such as a monotonous flat voice and idiosyncratic intonation, rhythm and stress.

Impairments in imagination (Wing 1993)

Children with autism may exhibit:

- an inability to play imaginatively with objects or toys or with other children or adults; some children with autism have a limited range of imaginative activities (copied from TV programmes, for example) that are repetitive and rigid

- a tendency to select for attention minor details in the environment instead of an understanding of the meaning of the whole scene

- lack of understanding of social conversation, literature (especially fiction) and subtle verbal humour.

The ways in which any of the features are manifested vary from one child to another, and for the same child different aspects of the behaviour pattern may vary at different ages. Usually no one person has all the characteristics at the same time or at the same degree of severity.

According to Wing (1993), the Triad of Impairments is always accompanied by the repetitive stereotyped activities, which can take simple or complex forms. Wing (1993) classifies these behaviours into four groups:

1. Examples of simple stereotyped activities: flicking fingers, objects; spinning objects or watching objects spin; tapping or scratching on surfaces; feeling special textures; rocking; head banging or self-injury; teeth grinding; producing noises, etc.

2. Examples of complex stereotyped activities involving objects: intense attachment to particular objects for no apparent purpose; a fascination with patterns, sounds, etc.; arranging objects in lines or patterns, etc.

3. Examples of complex stereotyped activities involving routines: insistence on following the same route to certain places; bedtime ritual; repetition of a sequence of odd body movements.

4. Examples of complex verbal or abstract repetitive activities: fascination with certain topics; asking the same series of questions and demanding standard answers.

All these characteristics (the Triad plus repetitive stereotyped activities) are considered to be primary. Additionally, secondary characteristics are enumerated, which are common but *not* essential for diagnosis, such as: language problems, abnormalities of visual inspection and eye contact, problems of motor imitation and motor control, unusual responses to sensory stimuli, inappropriate emotional reactions, various abnormalities of physical functions and physical development (erratic patterns of sleeping, eating and drinking; resistance to the effects of sedatives and hypnotics; lack of dizziness after spinning round; unusual symmetry of face), special skills (contrasting with lack of skill in other areas) and behaviour problems (Wing 1993).

Some children and adults with ASDs display extremely challenging behaviour (aggression, self-injury, etc.). Some people with autism display remarkable abilities in drawing, music, calculation, etc. Some autistic children are very good at assembling complex jigsaw puzzles, even when the puzzles are upside-down. Some begin to read exceptionally early, even before they start to speak.

HFA, LFA, 'mild autism', 'severe autism', etc.

As autism is a spectrum disorder and its manifestation varies from individual to individual, it is no wonder, therefore, that many 'non-official' but widely accepted descriptions have emerged: high-functioning autism (HFA), low-functioning autism (LFA), 'mild autism', 'moderate autism', 'severe autism', 'autistic traits', 'autistic tendencies'. It is necessary to note that these terms are subjective. There are no clinical definitions of words such as 'high-functioning', 'low-functioning', 'mild' or 'severe' autism. However, because autism is so wide ranging, professionals may use terms like these to describe where on a continuum they believe an individual's abilities may lie (see Box 1.2).

Box 1.2 A way to look at ASDs

A U T I S M   S P E C T R U M

Classic autism	'Moderate' autism	HFA	AS
Kanner autism		'Mild' autism	
LFA			
'Severe' autism			

At present there are no widely accepted diagnostic guidelines for HFA. However, most researchers agree that it is appropriate to refer to somebody as having HFA if they meet the criteria for autism and have a Full Scale IQ above 70.

Asperger syndrome and autism

The issue of whether autism and AS are different conditions has been debated for many years. It was Wing (1981) who brought AS to the attention of the clinicians. She emphasized that there was no evidence for a distinction between AS and autism. However, her account of AS has inspired many researchers to investigate the possible differences between the two conditions.

In spite of separate diagnostic classification the controversy still exists as to whether AS is a syndrome in its own right or a form of autism, namely HFA, or 'mild autism'. Those who believe that AS is *not* a form of autism cite the current diagnostic classifications, which state that AS is a distinct diagnosis. Disagreement will continue until much more is known about the causes of ASDs. However, whatever the label, both autistic and AS individuals need support and services throughout childhood and adulthood, if the long-term outcome is to be significantly increased (Howlin 1997). It is important to remember that individuals with ASD differ as much from one another as they do from non-autistic people. They have their own personality, strengths and weaknesses.

For 'horizontal reading':

2.1 – pp.77–96
3.1 – pp.179–186
4.1 – pp.233–240

1.2

Diagnosis

At present there are no medical tests like brain scans, x-rays or blood tests that can identify autism. The diagnosis is made on the basis of certain behavioural manifestations. There are two standardized classification systems that are internationally recognized and used for diagnosis of autism:

- ICD-10 (the *International Classification of Diseases,* 10th edition) produced by the World Health Organization in 1992

- DSM-IV (the *Diagnostic and Statistical Manual of Mental Disorders,* 4th edition) by the American Psychiatric Association, 1994.

Since both the ICD and the DSM were modified in the early 1990s, there is a high degree of correspondence in the current criteria used in the two systems, in contrast to the earlier editions. As there are no medical tests to identify autism and children with ASDs cannot usually be distinguished by their physical appearance, both systems identify these disorders by clusters of particular behavioural symptoms. The behavioural descriptions of autism in these two main classification systems are based on Wing's Triad of Impairments. In DSM-IV and ICD-10, autism falls under the category of pervasive developmental disorders (PDDs). In both systems separate categories are provided within the class of PDDs (see Table 1.1).

The diagnostic criteria for autism disorder in ICD-10 and DSM-IV are very similar. According to ICD-10, in order for a diagnosis of autism to be made the person needs to exhibit problems in three broad areas: reciprocal social interaction, communication, and restricted, repetitive and stereotyped patterns of behaviour, interests and activities. At least eight of the specified items must be fulfilled. The age of onset of these symptoms has to occur before three years. According to DSM-IV, the individual needs to exhibit

Table 1.1 PDDs in ICD-10 and DSM-IV

ICD-10	DSM-IV
Autism disorder	Autistic disorder
Rett's syndrome	Rett's disorder
Other childhood disintegrative disorder	Childhood disintegrative disorder
Asperger's syndrome	Asperger's disorder
Atypical autism	Pervasive developmental disorder not otherwise specified (PDDNOS)

qualitative impairments in the same areas: social interaction, communication and stereotyped patterns of behaviour. The person needs to exhibit six symptoms in these areas with at least two symptoms indicating social interaction and one symptom in each of the communication and stereotyped patterns of behaviour categories. The symptoms should be present by 36 months of age.

However, autism can occur in association with other disorders such as metabolic disturbances, epilepsy, visual or hearing impairments, Down syndrome, dyslexia, cerebral palsy, attention deficit disorder (ADD), attention deficit hyperactivity disorder (ADHD), etc. In this case, dual diagnosis is made. It is important not to overlook autism in children with multiple disabilities. Many children with autism have general intellectual disabilities. Jordan (2001) states that, in fact, the more severe the general intellectual disabilities the more likely it is that the child will have autism. In adolescence and adulthood, ASDs may be complicated with the development of psychiatric problems, such as depression, mood disorders or severe anxiety.

Asperger syndrome

The criteria for Asperger syndrome follow the same lines as, and, in fact, overlap to some degree, the criteria for autism.

Similarities and differences between autism and AS

The following descriptions analyse the similar and different diagnostic features between autism and AS, which may help to differentiate these two conditions.

Similarities

Both autism and AS are defined in the DSM-IV and ICD-10 as PDDs. This means there are similarities between these two conditions, namely impairments in interaction, communication and restricted behaviours and interests.

Differences

Differences are seen primarily in the degree of impairment and the number of symptoms. For example, a person with AS usually exhibits fewer symptoms. Although the criteria of social interaction for autism and AS are identical, the manifestations of social impairments in these conditions are different. The social deficits of AS are less severe than those associated with autism. Individuals with AS, though isolative, may express a great interest in meeting people and making friends. However, their approaches are often awkward and inappropriate, and their 'blindness' to other people's feelings and intentions lead to their failures in making any permanent friendship. Because of this, frustration, depression and sometimes aggression may develop. AS may also be distinguished from autism on the basis of patterns of attachment in early childhood. AS children exhibit adequate attachment to family members and show some desire to interact with their peers (though inappropriate and odd). In autism, attachment is more atypical and children tend to be withdrawn and aloof (Klin and Volkmar 1996). Although the criteria of restrictive, repetitive and stereotyped patterns of behaviour, interests and activities for AS and autism are identical, it appears that these characteristics (with the exception of an encompassing preoccupation with an unusual and circumscribed topic) are less pronounced in AS.

In contrast to autism, in the definition of AS there are no symptoms in the area of impairments of communication. However, although significant abnormalities of speech are not typical to AS, for example, researchers (Klin *et al.* 1995) distinguish several areas of difficulty in aspects of verbal and nonverbal communication for individuals with AS:

- Non-verbal communication is clumsy and is poorly coordinated with verbal utterances.

- Speech prosody may be atypical, although not so rigid and monotonous as in autism. For example, individuals with AS may exhibit a very limited range of intonation patterns, with little regard to the communicative functioning of the utterance (humour, irony, etc.).

- Speech may often be overly formal, pedantic and long-winded. Conversations are usually factual, concrete and literal, and are often limited to idiosyncratic topics of personal interest; for instance, long monologues about train schedules, car makes, etc.

In addition, speech abnormalities such as echolalia and pronominal reversal, which are typical in autism, are usually absent in AS. While individuals with autism may have delay in, or total lack of, speech, individuals with AS *cannot* possess a 'clinically significant general delay' in language acquisition. Individuals with AS may, however, experience difficulty in receptive language – particularly in terms of irony, humour, sarcasm, etc.

Other common descriptions of the early development of children with AS include a certain precociousness in learning to talk ('He talked before he could walk'), a fascination with letters and numbers, hyperlexia, or spontaneous sight reading in young children with little or no understanding (Eaves 1996; Klin 1994). However, these behaviours are sometimes described for HF autistic children as well.

Tony Attwood (2000) believes that the language profile in AS is different. Whether or not individuals with AS were delayed in language acquisition is irrelevant. What is important is how they use language in a social context. Also, they are not skilled in translating their thoughts into speech. Quite often, their thoughts may be visualizations, which are not easy to convey in spoken communication but which may be conveyed by written or typed communication, drawings, etc.

Another distinction between autism and AS made in the DSM-IV and ICD-10 concerns cognitive ability. While some individuals with autism exhibit learning difficulties, by definition individuals with AS *cannot* possess a 'clinically significant' cognitive delay. Not all individuals with autism also have intellectual disabilities, but individuals with AS possess an average to above average intelligence.

In addition to the diagnostic criteria described in the DSM-IV and ICD-10, some researchers specify an additional symptom as an associated feature though not a required criterion for the diagnosis of AS, namely delayed motor milestones and presence of 'motor clumsiness' (Attwood 1998; Klin *et al.* 1995; Wing 1996). In individuals with AS acquisition of motor skills may be delayed. They often seem to be awkward, and exhibit rigid gait pattern, poor manipulative skills and significant deficits in visual–motor coordination. Ghaziuddin *et al.* (1994), however, question the inclusion of clumsiness as a differentiating symptom, after finding that subjects with AS were no more clumsy than subjects with high-functioning autism. The results of research by Manjiviona and Prior (1995) confirm this observation. Their study showed that 50 per cent of children with AS and 67 per cent of children with HFA were clumsy.

Another feature, frequently mentioned for AS, is what Asperger (1944) called 'sadistic traits' and 'delight in malice' – violence. Some researchers find no association between AS and violent behaviour (Ghaziuddin *et al.* 1994), whereas others consider violence to be more common in people with AS than in the general population and suggest that violent acts committed by individuals with AS may stem from deficits in empathy, or from the obsessional interests that are a hallmark of the syndrome (Scragg and Shah 1994).

The onset of AS, or at least its recognition, is somewhat later than that of autism. The outcome is reported to be more favourable than in autism (Klin and Volkmar 1996). It is interesting that early differences between autistic and AS children, seen at age four to five years, may decrease with age or disappear altogether by early adulthood (Gilchrist *et al.* 2001; Ozonoff, Rogers and Pennington 1991; Szatmari *et al.* 1995). Thus, the young children with autism may 'shift' to AS-type of development (Szatmari *et al.* 1995; Wing 2000).

The most important reason for recognition and proper diagnosis is not in order to label a child but in order to better understand how to help these children in a way that would allow them to cope with the condition and achieve their full potential.

Autism and AS can be confused with a number of conditions characterized by similar symptoms. Conditions which may be misdiagnosed for autism and/or AS are:

- mental retardation (intellectual disabilities)
- schizophrenia

- specific language disorders (elective mutism, developmental language disorder, etc.)
- Tourette's syndrome
- Landau-Kleffner syndrome
- Rett's syndrome
- disintegrative disorder
- William's syndrome
- obsessive-compulsive disorder
- depression.

In recent years, numerous diagnostic terms have been used to describe children with the features of AS, such as:

- schizoid personality disorder
- semantic pragmatic disorder
- non-verbal intellectual disability disorder
- developmental intellectual disability of the right hemisphere
- disorders of attention, motor coordination and perception (DAMP)
- pathological demand avoidance syndrome (PDA).

Some of the above 'disorders' have appeared only recently. Their 'separateness' from existing diagnostically valid disorders seems very controversial. If one of the aspects of complex disabilities has been focused on, you may originate dozens of 'new disabilities' out of the existing ones. There has been a debate whether these concepts describe different separate entities or (more probably) have limited their focus on different aspects of a heterogeneous group of disorders, such as, for instance, ASDs.

To make a diagnosis of autism, particularly in regard to its similarities with other conditions, it is necessary to make a comprehensive assessment, including a developmental history of the child (the pattern of behaviour that unfolds over time), psychiatric examination, psychological assessment and communication assessment. It is necessary to remember that a brief observation in a single setting cannot reveal a true picture of a child's abilities and behaviour patterns. Very often, at first sight a child with autism may appear to have mental retardation (intellectual disabilities), or problems with hearing. In this case, the parents of the child who know the meaning of his behaviour can help. They must not be ignored. Moreover, they should be encouraged to take part in the assessment. In addition, in structured situations with the staff the child knows, he may show no 'diagnostically significant' symptoms of ASDs. The child should be observed in different settings (especially, in unstructured environments) with different people, in order to get a full picture of his difficulties.

Early diagnosis

Early diagnosis is vital as the earlier treatments start, the better the prognosis. However, autism is very difficult to diagnose before the age of three as diagnostic behaviours (impairments in social interaction and communication) do not fully develop until later in childhood. Some autistic children are different from birth, others seem to develop normally until somewhere between one-and-a-half to three years, then autistic symptoms start emerging. Some autistic children reach developmental milestones (crawling, walking, talking) earlier than an average child, whereas others are delayed.

There have been attempts to develop diagnostic tools that can indicate autism at earlier stages (before the age of two). In order to achieve this, some other behaviours specific to autism should have been identified. In most cases, the behaviours – precursors of possible social impairments – have been chosen (pretend play, motor imitation, joint attention). An example of one such tool is the Checklist for Autism in Toddlers (CHAT) developed by Baron-Cohen, Allen and Gillberg (1992). The CHAT is a screening instrument which is designed to identify children aged 18 months who are at risk of developing social and communication disorders. It is a short, easily applied questionnaire, which is filled in by the parents and a health care worker at the 18-month developmental check-up. CHAT consists of two parts: the first nine questions are to be answered by the parents, and the last five are observations made by the primary health worker. The key behaviours, which, if absent at 18 months, put a child at risk of developing a social-communication disorder, are:

- joint attention, including pointing to show and gaze-monitoring
- pretend play.

Another simple measurement done during a paediatric check-up has the potential to provide an earlier indication of autism. It has been reported (Courchesne,

Carper and Akshoomoff 2003) that at birth autistic infants have smaller head circumference (on average, in the 25th percentile) than normal and then, by 6 to 14 months, there is a sudden and dramatic burst of growth (in the 84th percentile). Courchesne *et al.* (2003) used high-resolution brain scans to look at brain growth. It seems the larger the head size and brain overgrowth, the more severe the autism. (However, it should be mentioned, 6 per cent of normally developing children showed accelerated growth in head circumference from birth to between 6 and 14 months; and 41 per cent of autistic children did not have abnormal head growth.)

Unlike autism, the symptoms of Asperger syndrome are typically traced later in childhood.

Prevalence of autism: the autism epidemic?

When first identified in 1943, autism was considered as a 'rare disorder' (Kanner 1943). For many years, the most cited statistic has been that autism occurs in four to five out of 10,000 births. The prevalence in boys is reported to be four times higher than in girls. Since then there have been a number of studies giving rates of prevalence from 3.3 to 16 per 10,000. Wing and Gould (1979) examined prevalence of autism in children born between 1956 and 1970 in the former London Borough of Camberwell. They looked at children whose IQ levels were below 70 and found the prevalence rate of 20 per 10,000. Ehlers and Gillberg (1993) examined children with IQ of 70 or above in mainstream schools in Gothenburg and found a prevalence of 36 per 10,000 in children born between 1975 and 1983. They also found another 35 per 10,000 with social impairments of the autistic spectrum type. Adding figures from both studies gives a prevalence of 91 per 10,000, nearly 1 per cent of the general population. Based on their study in Karlstad, Sweden, Kadesjo, Gillberg and Hagberg (1999) report a prevalence for all autistic spectrum disorders, for all levels of IQ, of 1.21 per cent.

There arise questions: is the increase in the incidence of autism real, or merely an increased awareness? If there is a true increase, what causes it? There are several possibilities that could account for an apparent increase of autism:

- the definition of ASDs is broader now than original 'early infantile autism' described by Kanner

- there is a greater awareness of the condition and more accurate diagnostic tools

- many people who would be diagnosed with ASDs today were labelled as mentally retarded, imbeciles, schizophrenics, etc. in the past

- there is a real increase with no known causes yet.

AS prevalence

The initial epidemiological research suggests that one person in 250 has signs of AS; however, this estimate may be far too low. Like autism, AS is considered to be more common in males than females; usually the ratio 10 to 1 is reported. However, it may well be that females; may go undiagnosed longer or not at all, as girls usually have better developed language and social skills. There may be more females with undiagnosed autism or AS.

Is there any increase in the incidence of AS at present? There is an increase in *diagnosis* of AS. But is it a seeming or real AS epidemic? The answer to this question is nearly impossible because many adults have been diagnosed or self-diagnosed and, possibly, many more are 'still there' – either unwilling to be 'labelled' or experiencing problems with getting the diagnosis. In his book on Asperger syndrome, Tony Attwood (1998) outlined six possible factors (pathways) that might contribute to the increase in children and adults being diagnosed with AS:

1. Diagnosis of classic autism in young children who (with the intensive early intervention) progress along the autism continuum to the point where the descriptions of Asperger, rather than Kanner, more accurately describe their profiles of abilities.

2. The AS features may not be obvious till the child first starts school. The child then is referred for a diagnostic assessment.

3. There is an atypical expression of another syndrome that may mask and delay a dual diagnosis.

4. Diagnosis of a relative with autism or AS may lead to the identification of others within the family who share the same characteristics.

5. A secondary psychiatric disorder, especially depression, anxiety and panic attacks, developed in adolescence or adulthood may lead an experienced psychiatrist to screen the patient for AS and

thus reveal the primary problems of seemingly psychotic symptoms.

6. Residual AS in an adult when an adult (usually a relative of an autistic child) reads about AS and may recognize themselves and realize that this could explain their relationship problems.

For 'horizontal reading':

2.2 – pp.97–103
3.2 – pp.187–190
4.2 – pp.241–255

Causes

The Triad of Impairments describes the *behaviours* which help us to recognize autism. It does not tell us *why* autistic people exhibit them. These 'diagnostic behaviours' are the tip of the iceberg and unless we know 'what is under the water', there will not be adequate explanations of the displayed impairments and no straightforward guidance of what to do about them (see Figure 1.2).

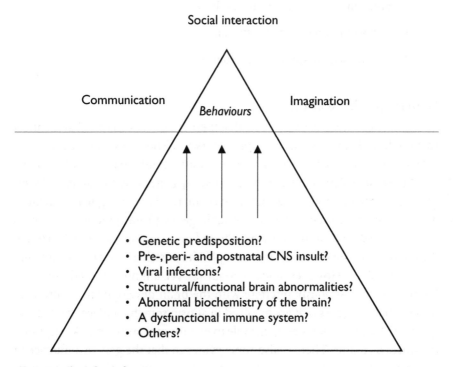

Figure 1.2 The Iceberg of Autism

What causes autism? This is a very difficult question. Since Kanner's time many theories have emerged to account for possible causes of autism, however, we still have no definite answer. The only fact we know for sure is that the so-called 'refrigerator mother' theory, i.e. autism is the result of a psychological withdrawal from what the child perceives as a cold and hostile environment, popular in the 1950s and 1960s, is absolutely wrong. The most popular theory now is a biological one – autism is the result of an injury or dysfunction to the central nervous system which causes abnormal brain development, though the nature and the cause(s) of the brain abnormalities remain the subject of controversy. Organic brain defects can be caused by one or several biological factors, such as:

- genetic predisposition
- pre-, peri- and postnatal CNS insult
- viral infections
- structural and/or functional brain abnormalities
- abnormal biochemistry of the brain
- a dysfunctional immune system
- others (which are yet to be found).

Genetic predisposition

The studies of autism in twins show that there is a greater chance that identical twins will both have autism than fraternal twins. They suggest that autism (or at least a higher likelihood of some brain dysfunction) can be inherited. Some researchers speculate that from three to twenty genes may be associated with autism. Another hypothesis is that what is inherited is an irregular segment of genetic code or a small group of unstable genes (from three to six). Genes possibly involved in autism have been found on chromosomes 2, 6, 7, 16, 18, 22 and the X chromosome. In most people, the unstable genes may cause only minor problems. However, under certain (as yet unknown) conditions, the faulty code may seriously interfere with the brain development. It also may well be that the genes that are involved in autism somehow place that baby at greater risk or make it more vulnerable to environmental events, like exposure to viruses or toxins. There is also some evidence that the genetic influence in autism may be a weakened immune system. In addition, autism is also associated with other genetic disorders (fragile X syndrome, taberous sclerosis, neurofibromatosis, Rett's syndrome, etc.) as they appear more frequently in children with autism and their families. Other problems (dyslexia, depression, etc.) are quite common in families with an autistic child.

Pre-, peri- and postnatal CNS insult

During pregnancy, anything that disrupts normal brain development may lead to lifelong effects on the child's sensory, language, mental and social functioning. These may include the mother's illness during pregnancy, problems during delivery (for example, lack of oxygen to the baby), or soon after the birth (asphyxy, reanimation of the child, postnatal encephalitis). It has been reported (Bolton *et al.* 1994) that the genetic abnormalities are likely to increase the incidence of pre-, peri- and postnatal complications and that autistic children with the greatest genetic liability also suffer the most prenatal and delivery problems, suggesting that obstetric complications are a result, not a cause, of autism.

Viral infections

There is evidence that viral infections, particularly at the early stages of pregnancy, may lead to a variety of developmental disorders, including autism. The infections that have been reported in association with autism are the rubella (or German measles) virus, cytomegalovirus, herpes simplex virus and candida albicans. Recent concerns have been raised about vaccinations (especially MMR) as being a possible cause (Wakefield 1998).

Recent concerns have been raised about MMR in particular as being a possible cause of autism (Wakefield 1998). The MMR immunization is designed to protect against measles, mumps and rubella and works by stimulating the immune system to produce antibodies against these three viruses. It is usually given in two doses: the first to children of 12 to 15 months, a second at three to five years. The majority of children receive the vaccination without any obvious side-effects, but some become seriously ill within a few days or weeks. They may begin to behave strangely, scream, develop bizarre eating and sleep patterns, stop talking and withdraw from any social interaction. This may be accompanied by bloating, bowel disturbances, incontinence and abdominal pain. Other people insist that the MMR vaccine is safe. However, the jury is still out. Some research studies indicate that toxins (for example, mercury) and pollution in the environment may also be linked to developing autism.

Structural and/or functional brain abnormalities

It is generally accepted that autism may be caused by (even if very subtle) abnormalities in brain structure or functions. However, as autistic symptomatology is so broad, it is difficult to find a brain region (or regions) as a possible site of pathology. There has been extensive research to find out how a brain with autism differs from the normal brain. The results are wide-ranging: abnormalities in different people with autism have been located in different parts of the brain. As yet, no abnormality specific for autism has yet been found. Of those reported, differences have been described in the cerebral cortex, the brainstem, the limbic system (the amygdala and hippocampus) and the cerebellum. However, each of the differences has been seen in some but not all the people with autism who were tested. The most common observation reported by researchers such as Piven *et al.* (1995) is that the volume of total brain tissue and lateral ventricles in brains of autistic individuals are on average greater than that of normal individuals. The authors hypothesize that perhaps there is a failure of neurons to die off normally during early development.

Bauman and Kemper (1994) found reduced neuronal size and increased cell-packing density in the limbic system (the part of the brain that is involved with emotional responses). Based on the findings of their studies, Bauman and Kemper suggest that high-functioning autistic individuals may have more pronounced abnormalities in the amygdala (a part of the brain responsible for processing emotions and behaviour). Low-functioning autistic people appear to have more extensive abnormalities in other limbic systems, particularly the hippocampus. This disparity may reflect differences in timing of the appearance of the underlying defect during brain development. Courchesne *et al.* (2003) present more evidence that brain growth abnormalities begin early, even before birth. Infants who later develop autism have a reduced head circumference at birth compared to non-autistic babies, but undergo a rapid spurt in growth during the first months and years of life. By the age of three, when behavioural symptoms of autism are beginning to emerge, autistic brains are considerably larger than normal. The cause of the small brain size at birth is unknown, but the abnormally accelerated brain growth probably reflects an excessive number of brain cells, the failure of the brain to prune the hundreds of synapses that connect one neuron to another, or both. In the normally developing brain, unneeded and unused synapses are pruned away. In contrast, autistic babies seem to suffer from the neurological equivalent of electrical overload – too many impulses, sensations and thoughts in their brain (Courchesne *et al.* 2003). This study confirms the biological origin of autism and gives some evidence that environmental factors cannot be the causes of the condition, though they likely aggravate the manifestation of it. This hypothesis is very plausible in some (but not all) cases of autism, as the abnormally high rates of brain growth were observed in 59 per cent of autistic cases and 6 per cent of non-autistic ones (Courchesne *et al.* 2003). Another interpretation of the results may be that the high rates of brain growth from birth to two years of age are necessary antecedents of autism, but that an additional trigger is needed to induce the actual expression of the condition (Courchesne *et al.* 2003). The findings of these studies indicate the necessity of early intervention for better outcome. If interventions start early, before the brain becomes hard-wired with the circuits underlying autism, we might get a better outcome for a child (even if the child still remains autistic).

Abnormal biochemistry of the brain

Differences in neurotransmitters have been researched. High (or sometimes low) levels of serotonin have been found in a number of people with autism, but no consistent abnormalities specific to autism have been revealed yet. It has been proposed that autism, as well as some other related conditions, may be the consequence of metabolic abnormalities like the incomplete break-down of certain proteins, particularly, but not necessarily exclusively, gluten from wheat and casein from dairy products, that result in production of peptides which enter the bloodstream and cross the blood–brain barrier ('leaky gut syndrome') (Shattock and Savery 1996). There is some evidence that candida albicans overgrowth may cause toxins to be released into the body and cause some difficult behaviours common in autism (for instance, hyperactivity, irritability, aggression) and other health problems (headaches, constipation, diarrhea, skin rashes, etc.). It has been hypothesized that candida overgrowth may be caused by antibiotic treatments in early infancy.

A dysfunctional immune system

Some evidence links autism to immune system abnormalities (Gupta, Aggarwal and Heads 1996). A dysfunctional immune system (often associated with autism) is thought to be damaged by a viral infection, an environmental toxin or a specific genetic influence.

Despite some intriguing and promising findings, the aetiology of autism is actually unknown. Several conceptual models have been put forward, but none can account for all cases of autism. For example, in some children autism can be explained by structural abnormalities in the brain, in others by deficiency of the immune system. So the most reasonable model proposed so far is 'the final common pathway', according to which various possible causes of autism all lead to the same clinical picture of its manifestation – impairments in social interaction, communication and rigidity of thought.

For 'horizontal reading':

2.3 – pp.104–112
3.3 – pp.191–196
4.3 – pp.256–259

Development

It is very important to know a detailed developmental history. An autistic child has very uneven development and often does not follow the typical patterns of child development. We may distinguish three types of development – normal (typical), delayed and atypical (deviant, idiosyncratic, uneven) development. In Figure 1.3, three children are five years old at the time of the assessment. Child A has typical development, child B displays delayed development, child C has autism. The development of normal children is even across all the aspects. Developmentally delayed children also show an even development, though they reach main milestones considerably later than typically developing children. In autism, development is very uneven – children may be well above average in some domains while delayed in others.

There may be several possible scenarios of development in autism. The child may start developing normally and then seem to stop; may have very well-developed skills in some areas and very poor in others; or may show the signs of future problems from birth.

Studies comparing developmental profiles of children with autism and children with other developmental disorders have shown that:

- motor skills of autistic children are relatively more advanced than social skills (DeMyer, Barton and Norton 1972; Klin, Volkmar and Sparrow 1992; Stone *et al.* 1999)

- some autistic children experience considerable problems in acquiring motor skills (motor imitation, coordination, speech articulation, etc.) (Jones and Prior 1985; Rapin 1996)

- praxis deficits during goal-directed motor tasks that do not require imitation may be present (Hughes and Russel 1993; Smith and Bryson 1998)

- atypical sensory modulation and motor behaviours, including rubbing surfaces, finger flicking, body rocking and absence of responses to stimuli (Rapin 1996), distinguish children with ASDs from children with other developmental disorders, even those with very low developmental levels (Adrien *et al.* 1987; Rapin 1996).

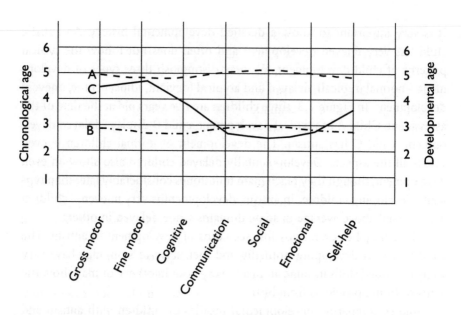

Figure 1.3 Three types of development: A – Normal (typical), B – Delayed, and C – Atypical (deviant, idosyncratic, uneven)

For 'horizontal reading':

2.4 – pp.113–125
3.4 – pp.197–201
4.4 – pp.260–264

1.5

Theories

One of the influential theories popular in the 1960s and 1970s was originated by Bruno Bettelheim who blamed parents (especially 'refrigerator mothers') for causing autism in their children. Bettelheim nurtured the possibility that the child with autism was basically intelligent but had withdrawn from social contact due to traumatic events in his environment, specifically the lack of a warm attitude from one or both parents (Bettelheim 1967). Neither Bettelheim nor his followers provided any evidence to support this psychogenic theory of autism, and after many years of carrying the blame for their children's withdrawal, the parents were 'acquitted' when new research showed the absurdity and harm of this approach.

Since that time there have been numerous attempts to account for autism and a number of psychological theories have emerged. These theories do not explain autism. Each one is able to shed some light on some aspect(s) of the condition but falls short of covering all the characteristics. This does not mean that they are without value. In a way, they are very useful. Some theoretical constructs may help understand the person's psychology and provide useful clues about possible treatments. Besides, they may stimulate a great deal of research that could lead to new findings and our better understanding of autism at all levels (biological, psychological and behavioural). However, if the data do not support the theory, we must be prepared to let the theory go and look for the explanation somewhere else. Unfortunately, this is not always the case. Sometimes a theory that originated several decades ago is being stretched beyond its limits in order to account for the whole autistic spectrum.

The selected theories represent the most influential schools of thought at present. Here they are not discussed in depth, however, and the reader can get more information from the books referred to at the end of the chapter.

Theory of Mind (ToM)

It has been noticed that autistic people find it hard to perceive the mental states of others (Baron-Cohen *et al.* 1985; Frith 1989). Simon Baron-Cohen (1995) suggests that the central feature of autism is an inability to infer another person's mental states; in extreme cases autistic children may have no concept of mind at all. This inability has been termed lack of Theory of Mind, or 'mind-blindness'. In one widely used ToM task, known as the Sally–Ann test (Figure 1.4), the child sees a doll named Sally watch another doll named Ann place a marble in her basket. Ann leaves, and Sally moves the marble from the basket into her box. When Ann returns, the child is asked where Ann will look for her marble: in the basket or the box? Normal children (and most children with Down syndrome) will correctly infer that Ann will look in the basket because she does not know that the marble has been moved. Most children with autism will say that Sally will look where they, not Sally, saw her marble hidden. Even those autistic individuals who give the right answer come to the solution differently from non-autistic ones. Non-autistic children when they do the test cannot in detail explain why, while autistic people who succeed readily give an articulate justification (Happé 1995). For non-autistic people the answer is spontaneous, while individuals with autism work out a solution logically. Such 'mind-aware' autistic people fail harder ToM tasks that test more difficult forms of mind awareness. Besides, unlike others, they do not use such skills in real life (Happé 1995).

Although lack of ToM can account for some typical social impairments in autism, it does not cause these behaviours. We may define an approximate place of the theory of ToM on the iceberg – it is somewhere halfway between the water and the tip of the iceberg. Like the Triad of Impairments, the Iceberg theory is very useful to interpret some 'autistic behaviours' but not to explain the causes of these behaviours.

Weak central coherence theory

In an attempt to explain 'non-social' features of autism (that could not be accounted for by the lack of ToM), Uta Frith (1989/2003) originated the theory of weak central coherence in autism. This theory focuses on the cognitive differences (both deficits and strengths) in autism. Frith suggests that in the normal cognitive system there is 'a built-in propensity to form coherence over as wide a range of stimuli as possible, and to generalize over as wide a range of contexts as possible' (Frith 2003, pp.159–160). In contrast, people

Figure 1.4 ToM: Sally–Ann test. Illustrations by Ian Wilson. Reproduced with permission.

with autism lack this 'built-in form to coherence'. The theory predicts that autistic individuals will have deficits in integrating information into a higher level of holistic information; that is, they may do well in Embedded Figures tests but find it difficult to 'see the whole picture'. Frith (1989/2003) believes that the theory of impaired (weak) central coherence can well account for the typical islets of abilities in autism as well as the inability to focus on meaningful information and ignore what is irrelevant that leads to the inability to make sense, to see meaning and structure in everything. The theory of weak central coherence has been developed further by Francesca Happé (1999a,b), who concludes that central coherence may form a continuum of cognitive style, from 'weak' to 'strong' – with autistic people falling at the extreme 'weak' end.

Quite a few studies have questioned the proposition of universal weak central coherence in autism (see, for example, Garner and Hamilton 2001; Ropar and Mitchell 1999, 2001; Ropar, Mitchell and Ackroyd 2003) and alternative explanations have been suggested (for instance, Bogdashina 2003; Mottron and Burack 2001; Plaisted 2001; Plaisted, O'Riordan and Baron-Cohen 1998). We may conclude that the theory of weak central coherence, while being useful in stimulating research, seems to be stretched too far in the attempt to account for *all* the aspects of autism by identifying a single universal denominator. This approach may hinder further explorations of such a puzzling disorder as autism. Some specialists are unaware of the pitfalls of the theory and alternative explanations and in their work focus on such notions as 'thinking in detail', or the 'fragmented world' of autism, leaving other aspects outside the scope of their interest (i.e. they themselves 'do not see the wood for the trees'). While 'fragmentation' is real, it is not present at all the stages of perception and functioning. Ozonoff *et al.* (1994) hypothesize that autistic individuals do indeed focus on details at the expense of seeing the big picture, but do this at a conceptual, rather than perceptual, level. To apply weak central coherence to all aspects of autism seems an unnecessary and not very useful simplification.

Deficient executive functioning

Another theory searching for a core deficit in autism is deficient executive functioning theory, originated by Sally Ozonoff (1995). Executive functioning refers to the ability to free the mind of the immediate situation and context to guide behaviours through mental models or internal representations. The executive functions include planning, organizing, monitoring progress towards a goal, and taking a flexible approach to problem solving. Sally Ozonoff has studied the impairment of executive functions in autism and found that behavioural peculiarities of autistic people in this area appear very similar to those of people who have suffered frontal lobe damage as adults. It is suggested (Belmonte 1997) that the deficit in people with frontal lobe injury seems to lie not with the ability to understand but rather with the ability to execute. An impaired capacity to generate new ideas and action plans will lead to limited spontaneous behaviour and repetitiveness (Turner 1999). The executive functioning theory can easily account for the lack of flexibility and the rigidity exhibited by people with autism, their difficulties in planning, and their problems with starting and finishing actions, but these executive functioning deficiencies are not exclusive to autism and, consequently, cannot be considered as autism-specific deficiencies.

Sensory perceptual theory

To identify the neural basis of autism, the studies have been conducted to investigate brain systems underlying cognitive functions (Ornitz 1983, 1985, 1989). Delacato (1974) suggests that autism is caused by a brain injury that affects one or more of the sensory channels, which makes brains of autistic children perceive inputs from the world differently from non-injured brains. Many autistic individuals seem to have sensory impairments in one or more of their senses. These impairments are different from blindness or deafness and are characterized by differences in perception. These may include an inability to filter information, fragmented perception, hyper- or hyposensitivities, sensory agnosia, etc. (Bogdashina 2003). Although the theory highlighting the sensory perceptual abnormalities as core features of autism has not been widely recognized, at present there is an increasing interest in these aspects of the condition. And it is worth considering here, for the logical structure of the whole book.

Unusual responses to the sensory stimuli were noticed from the very beginning of the official 'history' of autism. Kanner (1943) and Asperger (1944) described bizarre reactions of their patients to sound, touch, sights, taste and smell. Creak (1961) included unusual sensory perceptual experiences in the list of core symptoms of autism. Rimland (1964) emphasized the importance of exploring perceptual abilities of autistic children. Ornitz (1969, 1989) described disorders of perception common in autism and extended the notion of a disorder of sensory processing to the notion of sensory and information processing. This approach allowed him to clarify and identify separate stages and functions of sensory perception and consider information processing in terms of more discrete functions, such as attention, memory and learning. It was hypothesized that unusual sensory experiences were a primary characteristic feature of autism able to account for the basic symptoms of the condition, considered to be essential in the current diagnostic classifications. Thus, abnormal perceptions might give rise to high levels of anxiety, this in turn results in obsessive or compulsive behaviours, thus making the more commonly accepted criteria, in fact, secondary developmental problems (Delacato 1974). Though the syndrome of autism is far too complex a phenomenon to be explained by differences in sensory experiences, sensory perceptual problems do play an important role in autism (Bogdashina 2003), and the sensory perceptual theory is worth investigating further.

Other theories

Recently there have appeared other numerous theories aiming to explain autism. Here are just a few examples of these theories.

An 'experiencing self' theory

Powell and Jordan (1993) put forward the idea that the difficulty for autistic children of establishing an 'experiencing self' is one of the fundamental deficits of autism. Their idea arose from the identification of problems autistic individuals experience in 'personal episodic memory'. They can easily recall events and things happening to others, but find it extremely difficult to recall an event in which they have participated, if no cues are provided to trigger it (Jordan and Powell 1992). The mechanism for developing this sense of self has not yet been identified.

Autism as a disorder of affective and social relations

Hobson's (1989) theory is one of the intersubjectivity theories of autism. It develops further Kanner's original idea of autism as 'disturbances of affective contact' which is reflected in 'children's *inability to relate themselves* in the ordinary way to people and situations from the beginning of life' (Kanner 1943, p.242).

Autism as an extreme version of the male brain

In his book *The Essential Difference* (2003a) Simon Baron-Cohen proposed a provocative theory that autism can be understood as an extreme version of the male brain.

Baron-Cohen distinguishes two cognitive characteristics that differ in most men and women:

- emphasizing – a type of intelligence which is used to understand people (female feature)

- systemizing – a type of intelligence which is used to understand things and how they work (mostly male characteristic).

While most people possess both, some studies suggest that women seem to be slightly more empathic than men; that is, they are more likely to recognize, and respond to, the emotions of others. Men, on the other hand, are on average slightly better at understanding systems (for example, they are slightly better at mathematics, engineering and computer technology). According to Baron-Cohen, autism (which is more prevalent in males) can be an extreme version of the 'male brain', with good systemizing abilities but an inability to relate easily to people.

For 'horizontal reading':

2.5 – pp.126–137
3.5 – pp.202–207
4.5 – pp.265–283

1.6

Treatments

It has been estimated there are more than 450 different treatments for autism! And every year more new therapies appear. Some aspects of different therapies overlap. There is much debate about which of the available therapies are effective. Special reports on evaluation and comparison of different approaches have been prepared (Dawson and Osterling 1997; Jordan, Jones and Murray 1998). These reports conclude that no one approach has been proven to be the best approach for all individuals with ASDs, as autism is so variable and each particular child may benefit from a particular approach at a particular time. Besides, an inspired and dedicated teacher/carer can often succeed with whatever approach they believe in (Jordan *et al.* 1998). The following is a very brief look at some of the many approaches currently in practice.

General autism treatment (therapy) categories:

- Biomedical (medication, diet, food and vitamin supplements).

- Neurosensory (patterning – Doman–Delacato method, sensory integration therapy, auditory integration training, Irlen method).

- Psychodynamic (psychoanalysis, holding therapy).

- Interactive approaches (options, floor time).

- Behavioural/educational (ABA, TEACCH, daily life therapy).

- Cognitive approaches.

- Communication/language therapies (speech–language therapy, PECS, sign language, FC).

- Others (music therapy, dolphin therapy, etc.).

Note, however, that it is important to remember that there are no 'pure category' approaches, as these treatments use methods from other categories as well. Some approaches are very narrow, focusing on one or two specific aspects of autism (for example, AIT, Irlen method), others 'borrow' certain techniques from different approaches (for instance, TEACCH), still others use 'different names' to present the existing approaches as new ones (possibly adding some bits and pieces), for example SIT, Intensive Interaction, etc.

Biomedical (pharmacological) approaches

No medication can correct the brain structures or impaired functioning. However, researchers have found that some drugs developed to treat other disorders are sometimes effective. Medications used to treat anxiety and depression may be helpful for some autistic people with high levels of anxiety. (However, it is important to remember about possible side effects, and implement the drugs very carefully under constant supervision of a doctor.) These drugs include:

- fluoxetine (Prozac)
- fluvoxamine (Luvox)
- setraline (Zoloft)
- clomipramine (Anafranil).

Risperidone commonly used to treat schizophrenia has been used with autistic patients to control serious aggression, self-injury and ritualistic behaviours. While it has been reported successful in some cases, in other cases it does cause side effects including menstrual irregularities, weight gain, abnormal breast enlargement in males, heart palpitations, constipation, fatigue, low blood pressure and dizziness.

Piracetam has been used with autistic children with some positive effects – an increase in the attention span and general cognition capabilities, awareness and responsiveness to interaction. The main side effect seems to be hyperactivity caused by high-dose piracetam overstimulation.

To reduce hyperactivity in autism, stimulant drugs like Ritalin are often prescribed (typically used for children with ADHD). However, sometimes beta-blockers (for example, propranolol) may help reduce arousal and anxiety without the side effects often caused by Ritalin. We must remember, however, that any drug may cause unwanted side effects and should be administered with caution.

Vitamin B$_6$ with magnesium is said to stimulate brain activity and increase awareness, attention and general well-being. The prediction that high doses might help people with autism has not been scientifically confirmed yet, but quite a few successful anecdotal outcomes have been reported. Further study is needed.

There have been cases of individuals with ASDs who display food intolerance, food allergies and the possibility of candida albicans. These problems can be controlled through certain drugs and diets. Food intolerances and food sensitivities (quite common in autism) are addressed via special diets. Some individuals show dramatic changes in their behaviours after certain food items have been removed from their diets. It is believed that abnormal peptides (detected in the urine of autistic individuals) may be due to the inability to break down gluten (found, for instance, in wheat, barley and oats) and casein (dairy products) into amino acids. When these substances are removed from the diet, there may be positive changes in behaviour.

Neurosensory approaches

Patterning (Doman–Delacato method)

In the 1950s and 1960s, a group of researchers (Temple Fay, Carl Delacato, Glen and Robert Doman and others) at the Institute for the Achievement of Human Potential, USA studied the link between sensory processing problems and intellectual disabilities. This method of rehabilitation has become known as the Doman–Delacato method or patterning. This approach is based on the theory of hemispheric dominance and the relationship of individual sequential phylogenic development. The treatment is offered on the premise that there are significant developmental stages of neurological organization which cannot be bypassed, and the child must master the functional activities at different levels of development before moving on. According to this theory many cases of intellectual difficulties, behaviour disorders and autism are caused by brain damage or 'poor neurological organization' that can be effectively treated by 'retraining' the brain and 'patterning' the movements 'from outside' to 'organize' the way the brain works. As there has not been research evidence of complete 'recovery', the Doman–Delacato method was heavily criticized and the policy statement of the American Academy of Pediatrics was issued in 1965 that discredited the treatment altogether. However, strangely enough, many researchers have developed their treatments on the basis of some of the concepts of patterning and normalization of the senses (especially in the field of occupational therapy) without having been 'condemned' by official organizations. The trick that seems to allow these 'new' approaches to be accepted is to use the ideas without mentioning the name of their originators (see Chapter 4.6).

In the 1970s Delacato left the Institute to concentrate his research on the treatment of autistic children. He outlined his theory of autism and its treatment in his book *The Ultimate Stranger: The Autistic Child* (1974). It is based on the belief that children with autism are unable to deal with the stimulation coming into their brains from the outside world because one or more of their intake channels (sight, sound, smell, taste, feel) is deficient in some way. Delacato proposed a therapy aiming to stimulate the development of a disorganized nervous system. According to Delacato, neurological problems causing autistic behaviours ('sensoryisms') are treatable through rehabilitative processes.

While Delacato's treatment deals mostly with five senses (sight, hearing, tactility, smell and taste) *Sensory Integration Therapy* (Ayres 1979) (based on a similar theoretical foundation) was originally used to treat dysfunctional tactile, vestibular (balance) and proprioceptive (body awareness) senses. The goal of sensory integration therapy is described as facilitating the development of the nervous system's ability to process sensory input in a more normal way. Sensory integration approaches may be of various types:

- *multi-sensory integration* – the use of senses in an integrated way, i.e. the use of several sensory modalities simultaneously, for example look and listen, rather than being single-channelled

- *desensitization* that provides more tolerance, increases speech and eye contact and decreases stereotypical, self-injurious and aggressive behaviours. To achieve desensitization special sensory diets are prescribed that involve a planned and scheduled activity programme implemented by an occupational therapist. A sensory diet stimulates the 'near' senses (tactile, vestibular and proprioceptive) with a combination of alerting, organizing and calming techniques.

Treatments have been developed addressing processing problems of different sensory modalities. Visual problems are addressed via tinted glasses (Irlen method) or visual training (for example, wearing prism lenses and performing movement exercises).

Irlen method

Perceptual problems caused by light sensitivity were identified by Helen Irlen who worked with adults with dyslexia. Irlen called the cluster of symptoms of this dysfunction scotopic sensitivity syndrome (now known as Irlen syndrome) (Irlen 1989, 1991, 1997). It has turned out that similar symptoms are displayed by some autistic people who have visual processing difficulties. Irlen has developed methods to treat this visual dysfunction: the use of coloured overlays to improve reading and tinted glasses to improve visual perception of the environment. It is believed that tinted lenses (the colour of which is very individual for different people) filter out those frequencies of the light spectrum to which a person may be uniquely sensitive (Irlen 1997). This method seems to work for those autistic individuals whose visual problems are overwhelming and helps slow down the incoming visual information and reduce the overload. However, it does not 'cure' autism but rather provides tools to normalize 'reception' of visual information.

Behavioural optometry is based on the assumption that vision may be 'retrained' mechanically by the use of special prisms and eye exercises.

Auditory integration training (AIT)

This method is aimed at 'retraining' the ear to reduce hypersensitivity to sounds. There are two main types of AIT, the Tomatis method and the Berard AIT. The AIT procedure involves:

- audiometric testing to find out whether the person has 'auditory peaks' that can be reduced or eliminated by AIT

- the filtering out of sounds at certain selected frequencies in accordance with the individual audiogram; where an accurate audiogram cannot be obtained, the basic modulation system without specific filters is used

- the modulation of the music by alternatively dampening and enhancing, on a random basis, the bass and treble musical output; each session lasts for 30 minutes, two sessions a day for ten days

- another assessment of the person's hearing after five days to find out whether the auditory peaks are still present and whether there is a need to readjust filters. If the person has speech and/or language problems, after half the sessions the volume level for the left ear is reduced to stimulate the language development in the left hemisphere.

After AIT the person should perceive all the frequencies equally well and have no auditory peaks. Both the Tomatis and Berard methods have been reported to be beneficial in hypersensitive hearing, and have been used with people with autism, dyslexia, intellectual disabilities, ADHD and others. Some successful stories have been widely advertised, but in many cases the improvement is often short-lived and there is still much controversy in the reports of the AIT efficiency.

Psychodynamic therapy

Psychodynamic therapy is an umbrella term for a group of therapies with similar theoretical foundations. It is based on the belief that a person's feelings, emotions and behaviours are directly influenced by past events (for example, psychological trauma in infancy can have long-lasting effects in adulthood). Therefore, the main aim of the psychodynamic approach is the exploration of the patient's past in order to make connections between past events and present behaviours and feelings. It is believed that when these connections have been identified, the person can make conscious changes in the behaviours.

Psychoanalysis

Psychoanalysis as a treatment for autism was popular in the past (and still is, in some countries). Psychoanalysts consider parents (especially mothers) to be the cause of the condition in their children. The core assumption of the therapy was that it was possible to 'cure' autism if the child is removed from 'refrigerator parents', or parents are taught how to form 'proper bonding' with the child. Psychoanalysis has been proved to be ineffective (and sometimes even harmful) in the treatment of autism.

Holding therapy

In the late 1980s 'holding therapy' was advertised as a miracle cure for autism. Dr Martha Welch, the originator of the therapy, argued that faulty attachment between mother and child brings fear in the child and this, in turn, leads to the child's withdrawal and autism. When attachment is made more secure, the child can progress along his or her path of development. The holding therapy is seen as strengthening the bonds of love between a mother and her child which are the foundation of happy and healthy development. It is assumed that when held safely in its mother's arms, the autistic child learns to overcome the fear of direct eye contact and close attachment. This helps the child to release previously inhibited feelings of anger and rage. Despite the child's attempts to get free the mother holds the child firmly, supposedly giving the message that the mother's love is so strong that whatever he or she does, whatever his or her feelings are, she can take care of him or her. The experience of holding therapy has been traumatic for both the child and the mother but the parents were told this was the price of a 'cure'. There is no evidence whatsoever that forced 'holding' can create loving bonding between the child and the mother, to say nothing of a 'cure' for autism.

Interactive approaches

Interactive approaches highlight the importance of developing a relationship and communication between the child and the carers. At present there are several different interactive approaches: options, floor time, gentle teaching, and others.

Options

When their child Raun was diagnosed with autism and was given a very bleak prognosis, Barry and Samarhia Kaufman refused to accept the verdict. They formulated three areas of apparent dysfunction in their son: first, his ability to perceive and digest data from people and situations appeared to be severely inhibited. Second, Raun did not seem capable of using whatever information he could absorb in a manner meaningful to others. And third, he had designed internal systems to stimulate himself, which drew him further inside:

> All of Raun's sensory intake systems appeared to be intact, yet he could turn off his sight or hearing at will. He demonstrated extraordinary capabilities. He could cut off perceptions and successfully, as well as

selectively, nullify his sensory apparatus... Yet his reasons for throwing his internal switches on or off at any given moment remained a mystery. (Kaufman 1995, p.100)

The parents started to imitate Raun, hoping in this way to find some insight or understanding, and letting him know that they were with him. If he could not follow them, they wanted to follow him. Slowly Raun grew more responsive and alert and started to initiate and guide his own sessions. Now Raun (who is reported to have recovered from autism) is a passionate advocate of the 'options' approach ('Son-Rise') – a home-based treatment programme for autism, developed by Barry and Samarhia Kaufman (1986) based on their personal experiences with their autistic son.

Floor time

Stanley Greenspan (Greenspan, Wieder and Simons 1998) developed the concept 'floor time' – time when carers 'join the child's world' by imitating his or her activities and following the child's lead. Starting with this mutual, shared engagement, the carers try to draw the child into 'their world' by creating interactions ('opening and closing circles of communication') by taking turns, interpreting the child's seemingly meaningless behaviours as if they were communicative and meaningful. The primary goal of this intervention is to create sustained two-way communication which then leads to the child's developing social and cognitive skills.

Other intensive interaction approaches have sprung to life recently. They are based on the same principles and are described as a technique based on a primary infant/mother interaction (see, for example, Nind and Hewett 1994) but introduced as 'new approaches'.

Behavioural and educational approaches

The 'behaviourist' approaches follow Skinner's model of understanding behaviours by studying 'responses' to controlled 'stimuli' (Skinner 1971). According to this view, in order to modify undesirable behaviour, it is necessary to analyse its constituent parts which can be retrained by 'operant conditioning' – if the response is appropriate, it is rewarded; if it is inappropriate, it is punished or ignored. Behavioural modification approach are based on observation and recording of certain behaviours and highlighting environmental triggers that may be amended to change the behaviours. In the early days of behaviour modification, punishments were quite cruel – electric shock, cold water, etc. The most widely spread behavioural approach is ABA (or the Lovaas method). Other approaches 'borrow' some behavioural techniques and incorporate them into their programmes (for example, TEACCH, PECS).

Applied Behavioural Analysis (ABA)

ABA, sometimes referred to as the Lovaas approach, focuses mainly on early intervention (pre-school years). Dr Ivar Lovaas pioneered behavioural interventions for autistic children in the 1960s. The underlying principles of ABA are based on Skinnerian operant conditioning and behavioural discrete trials. The methods involve time-intensive, highly-structured, repetitive drills in which a child is given a command and rewarded each time he responds correctly. Behavioural discrete trial programmes start with achieving general compliance – training to get the child to sit in a chair, make eye contact and imitate non-verbal behaviour in response to verbal commands. Speech is taught as a verbal behaviour via verbal imitation, following one-step commands, receptive discrimination of objects, pictures, etc., and expressive labelling in response to questions. However, a discrete trial approach has proven to be limited – the language 'trained' during the discrete trial fails to be generalized to other environments and to be used spontaneously. It is an intensive (40 hours a week), home-based programme with one-to-one trial training. Parents and other adult helpers share the delivery of the programme. Usually, it consists of several stages:

- *The first year.* The programme focuses on reducing self-stimulatory or aggressive behaviour, developing compliance, encouraging imitation and play.

- *The second year.* More emphasis is placed on expressive language and interactive play.

- *The third year.* The emphasis moves to emotional expression, pre-academic tasks and observational learning.

Challenging behaviours are addressed by using such strategies as ignoring, time out and shaping. Lovaas recommends that intervention should begin as early as possible and ideally before four years. With intensive 40 hours a week and early intervention, it was claimed that nearly half of the children (47%) in his study achieved normal educational and intellectual functioning and were successfully mainstreamed into standard classrooms (Lovaas 1987). However, the analysis of the studies shows that these results demonstrate the effects of intensity rather than the treatment itself (Jordan *et al.* 1998). Besides, very often, behaviours learned in one setting cannot be easily transferred to another.

TEACCH

Division TEACCH (Treatment and Education of Autistic and related Communication handicapped CHildren) was founded at the University of North Carolina in 1972. It is a structured teaching approach based on visually mediated learning and structuring of the environment, time and activities to cue behaviour. This is a state-wide community-based programme for children and adults with autism and other related communication disabilities. The major goal of the programme is to provide continuity of services throughout the person's life. TEACCH philosophy is based on the recognition that autistic individuals perceive the world differently, use different thinking techniques and, therefore, have a different mode of learning.

Like ABA, TEACCH applies behavioural methods. There are, however, important differences in these two approaches:

- The philosophy underlying ABA methods is that normalcy is possible because all skills can be taught. TEACCH, on the contrary, emphasizes that certain difficulties (for example, language comprehension) are a lifelong deficit, hence the focus should be on functional skills (non-verbal communication, self-help and vocational skills).

- Unlike the Lovaas method, TEACCH is much less intensive and is seen as a lifelong learning ('from the cradle to the grave').

Daily life therapy (Higashi School)

'Daily life' therapy was developed by Dr Kiyo Kitahari at the Musashino Higashi Gakuen in Tokyo. This approach is based on age (rather than developmental) level and on group activities in order to prepare the child for integration into the mainstream. The Higashi method emphasizes vigorous physical exercises, arts, communication and social skills. This method has been adopted in a school in Boston, Massachusetts, and now is spreading into other countries.

Cognitive approaches

Cognitive approaches have been integrated into other educational approaches (for example, TEACCH). The strategies always start with a thorough assessment of each individual's strengths and weaknesses in order to find out the right level of challenge. The assessment includes:

- imitation
- perception
- fine motor skills
- gross motor skills
- eye–hand coordination
- non-verbal cognitive performance
- verbal abilities.

Identified domains of strengths are used to compensate the weaknesses. The teaching techniques take into account the preferred sensory modality (usually, but not necessarily, visual modality) and the necessity of structure and predictability.

Cognitive behaviour therapy seems to be an effective treatment for the mood disorders associated with Asperger syndrome. However, more research is needed to evaluate it and identify specific modifications for AS clients.

Language/communication

Speech–language therapy

Though autistic children have difficulties with language development and understanding, the traditional speech–language therapy has proven to be inefficient or even useless. They need to learn not how to speak the language but rather how to use language to communicate. There are several approaches designed specifically to develop communication skills. The most widely used methods are PECS and sign language.

Picture Exchange Communication System (PECS)

PECS was developed by Dr Andrew Bondy, a psychologist, and Lori Frost, a speech and language therapist in the Delaware Autistic Program, to help individuals with autism and other developmental disabilities acquire communicative skills (Bondy and Frost 1994). This system is based on principles of intentional communication and visual aids in development of communication. Though these principles had been worked out long before PECS was introduced, PECS presents them as an augmentative/alternative training package, to be used with children and adults with autism and other communication disorders in a systematic and prescribed way. The fundamental principle of the system is to teach children communication (not just language) from the very beginning. The main techniques used are identification of reinforcers to motivate a child's communication (usually food, drinks or favourite activities), prompting, shaping and fading.

Advantages of PECS and its differences from other pictorial systems of communication are:

- From the very beginning the interaction is intentional. (Children are taught to express their needs to adults who then meet those needs.)

- It is the child who initiates the interaction.

- Communication is functional and meaningful.

As the main goal of this approach is to teach spontaneous communication, direct verbal prompts such as 'What do you want?', 'Show me what you want' and 'What is it?' are avoided. From the very beginning children are taught such social and communicative skills as to approach and interact with another person spontaneously. There are several stages of introducing the PECS method, each stage building on the previous one. PECS has been proved successful for those who either do not use (and/or understand) speech or are echolalic. However, like with any other approach in autism, PECS does not work for every child.

Sign language

Sign language (e.g., Makaton) is often used with children and adults with autism. The advantages of sign language for autistic people are:

- signing is both visual and kinaesthetic

- signs can be taught through physical prompt and shaping that is beneficial for children with motor and executive function problems

- sign language is 'portable' and does not need any equipment
- sign language is a linguistic system and may stimulate acquisition of verbal language.

The disadvantages of sign language are:

- sign language is difficult for those who do not understand verbal language
- sign language is not understood by many people.

The outcomes of using sign language vary considerably: some children, after having acquired facility in sign language, learn to speak verbal language, whereas others never learn to use more than a few signs and remain mute.

Facilitated communication (FC)

FC is a method of providing physical and emotional support to individuals with severe communication problems as they type their messages. The FC technique has become widely known thanks to the work of Rosemary Crossley in Australia and Douglas Biklen in the USA. It is a very controversial approach, and to date there is a lack of quantitative research evidence validating FC. However, there are several qualitative studies indicating that some individuals with ASDs have developed independent communication skills via training in FC (Biklen 1990).

There are other therapies (for example, music therapy, dolphin therapy, etc.) which show some anecdotal success in improving social and communicative skills of autistic individuals but there is no therapy that 'fits' all autistic people.

Is there a cure?

There is a general consensus that there is no cure for autism, though there may be remarkable improvements in all aspects of functioning. Some sensational claims of 'recovery' from autism have both their believers and sceptics.

For 'horizontal reading':

2.6 – pp.138–161
3.6 – pp.208–219
4.6 – pp.284–294

1.7

Miscellany

Thoughts to Share

The 'Triad' or the 'Quartet'?

Working and living with autism I look for *logical* explanations in anything I come across. The central problem in autism is described as a Triad of Impairments affecting social interaction, social communication and imagination. This Triad is always accompanied by a limited, narrow, repetitive pattern of activities/behaviours (Wing 1993). I have always wondered, if these behaviours *always* accompany the Triad of Impairments, would it not be more logical to call it not the Triad but the Quartet of Impairments? In her (very good) book *The Autistic Spectrum: A Guide for Parents and Professionals* (1996) Lorna Wing explains that 'this aspect of autistic behaviour makes most sense if seen as the other side of the coin of impairment of imagination': if the person cannot enjoy social activities which involve creative thinking, etc., 'the only thing left is the reassurance of repeating those activities that do give some pleasure' (p.45). So, are the repetitive behaviours caused only by impairments in imagination? *Just a thought.*

Treating symptoms

The Triad of Impairments is very useful for recognizing and diagnosing ASD. However, it is important to remember that the Triad describes *behaviours* or *symptoms*. These behaviours are 'above the water' (Iceberg theory). The Triad gives clinicians a wonderful tool to identify people with ASDs and refer them to the services and treatments they need, but the Triad does not identify the causes of the behaviours. Nevertheless, most treatments have been developed to address the 'triadic' deficits, instead of 'digging deeper' and treating the possible causes. Instead of climbing around the top of the iceberg, shall we learn how to dive? *Just a thought.*

Is there a 'pure autism'?

In her book *Autism: Explaining the Enigma* (1989/2003), Uta Frith introduced a thought-provoking idea of 'pure autism' (Frith 1989) and the 'core of autism' (Frith 2003). According to the author, the abnormalities in (pure) autism are 'subtle and limited to some mental functions only, and again only to some aspects of these' (Frith 2003, p.205). All the rest is secondary. If we strip away various features that are not part of the core autism, we will see that

> most aspects of the ability to handle objects and to perceive the world through the senses are normal [in autism]; and so are the capacities to form abstract concepts, categorize events, understand spatial relation-ships, know about cause and effect, and make logical inferences...even in the core symptoms of social interaction and communication a great deal of competence exists. (Frith 2003, pp.205–206)

Uta Frith (2003) argues that as autism has a variety of manifestations and can co-occur with other developmental disorders, some impairments do not con-stitute the core part of autism and should be stripped away in the search for a common denominator. The impairments that should be excluded from the core part of autism are seen in children who 'do not have normal appearance, cannot move well, are clumsy when handling objects, have problems with sensory perception, do not speak, or have considerable problems in abstract thinking' (Frith 2003, p.206). This approach can lead to re-defining the con-dition altogether. Uta Frith (2003) revives the idea of the homunculus (the last visible self – self-aware self) as a common denominator of autism. The last visible self may be 'asleep or absent in autism' (Frith 2003, p.218). Shall we 'wake it up' or help them develop it, even if artificially, 'by inserting conscious and explicit rules' (p.218)? The problem with this last visible self as a common denominator in autism is that the self-aware self emerges only gradually in older children and adolescents, while autism is present from or even before birth. It seems unlikely that autism can be simplified to one subtle abnormal-ity. The brain studies so far have failed to locate the brain region, the damage to which could cause autism. Or is there a single definable denominator that is waiting to be found? *Just a thought.*

'Quasi-autism'/'Pseudoautism'

We can see 'autistic symptomatology' in cases of sensory deprivation or sensory impairments. These cases are often described as 'quasi-' or 'pseudo-autism'. The difference between 'true' and 'pseudoautism' lies in possible 're-covery' from 'quasi-autism' if appropriate sensory stimulation is provided, in contrast to 'true' autism where, despite stimulation, there is no complete 're-covery'. Well-known examples of acquiring pseudoautism (and recovering from it) are young Romanian orphans adopted by UK families. Michael Rutter and colleagues (1999) followed the development of 165 Romanian babies (most under 12 months of age) in the adopted families. These children suffered from physical and social deprivation in their home country, where they were kept in orphanages with minimum care and human contact. On the arrival to the UK, the children were assessed and many 'autistic symptoms' were reported, including preoccupation with sensations of smell, taste and touch, impaired language development and social unresponsiveness. With the intervention they received from their adoptive families, the majority of these children showed a remarkable 'recovery' and were indistinguishable from normally developing children of their age. Those who were over 12 months old when they arrived in the UK (i.e. those who experienced deprivation for much longer), however, remained slow and idiosyncratic in their development and could not easily catch up with their peers. Is it possible that timing deter-mines if the impaired (by sensory deprivation) development may become irre-versible?

Another example of pseudoautism is the development of visually/auditory impaired children. Young children who are congenitally blind display such 'autistic' symptoms as impairments in social interaction, commu-nication, idiosyncratic language development, and stereotyped movements (Cass 1996; Gense and Gense 1994). The distortion of auditory input during a critical phase of early development may be one of the causes of impairments in language, thinking and communication development (Tanguay and Edwards 1982). Bearing these examples in mind, is it possible that babies born with distorted sensory perception and/or who learn very early in life to protect themselves from painful and overwhelming stimulation by self-imposed sensory deprivation may develop symptomatology of autism? The timing of intervention may play a crucial part in the child's development and type of autism. *Just a thought.*

Is disability a cultural phenomenon?

Can low-functioning autistic individuals live independently?

Despite the fact that autism was first officially identified and described in 1943 (Kanner), it is common knowledge that autistic people existed well before that date. Now, we try to identify autism in history using the clinical and non-clinical descriptions available. One of the most famous cases is that of Victor, the 'wild boy of Aveyron'. Thanks to detailed accounts of Jean Marc Gaspar Itard we learn the fascinating history of a boy who was found in a forest in France. The boy was first seen in 1797 in the woods near Lacaune. The villagers caught him twice in 1797 and 1798, but the boy managed to escape. He was captured again in early 1800, and this time was held. The boy (thought to be about 12 years old) was examined and labelled as 'idiot'/'imbecile'. Itard, a young physician at the time, took on the challenge of studying Victor's condition and rehabilitating him. Based on Itard's reports on the boy's descriptions and reactions to intervention and other papers written about him, it has been suggested that Victor might have had autism (Frith 2003; Lane 1977). As Victor never acquired speech (just a few words to ask for food), and maintained his autistic behaviour that could not be much improved despite systematic education, he would have been described today as 'low-functioning'. The question is, how could a low-functioning autistic boy survive alone for at least two years in the wild and could not live independently in a society, among people? Did social rules and conventions disable him? *Just a thought.*

Are high-functioning people with autism and AS disabled by society?

Concept of disability is relative to a particular environment, both cultural and biological. If environmental expectations change, or they are put in a different environment, people with HFA/AS may not necessarily be seen as disabled (Baron-Cohen 2000). In the present society, to be successful means to be able to socialize and talk 'sweetly'. Many employers, especially in non-industrial and non-technological fields, prefer 'sweet-talking', polite, politically correct employees. They might not be very clever, but pleasant in company. As such institutions 'do not deal with rocket science', it does not matter if the employees are incompetent in their field, it is more important that they comply with social rules. In this context, people with high-functioning autism and AS have no chance to succeed. They may be capable and inventive, but still they will be 'socially disabled' and, hence, unemployed in the field of their expertise. *Just a thought.*

Increase in prevalence of ASDs – a positive selective process?

Professor Simon Baron-Cohen (2000) gives a very interesting (if controversial) interpretation of the possible increase in the prevalence of ASDs – as an evolutionary change to accommodate the changes in the environment. The computer revolution in the twentieth century has created demands in abilities to systemize and logically solve problems (which is exactly what people with high-functioning autism and AS are good at). Therefore, the genes carrying advantageous cognitive profile (HFA/AS) may be positively reinforced (Baron-Cohen 2000). This hypothesis is supported by the findings of Dr James Flynn, whose research provided evidence for rising IQ scores of abstract and visuo-spatial skills in many countries. (His original report analysed the trend of rising IQs in 14 countries – Flynn 1987.)

'Recovery' from autism

There have been reported cases of full recovery from autism following different treatments (for example, Kaufman and Kaufman 1986; Maurice 1994; Stehli 1991). These seem to contradict widely accepted assumptions that autism cannot be cured. To defend this assumption some researchers argue that those who 'recover' might be misdiagnosed in the first place, and actually were not autistic. Others claim the recovery is possible, as these children have become indistinguishable from their normally developing peers. However, how can we account for many adults who are diagnosed only in their thirties or forties (and who have been 'indistinguishable' from their peers and did not know they were autistic before the diagnosis)? As they were born with ASD but not diagnosed, they did not think they were autistic/AS. They 'discover' their condition only late in life and the diagnosis helps them understand the (invisible to others) difficulties they have experienced. Are they 'self-recovered' in childhood but feeling they are still 'ill' in adulthood? *Just a thought.*

For 'horizontal reading':

2.7 – pp.162–173
3.7 – pp.220–226
4.7 – pp.295–300

Further Reading

Some sources of information are more reliable than others. The research on autism brings new information every year and what was a fact yesterday may well be a myth today or tomorrow. The following resources provide a good starting point for gaining information but it is important to update your knowledge and follow research findings in journals that provide the latest data in the field of ASDs.

General information on ASDs

There have been published (and will be published) numerous 'Complete Guides' of autism. However, if it had been possible to write a *complete* guide, one would not need more than one! Unfortunately, it is impossible. All existing 'guides' usually cover the same information (sometimes, in the same order: 'what is autism', history, diagnosis, causes, theories, treatments, practical recommendations, etc.), the differences being in writing style, anecdotes and the date of publication. Most recent ones are likely to contain information about the latest research. One must be aware, however, that these books are written for those with no or very little knowledge of autism, and simplified to make them easy to read. Some information may be incorrect or just speculative to make it an interesting read for the general public. For example, such statements as 'Some or all of their [autistic] senses are one hundred times more sensitive than in others, and therefore, they process the environment differently from neurotypicals' is a new myth about autism. It is true that many (if not all) autistic people experience sensory processing problems, but to limit them to hypersensitivities is very misleading, to say the least. And to rate the sensitivities at one hundred times may be both overestimated and underestimated. These 'complete guide' books are useful to get a brief overview of the condition. But one guide is enough, whichever you choose. It is a good starting point for those who are new to the field of autism. For more detailed information it is better to look for books devoted to specific aspects of ASDs.

There are hundreds (if not thousands) of books on autism. But as one professional (who has read many and is always looking for new information) told me once,

> It's so difficult to find an autism book with something new. About 95 per cent of books describing autism contain the same information 'wrapped up' into different formats. You take 100 books, read one, put 94 aside, and enjoy the five that are left (personal communication).

The following books are outstanding:

Wing, L. (1996) *The Autistic Spectrum: A Guide for Parents and Professionals.* London: Constable.
It is a classic book on ASDs and well worth reading. It is always better to get information first hand. Lorna Wing is one of the most recognized experts of ASD who has 'shaped' the definition and diagnosis of the condition. The book is non-technical with explanations and practical recommendations.

Baron-Cohen, S. and Bolton, P. (1993) *Autism: The Facts.* Oxford: Oxford University Press.
In a non-technical way, this book gives a simple summary of autism and explains what is known about the condition in a very traditional, 'classic' manner. It covers the recognition and diagnosis of autism, its possible causes, psychological problems, treatments and educational approaches available.

Attwood, T. (1998) *Asperger's Syndrome: A Guide for Parents and Professionals.* London: Jessica Kingsley Publishers.
A good starting point for acquiring knowledge about AS. The book provides a description and analysis of AS characteristics and practical strategies to address challenging behaviours. It covers such issues as diagnosis, social behaviour, language, interests and routine, motor clumsiness, cognition and sensory sensitivity. The last chapter answers the questions most frequently asked by those who live or work with individuals with AS.

Waterhouse, S. (1999) *A Positive Approach to Autism.* London: Jessica Kingsley Publishers.
Another book (out of the 5%). This book discusses the same issues (the symptoms, behaviours, possible causes, diagnosis, and treatments), *but* the information provided is well-researched and referenced, and the author does not 'go with the flow', but investigates the condition, discusses theories and ideas, and puts forward hypotheses. She does not limit her exploration with a few issues, nor does she just describe different aspects.

Stella Waterhouse discusses many facets of autism and connects seemingly unconnected problems in order to provide a holistic picture of the syndrome.

Peeters, T. and Gillberg, C. (1999) *Autism: Medical and Educational Aspects.* London: Whurr Publishers.
A highly readable, informative and accessible book which introduces the medical background to autism and discusses current educational approaches to helping children with ASDs.

Howlin, P. (1998) *Children with Autism and Asperger Syndrome: A Guide for Practitioners and Carers.* London: John Wiley and Sons.
The book is a practical treatment guide for people working with children with autism and AS. It covers general information, diagnostic criteria, causes, a brief overview of educational approaches, family issues and the range of provisions available for children.

Happé, F. (1994) *Autism: An Introduction to Psychological Theory.* London: UCL Press.
This book provides a very good account of the three dominant theories of autism – Theory of Mind, weak central coherence theory and executive dysfunction.

Theory of Mind

Baron-Cohen, S. (1995) *Mindblindness: An Essay on Autism and Theory of Mind.* Boston: The MIT Press.
The book presents the Theory of Mind explanation of autism.

'Extreme male brain' theory

Baron-Cohen, S. (2003) *The Essential Difference.* London: Penguin Books.

(For specific information on different treatments see Further Reading in Part 4.)

Part 2
Autism from the Inside (Internal View)

Definitions and Classifications

There is agreement among autistic individuals that autism is a spectrum condition. However, the spectral character of autism is seen differently – not as described behaviours but rather as identified underlying problems. It is recognized that autism may affect different combinations of functions within all people with the condition. For example, in some people it may bring difficulty with emotional information, while in other cases it may cause problems with language, sensory processing or there may be combinations of these (Williams 1996). Autism never manifests itself in the same way twice, as there are many types of it (O'Neill 1999). Sometimes ASDs are viewed as many 'autisms' caused by different problems but leading to the same behaviours 'on the surface' and there may be different types of autism in different individuals, and sometimes more than one type of autism present in the same person (Williams 1996). According to Donna Williams (Undated, c), for example, autism can be about severe sensory-perceptual issues which can constitute a very different sensory perceptual and cognitive reality; or autism can be about being controlled by involuntary behaviours and extreme impulse control issues that dictate the nature of interaction and communication. Donna does not see 'autism' (as a collection of symptoms) but rather compounding collections of autism-related problems and different adaptations and compensations to different types of autism-related problems, when any problem affecting one system of functioning will cause a weakening in another system as it tries to compensate (Williams 1996). Temple Grandin (2000) subdivides autism into two broad categories – Kanner/Asperger types (here: HF autism) and the epileptic/regressive types. High-functioning types can range from individuals with rigid thinking patterns to people with more normal thinking patterns with lots of anxiety and sensory sensitivity problems, while individuals with the regressive/epileptic types often have more obvious neurological problems, and their ability to understand speech is poor. Many regressive/epileptic children are labelled low-functioning and have low IQ scores. Some may be retarded, but others may receive a low-functioning label because their sensory processing problems make communication difficult (Grandin 2000). Jared Blackburn (1999) suggests there may be cerebellar-attentional, primary-sensory and miscellaneous brain damage types of autism.

In contrast to the continuum of social impairments in autism, Temple Grandin puts forward another type of continuum – at one end of the spectrum, autism is primarily a cognitive disorder, and at the other end, it is primarily a sensory processing disorder:

> At the severely impaired sensory processing end, many children may be diagnosed as having disintegrative disorder. At a midpoint along the spectrum, autistic symptoms appear to be caused by equal amounts of cognitive and sensory problems. There can be mild and severe cases at all points along the continuum. Both the severity and the ratio of these two components are variable, and each case of autism is different. (Grandin 1996a, p.58)

It is worth considering the problem of the definition of autism from the perspective of those who have it. We may roughly classify the definitions of autism suggested by autistic individuals into three groups:

- neutral descriptions
- descriptions emphasizing positive characteristics
- descriptions emphasizing negative characteristics.

The way autism is defined (neutral/positive/negative descriptions) depends on the attitude of the person to the condition, which, in turn, depends on the acquired compensatory strategies and adjustment of the environment. Very often, a positive attitude is not the attempt to idealize the condition, but rather the attempt to understand it, cope with it and take advantage of it. For example:

> After years of torment, rejection, and abuse from many people, I've learnt to feel pride in my differences. I've chosen to develop my own self. I am not a girl to follow others, nor am I a leader. I go my own way. I know that I'm very unique, and that fact makes others wonder about me, or even fear or condemn. Society has always tried to convert those

who stand out from the crowds. Yes, despite the abuse, I prefer to be who I am, for being different can be marvellous. (O'Neill 2000)

Many autistic individuals describe both positive and negative sides of having ASDs. It is interesting that negative effects are often attributed to environmental factors (see Chapter 2.7).

It should be noted that one and the same person may give both positive and negative definitions of the condition due to their particular circumstances at the time. The fact is, depending on strategies and adaptations the person acquires and the support they get, they may experience autism differently – sometimes it may feel comfortable, and at other times it may be very frustrating. In contrast to official definitions of autism as outer behaviours (the more 'bizarre' behaviours the person exhibits, the more severe the autism is seen to be), for autistic people autism is inner reality and it can appear (on the surface), disappear and reappear in varying degrees in different circumstances. Autism as an experience is described as a very complex interplay between identity, personality, environment, experience and the equipment with which to make sense of that experience (Williams 1998).

Some examples of definitions of all three categories are given in Box 2.1.

Box 2.1 Definitions of autism

Neutral descriptions

> Autism is a way of being. It is *pervasive*; it colors every experience, every sensation, perception, thought, emotion, and encounter, every aspect of existence. It is not possible to separate the autism from the person – and if it were possible, the person you'd have left would not be the same person you started with. (Sinclair 1993, p.3)

> Autism is a kind of dyslexia of the environment; it goes beyond social and communication problems and includes all sensory processing. (An adult with ASD, personal communication)

Like many adults I see autism as much as a maladaption of society to my specific cognitive style as myself being ill-adapted to that society. (Arnold 2004)

ASD implies pervasive developmental delays. This means that...children with ASD may be delayed in their starting of a stage [of development] and in their completion of a stage. Children and adults with ASD...'catch up' over time and the gap between [autistic and non-autistic people] diminishes with age. (Lawson 2001, p.23)

Positive descriptions

I believe Autism is a marvellous occurrence of nature, not a tragic example of the human mind gone wrong. In many cases, Autism can be a kind of genius undiscovered. (O'Neill 1999, p.14)

To me, autism is home. It is a place where I belong. I always have. It is protection against overwhelming sensory information coming at me from all over, and the too high and too demanding expectations from my parents and family to be 'normal'. It was, and always has been, a buffer between me and their utter incomprehensibility... Now, yes, the problems I have with communication (especially speech) are a nuisance sometimes, but they are a part of me, and I have lived with them for so long that they have become comfortable. (Kim 1999)

Negative descriptions

Autism is something I cannot see. It stops me from finding and using my own words when I want to. Or makes me use all the words and silly things I do not want to say... Autism makes me feel everything at once without knowing what I am feeling. Or it cuts me off from feeling anything at all... Autism makes me hear other people's words but be unable to know what the words mean. Or autism lets me speak my own words without knowing what I am saying or even thinking... Autism cuts me off from thoughts and curiosity, and so I believe I think nothing or am interested in nothing.

> Or autism makes my mind almost explode with the need to
> reach out and say what I think or show what I am interested
> in…but nothing comes out…not even on my face, in my
> eyes, or from my words… Autism cuts me off from my own
> body, so I feel nothing. Autism also can make me so aware of
> what I feel that it is painful… Autism makes me feel some-
> times that I have no self at all, and I feel so overwhelmed by
> the presence of other people that I cannot find myself.
> Autism can also make me so totally aware of myself that it is
> like the whole world around me becomes irrelevant and dis-
> appears… Autism is like a seesaw. When it is up or down I
> cannot see a whole life. When it is passing through in the
> middle I get to see a glimpse of the life I would have had if I
> were not autistic… Autism is just an information-processing
> problem that controls who I appear to be. (Williams 1999c,
> p.207)

As autistic individuals differ from each other as much as their non-autistic
peers, there are as many 'autistic' definitions as there are autistic individuals.
However, in all the diversity of the descriptions one can find certain points
that run through *all* the accounts. And surprise, surprise, they do not see it as a
Triad of Impairments but as information processing problems, cognitive and
sensory perceptual differences. In short, autism is seen as a fundamentally different way of being – perceiving, interpreting and thinking.

How does the Triad of Impairments fit in in this construct? Unfortunately,
the Triad of Impairments, while being useful for diagnosis and recognition of
autism from the outside, has brought many misconceptions of the condition.
Often 'impairments of social interaction, communication and imagination' are
interpreted as 'inabilities' to interact, communicate and imagine. However, if
we look at these 'impairments' from the point of view of 'fundamentally
different ways of being' we will see a different interpretation of the same
behaviours.

Social interaction

Autistic people do interact and form relationships but of a different nature. Many of them have a strong desire to be with other people, to express themselves and to be understood. Although some of them want friends desperately, they often find that the people with whom they interact find their interests somewhat strange. Since their world is so different from that of non-autistic people, they often have a hard time in 'normal' social relationships that come from ideas learned in early childhood. These ideas are not necessarily logical for autistic people and are a sort of 'fantasy' which they do not understand well. Therefore, they may do and say many things that violate most people's social context without realizing that there is something they are violating. The social isolation that results from this increases their loneliness and feelings of being different (Joan and Rich 1999).

> I took the social life as seriously as I took my [university] course but unfortunately, I found that the social chemistry was quite a lot harder than the study of biomolecular forces when applied to enzyme kinetics. It seemed as if everything I did was wrong, or at least someone would have the knack of making it look wrong. (Segar Undated)

Let us look at the four subgroups of individuals with ASDs, shifting the emphasis to the way they experience the world and their attempts to interact.

The aloof group

These are individuals who have given up trying to understand the confusing, incomprehensible and often threatening world around them. They learn early in life to shut down painful stimuli, thus creating self-imposed sensory deprivation. If there is no appropriate intervention they may stay at this stage well into adulthood, unwilling and with time unable to leave the 'sanctuary' of autism. Their world becomes what Donna Williams calls 'simply be' – the world without words, but rich in experiencing of sounds, patterns, colours and textures.

The passive group

They may passively accept interaction but, as their development is so different, they do not comprehend social rules imposed on them by the society. There is little, if any, desire to communicate as the communication systems are so different. Their 'communicative messages' may go unnoticed and/or misunderstood.

The active but odd group

They are willing to interact and be accepted, but they interact using cognitive mechanisms available to them (and different from non-autistic people). They learn to mimic appropriate facial expressions, body language, gestures, and verbal responses. They use a stored and rehearsed repertoire of 'social' stuff (often in the form of different faces/characters) (see, for example, Williams 1999b) triggered by environmental stimuli. They may appear high-functioning, nearly 'normal', but at the cost of losing the ability to 'be' (Williams 1999c). Some individuals are desperate to 'fit in' and to be accepted as 'normals'. A subgroup of 'active but odd', that seems to be opposite to the 'I-want-to-be-normal' individuals, but, in fact, reflects the same 'active but odd' characteristics from a different angle, are autistic individuals who develop the idealized concept of autism as a superior condition to 'neurotypicality'. They expect and *demand* others (NTs and their fellow autistics alike) to change their views on the condition to accommodate the environment to their (superior) differences. Any suggestion that there may be deficits/dysfunctions/problems in autism sends them to the state of rage ('How dare you to say that autistic people may have deficits/that they are less than perfect!'). Fortunately, this group is not numerous, but (unfortunately) it is very 'noisy'. However, it is important to recognize that their stance is rooted in low esteem and insecurity. In fact, they are very vulnerable, and need much more support than the other groups, in order to overcome the rigidity of their thinking, negativism towards other people, and inability to see (and accept) different perspectives.

The logical group

These individuals have learned to 'survive' in a 'foreign culture' without losing their own selves (Sinclair 1992; Williams 1999c). They have developed their own strategies to work with overload and fragmentation of the perception, to communicate meaningfully while being 'meaning-blind', to learn social rules by rote and avoid situations they cannot cope with. It is this group that tries really hard to understand non-autistic ways of being and very real differences in perceiving and interpreting the world. It is this group that is willing to educate the world about these differences in a desperate attempt to create harmony between the autistic and the non-autistic populations by mutual respect and cooperation. It is interesting to note that despite different nationalities and cultures, 'their world' concepts, strategies, experiences, and even made-up words to describe them are very similar. When they meet they feel a sense of belonging, of being understood, of being normal. The way they think, communicate and interact is normal in their company (Williams 1999c). Not only do they generally find each other's concepts comprehensible but also many have spontaneously come up with the same signs, words and gestures to describe the same sensory-emotional experiences. Thus, for instance, Donna Williams, who grew up in Australia, had no problems while communicating certain concepts to an autistic woman in the UK (Williams 1998).

With development and proper support people with autism may shift from one group into another. The opposite is true, as well – with lack of support and understanding they may stay at the stage they are and/or 'become unreachable' without any motivation to 'enter the world of NTs'.

Social communication

Non-autistic people are often puzzled by the 'odd' communication expressed by autistic individuals. However, autistic individuals may be equally puzzled by their non-autistic communicative partners. It is often not so much that an autistic person has no regard for their rules as that the person cannot keep up with so many rules for each specific situation (Williams 1996). Sometimes they are not aware of social cues because of the same perceptual problems which affect their understanding of other aspects of the environment. For example, visual processing problems may prevent the person from learning to recognize and interpret facial expressions. They may have to develop a separate translation code for every person they meet. Even if they can tell what the cues mean (because they have learned them theoretically), they may not know what to do about them. For example, the first time Jim Sinclair ever realized that someone needed to be touched was when he encountered a grief-stricken, hysterically sobbing person. Jim could see that the person was upset but he could not figure out that there was *something* he could do to help in this situation. Just because the person does not know what to do in certain social situations (due to different cognitive strategies the person uses instead of basic instincts that he does not develop intuitively) does not mean that the person does not care (Sinclair 1992a).

Establishing communication and understanding between any two people with different experiences and perceptions involves developing a common language. As an autistic person's experience and vocabulary (verbal and non-verbal) may be idiosyncratic, a great deal of effort must be taken on both sides to develop this common language (Sinclair 1989). Communication is a two-way process, and it takes two people to mess up a conversation. Not all the problems are caused by autistic people. NTs have a lot to learn about the art of communication with people who do not converse in the same way, whether it is verbal or non-verbal language (Bovee Undated). Many autistic individuals find it strange that if there are a few people present one is expected to talk about anything, even if they have nothing in common. It is being polite for the sake of politeness. However, some people do not need 'empty' social contact; they may be bored but they do not feel lonely. Isn't it more logical to communicate only with those who are interested in you as a person? For example:

> People seem to expect me to notice them and relate to them no matter who they are, just because they happen to be there. But if I don't know who people are, I don't know how (or why) to talk to them. I don't have much of a sense of people-in-general as things to be involved with. And I don't know how to have prefabricated relationships; if I happen to be involved with some person-in-particular, I practically have to learn to talk all over again to develop a common language with that person... I relate only as myself, only in ways that are authentic to me. I value people only as themselves, not for their role or status, and not because I need someone to fill empty spaces in my life. Are these the severe deficits in communicating and relating that I keep reading about? (Sinclair 1992a, pp.300, 302)

And again, it is very logical – what is the point of smiling and being polite if you do not like the person? Isn't it better just to ignore him or to leave? Or to say 'I'm fine' when you are not? Should you lie to 'get it right'?

The impairments of communication in autism are better described as qualitatively different ways to interact, communicate and process information which do not coincide with conventional ones. It is important to remember that:

> [Non-autistics] can be ignorant of the autistic's struggles to communicate. In this case, more care must be taken to learn how to interpret autistic languages... Communication in Autism is not a 'failure'. It is

not non-existent. It's simply different, in some way eccentric in an interesting way, and in some cases dormant. (O'Neill 1999, p.47)

However, people with autism do have deficits in social communication, but of a different nature. These deficits may be very severe and may make the person very vulnerable and dysfunctional in certain situations. These are deficits in the inability to recognize people who are not sincere (though *very* polite), who do not value them as unique individuals (while talking about equality and person-centred approaches), etc. It is hard for them to recognize, for example, when someone is lying, or just to learn what lying is (Sinclair 1992a). Autistic people may be confused and do not understand how somebody could have bad intentions, yet still act in a friendly way on the outside. Their social naiveties, innocence and literalness prevent them from being able to distinguish between foe or friend in many cases (O'Neill 1999).

Imagination

Bearing in mind that autistic cognitive processes are qualitatively different relative to the cognitive processes of the non-autistic population, the creativity and imagination of the person with autism would be qualitatively (and contextually) different as well (Bogdashina 2004). For example, visual thinking has enabled Temple Grandin to build entire systems in her imagination (Grandin 1996a). The extremely vivid imaginative powers and enormous creativity of people with autism are seen in poetry and prose, music and art (Kochmeister 1995; Lawson 1998; Williams 2003).

Other misconceptions resulting from a literal (one-sided) interpretation of the Triad are:

- 'autistic people lack empathy'
- 'autistic people lack emotions'
- 'autistic people lack a sense of humour'
- 'autistic people have bizarre responses to sensory stimuli'.

'Autistic people lack empathy'

If empathy means 'the power of identifying oneself mentally with (and so fully comprehending) a person', it is therefore much easier to 'empathize' with (i.e. to understand the feelings of) someone whose ways of experiencing the world are similar to one's own than to understand someone whose perceptions are very different. But if empathy means being able to understand a perspective that is *different* from one's own, then it is not possible to determine how much empathy is present in each person without first having an adequate understanding of each person's perspective and of how different those perspectives are from each other (Sinclair 1989).

Empathy is a two-way process. As there are no common or shared experiences, it is not just an autistic person who may have difficulty empathizing with others, but others may have difficulty empathizing with an autistic person (Myers, Baron-Cohen and Wheelwright 2004). The ignorance demonstrated by many non-autistic people sometimes makes them appear far from having empathy themselves (Williams 1996). The autistic person may *appear* to others to be distant and unsympathetic. However, it is not the case. They must be allowed to consider the problems and feelings of others with the tools they have at their disposal, often in abundance (Sinclair 1999). Many AS and autistic individuals easily pick up the distress or happiness of others. Lack of empathy?

> I have a great deal of affection. I don't understand people, but I like them. I care about them. I don't always understand why people are upset by certain things – sometimes I wonder how they could be so stupid – but it does bother me if I know they're upset. (Blackburn 1999)

Many autistic people have a strong sense of social justice and a great deal of compassion for others (Perner Undated, a). One of a great number of examples of empathy in autistic people is that of a nine-year-old AS boy, Cameron McAllister (USA), who after seeing the horrendous images of destruction brought about by the tsunami of 26 December 2004 on TV told his father that he wanted to cash in his precious penny collection and send the money to those in Indonesia, because they needed it more than he did.

'Autistic people lack emotions'

People with autism may not show emotions in a traditional way but this does not mean they have no emotions. In fact, they show their emotions with a greater intensity. Autistic people do have problems recognizing emotions in NTs but they do not lack them:

> Autistic people can feel deep love for others. They can feel deep sadness and ecstasy. They are able to feel the entire rainbow of emotions that

exists, including jealousy and envy. They can't always name or define their individual emotions, and the myriad of simultaneous feelings can seem confusing. (O'Neill 1999, p.36)

'Autistic people lack a sense of humour'

It is not a sense of humour they lack, but rather social skills to recognize when others are joking, signal that they are joking, or appreciate jokes which rely on an understanding of social conventions (Sainsbury 2000a). Autistic people may not understand non-autistic jokes, but 'they lack a sense of humour'? – Don't make me laugh! Look, for example, at how they define non-autistic people – neurotypical syndrome. Lack of humour? I don't think so.

What is NT?

Neurotypical syndrome is a neurobiological disorder characterized by preoccupation with social concerns, delusions of superiority, and obsession with conformity. Neurotypical individuals often assume that their experience of the world is either the only one, or the only correct one. NTs find it difficult to be alone. NTs are often intolerant of seemingly minor differences in others. When in groups NTs are socially and behaviorally rigid, and frequently insist upon the performance of dysfunctional, destructive, and even impossible rituals as a way of maintaining group identity. NTs find it difficult to communicate directly, and have a much higher incidence of lying as compared to persons on the autistic spectrum. NT is believed to be genetic in origin. Autopsies have shown the brain of the neurotypical is typically smaller than that of an autistic individual and may have overdeveloped areas related to social behavior. (Muskie 1999)

Ironically, many non-autistic people do not understand the humour of AS individuals. As one AS person puts it, 'They [non-autistic individuals] lack the intellectual firepower to understand it… How disillusioning it is that many people just don't get [this] gift!' (Perner 2002, p.4).

'Autistic people have bizarre responses to sensory stimuli'

Bearing in mind the differences in perception, cognitive mechanisms and adaptive strategies they acquire, their so-called 'bizarre responses' are normal (from their perspective). When sensory information is unreliable, it is hardly surprising that they try to bring predictability and some order to the chaos in which they live:

A lot of self-stimulations, including rocking the body, swaying, flapping the hands, rubbing the skin, and countless others, are pleasurable, soothing connections with the senses. They help ground the autistic person, provide rhythm and order, calm, and simply feel good! (O'Neill 1999, p.33)

These and similar misconceptions of the condition have originated from the 'lack of imagination' of non-autistic people, who (wrongly) assume that the only way to perceive, react and respond to the environment is a 'normal' (non-autistic) way. However, differences in perception, cognitive functioning in autism (not mentioned in the Triad) and adaptations they acquire bring differences in responses and expressions that are 'normal' from an 'autistic' point of view. Many authors with ASDs question these well-established misconceptions and feel that 'lack of empathy/imagination' is more typical for non-autistic individuals.

Taking three of the recognized features of autism (impairments in social interaction, communication disorder and bizarre behaviours) Donna Williams focuses on a few specific problems that can result in all three of these features. She groups them into three basic types of problem (Williams 1996):

1. *Problems of control* (are about being able to respond with intention to the world and/or oneself):

   - compulsion
   - obsession
   - acute anxiety.

2. *Problems of tolerance* (are about being able to stand the world and/or oneself):

   - sensory hypersensitivity
   - emotional hypersensitivity.

3. *Problems of connection* (are about being able to make sense of the world and/or oneself):

   - attention problems
   - perceptual problems

- system integration problems
- left–right hemisphere-integration problems.

According to Williams (1996), problems of connection (or information processing problems) are at the root of some kinds of problems of tolerance and problems of control (see Figure 2.1).

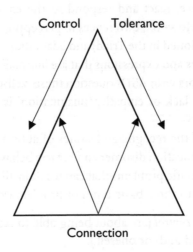

Figure 2.1 Another way to look at the Triad of Impairments in autism (based on Williams 1996)

Stereotyped behaviours that 'always accompany the Triad of Impairments' are seen by autistic people as their compensatory strategies to regulate their sensory systems and cope with sensory overload. Routines and rituals bring some predictability to an otherwise incomprehensible world.

Unlike the most recent trend to interpret stereotypies as attempts to communicate, it is not always necessarily so. Some do these sorts of things out of frustration caused by being unable to communicate. However, there may be other reasons for stimming, different for each individual and for different situations (Blackburn 1999). Self-stimulatory behaviours may serve several purposes and one and the same behaviour may have different underlying causes. Some examples of different functions of stimming are:

- *defensive:* in order to reduce the pain caused by hypersensitivities; for example:

  > This behaviour is an attempt to eliminate a sensory assault that interferes with functioning. (Shore Undated)

- *self-stimulatory:* to improve the input in the case of hyposensitivity; for example:

  > You may observe the same autistic person rubbing sandpaper on his bare arm, or banging his knuckles sharply into a solid wooden dresser, then peering at them as if to say, 'Oh, hello, hand. So you do belong to me, then'... A lot of self-stimulations, including rocking the body, swaying, flapping the hands, rubbing the skin, and countless others, are pleasurable, soothing connections with senses. (O'Neill 1999, p.33)

- *compensatory:* to interpret the environment in the case of 'unreliable' sensory information (fragmentation, distortions); for example:

  > I was coping in a world where other people effectively realised nothing of that. I reacted to all this bombardment and confusion with those physical movements, silence and strange sounds which are generally lumped together as 'autistic behaviours'. (Blackman 2001, p.19)

- *out of frustration;* for example:

  > Sometimes head banging and knuckle nibbling, tantrums, or outbursts happen as a way of letting someone know enough is enough! (Lawson 2001, p.78)

- *just pleasurable experiences* that help to withdraw from a confusing environment; for example:

  > Rocking and spinning were other ways to shut out the world when I became overloaded with too much noise. Rocking made me feel calm. It was like taking an addictive drug. The more I did it, the more I wanted to do it. (Grandin 1996a, pp.44–45)

Characteristics of autism defined as secondary in mainstream research literature seem to be primary for autistic people. Such features as, for instance, unusual responses to sensory stimuli are often seen as the core description of autism. Besides, from the 'autistic' perspective, these responses are 'normal' (not 'unusual' or 'bizarre') because they are caused by different sensory perceptual processing.

HFA, LFA, 'mild autism', 'severe autism', etc.

Temple Grandin (1996a) explains the difference between LFA and HFA with the help of a 'sensory processing continuum', at the one end of which is a person with AS or HFA who has mild sensory problems, and at the other end of the spectrum is the low-functioning person who receives jumbled, inaccurate sensory information. Children who are echolalic may be at the midpoint in the sensory processing continuum.

According to Grandin (1996a), the world of the non-verbal autistic person is chaotic and confusing. A low-functioning adult who is still not toilet-trained may be living in a completely disordered sensory world and may have no idea of his body boundaries, and sights, sounds and touches may all be mixed together:

> It must be like seeing the world through a kaleidoscope and trying to listen to a radio station that is jumped with static at the same time. Add to that a broken volume control, which causes the volume to jump erratically from a loud boom to inaudible. Such a person's problems are further compounded by a nervous system that is often in a greater state of fear and panic than the nervous system of a Kanner-type [here: HF] autistic. Imagine a state of hyperarousal where you were being pursued by a dangerous attacker in a world of total chaos. Not surprisingly, new environments make low-functioning autistics fearful. (Grandin 1996a, p.59)

Severe auditory problems may prevent the child from developing an understanding of speech. The constant stress of the jumble of unprocessed sensory stimuli will cause a semi-permanent state of overload. The child may show many forms of stimming, including self-injury, in an attempt to vent some of the stress from the confused senses (Klein Undated, d).

There are mild and more severe forms of different types of problems in autism, but what is seen from outside is not necessarily a true degree of 'severity', but rather the degree of adaptations and compensations which the person has developed. Some people may *appear* to be mildly affected because they have managed to cope with their problems despite a greater degree of impairment – they function at a higher level of their actual abilities. On the other hand, some people may *appear* severely affected by autism while, in fact, they function at a lower level of their abilities due to a lack of motivation and encouragement to develop functional adaptations (Williams 1996). That is why sometimes people labelled low-functioning may have a milder degree of impairment than another who is deemed to be high-functioning and vice versa.

Another interesting perspective with which to approach this issue is to look at it from the point of view of a person's 'true sense of self'. Are people who do not fight their differences and do not want to be 'indistinguishable from normal people' low-functioning, in contrast to those who have learned to copy others without being able to express themselves (often referred to as high-functioning)?

If we draw a boundary between LFA and HFA depending on the results of IQ tests, it will be misleading from the perspective of autism. Autistic people with high IQ may show good academic achievements, but does it make them high-functioning in the 'social world' they do not understand? As Ros Blackburn, an adult with autism, points out, her abilities are her greatest disabilities. Because she is verbal and intellectually able, people assume she does not need any support in social and everyday situations. Her high verbal and non-verbal IQ does not reflect her difficulties (such as crossing the road on her own, making a meal or conducting social 'chit-chat'). It is a paradox of 'high-functioning' autism – they are disabled by their abilities because their 'normal behaviour' appearances mask their very real (invisible to outsiders) difficulties.

Asperger syndrome and autism

It is interesting to consider what AS and HF individuals themselves think about differentiating these two conditions. This analysis is not just an exercise to consider similarities, differences and specific features of autism and AS. It is important in order to better understand how to help each particular individual in a way that will waste fewer resources (including mental and emotional energy) and have a more consistent degree of 'success' (Williams 1996).

Donna Williams, a HF person with autism, analyses the similarities and differences between herself and someone with AS, from her (autistic) perspective. She has no doubt that certain distinctions between these two conditions do exist. Besides, she distinguishes not only high- and low-functioning autistic people, but also high- and low-functioning people with AS, and gives some clues as to how to differentiate them. According to Williams, there are non-verbal low-functioning people with AS who are (wrongly) labelled autistic but who, unlike non-verbal low-functioning autistic people, have excellent receptive language, can approach others in a directly confrontational way and have only minor sensory-perceptual problems. By contrast, children with autism with the same low-level functioning often have markedly poor receptive language (both visual and auditory), have problems with connected body sense and body perception and often cannot initiate a direct and personal action with another person. Donna Williams further explains that both people with autism and those with AS may have poor language skills, but there is a great difference between these groups: one may be a case of lack of social instinct in spite of capacity, the other may be a case of inability or extreme difficulty in developing or using social skills in spite of intense social instinct (Williams 1996). HFA people seem to prefer to indulge in sensory repetitive activities (flapping things, etc.); AS individuals tend to display verbal obsessions (talking about their favourite topics) and thinking 'non-stop' about their projects (see Box 2.2).

Box 2.2 AS vs. autism (modified from Williams 1996)

Similarities
Both autism and AS have similar underlying problems.

Differences
- *The efficiency with which the information is processed.* In autism, in contrast to AS, the processing of incoming information is less efficient.
- *Accessing of stored information and monitoring of expression.* In autism, in contrast to AS, voluntary accessing of stored memories and the monitoring of the expression of thoughts are less efficient.

- *Sensory perceptual problems.* In contrast to autism, AS people have minor sensory perceptual problems.

- *The way to compensate for problems.* In autism, attempts to compensate for sensory/cognitive differences are mostly involuntary (for example, self-stimulatory behaviours) and hence often 'socially inappropriate', while people with AS seem to have voluntary strategies and a greater reliance on stored 'socially acceptable' behaviours and responses. Even if these responses look formal and stilted, they are still easily comprehensible in a non-autistic environment.

- *Language.* Though both autistic and AS people may be non-verbal, individuals (especially children) with autism have poor receptive language both visually and auditorily, while AS children's receptive language is good.

    Though both may have problems with expressive language, AS people have an intense social instinct and desire to communicate.

    AS individuals can tolerate a direct approach, while autistic individuals communicate better indirectly.

- *Different causes of need for acceptance.* AS people want social contact and acceptance in order to be appreciated. They are proud of their achievements and are easily embarrassed if they do not meet the expectations of certain situations. People with autism need acceptance as a guarantee of making others more predictable and avoiding being hurt.

Some HF/AS people see AS as the milder end of the autistic spectrum; and the only difference between AS and autism seems to be the severity of the condition, which includes sensory problems (Klein Undated, c). Schneider (1999, p.117), for instance, calls AS 'the highest functioning form of autism, so HFA is a subset of autism and AS is a subset of HFA'. Like autistic individuals, AS children may have speech delay, but these delays are not caused by auditory processing problems (typical for non-verbal or speech-delayed autistic children) but rather may be related to motor coordination difficulties. It is likely that AS children with delayed speech develop receptive verbal ability, thus allowing the brain to develop much as if the child were verbal (Klein Undated, d).

For 'horizontal reading':

1.1 – pp.21–28
3.1 – pp.179–186
4.1 – pp.233–240

2.2

Diagnosis

The autism umbrella is vast. It is a fluid diagnosis, with no definite beginning and no certain end, and with a wide range of abilities and disabilities (Willey 1999). Many autistic authors feel that the existing standardized diagnostic systems (ICD-10 and DSM-IV) and numerous checklists and questionnaires developed by clinicians to 'detect' autism contain the original error of a mis-understanding of the condition, i.e. looking at autism as a collection of behavioural symptoms described as deviations from the norm. However, such important (from the point of view of many individuals with ASDs) signs of autism as differences in sensory perception have never been included in a list of the 'core features'; at best they were mentioned as side comments, not necessary for diagnosis (Morris 1999). If we put the Triad on its feet and approach autism from an autistic perspective, the diagnostic criteria would look differently.

Unfortunately, using 'surface behaviours' (ICD-10 and DSM-IV) for diagnosis of autism, instead of underlying causes, makes it impossible to enumerate *all* possible manifestations of the condition, because the adaptations and compensations the person acquires differ from one individual to another. This brings undesirable side-effects if the criteria is being used by an inexperienced clinician who 'follows the prescribed textbook to the letter'. In this case many autistic people (especially with HFA and AS) are turned away when approaching GPs, psychologists or therapists for referrals for a diagnosis because they 'cannot possibly be autistic'; that is, they do not fit (stereotyped) descriptions in the manual. For instance, they may be sent away because they show too much emotion, or have eye contact, or smile when talked to, etc. Donna Williams writes about a woman who has an autistic son and whose mother has AS, who approached a professional with a view to getting a diagnosis for herself for problems she shared in common with her son and mother. She was turned away because she cried during the consultation and was, therefore, considered to have expressed too much emotion to have been autistic. Other people have been turned away because they have a wider range of interests or more acquaintances than the stereotypes portray or because, like many people diagnosed with Asperger Syndrome, they complain of having an overactive imagination that distracts them all the time. (Williams 1996, p.12)

There are hundreds, if not thousands, of children and adults who (having autism) have been seen by unqualified and inexperienced professionals and have been denied diagnosis because the 'specialists' could not read between the lines and, seeing a smile on the child's face or a tear in her mother's eye, make their verdict – 'The child (the woman) cannot be autistic! Look, he smiles/is being friendly/gives eye-contact, etc.'

Many autistic adults look perfectly 'normal'. They have developed individual strategies, adaptations and compensations to get them through life. This is especially true for women with high-functioning autism or AS who may be more able to learn social skills by imitation (often without real understanding). They often go undiagnosed (and, hence, denied professional support) because they cannot find a specialist. (Unfortunately, professionals like Tony Attwood or Digby Tantam are still rare!) The only accurate way to diagnose autism in an adult is to interview the person and his or her parents and teachers about early childhood development and specific behaviours (Grandin 1996a).

Different diagnostic features between autism and AS

In early development differences may be more apparent. However, some people may display symptoms of autism in early childhood but develop into an AS adult. For example, Wendy Lawson who was diagnosed with AS in her forties did not talk until she was four years old (that, according to diagnostic classifications, would indicate autism) (Lawson 2001). Temple Grandin had delayed abnormal speech development and some other symptoms of 'classic autism' at the age of two, but as an adult she would be more accurately diagnosed as having AS, as she has greater cognitive flexibility and can pass a simple ToM test. Though her sensory oversensitivities are still worse than in AS, she has no sensory mixing and jumbling problems (Grandin 1996a).

Thinking may become less visual as one moves along the continuum away from classic Kanner's [here: HFA] syndrome (Grandin 1996a). However, not all autistic people agree that a child with autism may develop into an AS adult, but insist that a low-functioning child with autism may grow into a high-functioning adult with autism.

Differential diagnosis

There are conditions that share some characteristics of autism but are not included in ASDs. People with these conditions and without an official diagnosis of autism are often referred to as autistic cousins (AC) (see Box 2.3). This term is primarily used by the autistic community on the Internet.

Box 2.3 Autistic cousins

Schizoid personality disorder

Obsessive-compulsive disorder

Tourette's syndrome

Attention deficit disorder/Attention deficit hyperactivity disorder

---

Conditions which may be misdiagnosed for autism/AS

There have been reported many cases when autism was misdiagnosed for other medical/psychiatric conditions, most common being schizophrenia and mental retardation (intellectual disabilities).

Schizophrenia

It is enough to say that for many people with AS the first diagnosis was schizophrenia. It happened more often in the past when experience of diagnosing AS was limited to a few professionals. Dozens of AS individuals spent years in psychiatric hospitals severely drugged.

Mental retardation / Intellectual disabilities

Autism (especially severe autism) is often associated with mental retardation (intellectual disabilities). However, it is a myth that severely autistic people are all mentally retarded. A single individual can be both low-functioning and high-functioning in different areas (O'Neill 1999). Some may be retarded, but others may receive a low-functioning label because their sensory processing problems make communication difficult (Grandin 2002). Many autistic individuals disagree with much of what professionals think they know about the 'intellectual abilities' of people with ASDs. They argue that while it may seem that autistic people do not understand things, this is not true. The real difficulties occur in speed and style of processing, storing and retrieving information (Kochmeister 1995). Obviously, some autistic individuals may be mentally retarded, just as are some non-autistic people. However, poor results of the IQ tests may be explained by different reasons. Due to certain perceptual and cognitive differences, the autistic person either may not understand what is expected from him or he cannot access his 'mental database' at the moment of testing. Besides, very often, smart autistic individuals are bored or even offended by the questions of the examiner and may give incorrect answers on purpose or refuse to cooperate altogether (Bogdashina 2004).

Donna Williams (1996) insists that mental retardation should never be assumed because, even if someone is functionally retarded and seemingly incomprehensible and uncomprehending, this says nothing about their intellectual capacity. It may merely be that an intelligent and potentially able person has had no form of self-feedback through which to discover all their knowing, blocked by problems of conscious processing, accessing and monitoring and exacerbated by information overload. As autistic individuals have different information-processing strategies and styles, they might struggle with tasks presented in a conventional, non-autistic way (for example, a person using only one sensory channel to process information for meaning may be presented with multisensory information). If non-autistic people find themselves in the same situation (using their cognitive mechanisms to complete the task in an 'autistic way'), they could be considered idiots in the autistic world, too (O'Neill 1999), and appear to be thoroughly 'subnormal' by 'autistic' standards (Williams 1996).

> A misdiagnosis doesn't help anybody, nor does a misplacement. Too many people with 'autism' have been testimony to ignorance and arrogance or lack of services or funding. Too often these things have

resulted in hammering square pegs into round holes. The dumping of people with 'autism' into other categories such as 'emotionally disturbed', 'mentally ill' or 'intellectually retarded' doesn't help the people with 'autism'. (Williams 1996, p.22)

Autism rarely (if ever) occurs in a 'pure' form. It often co-occurs with other conditions, such as digestive and immune system disorders, epilepsy, mood disorders, Tourette's syndrome, dyslexia, scotopic sensitivity syndrome and obsessive-compulsive disorder (Williams Undated, b). The inability of non-autistic people to understand people with autism can also create a very high degree of mental and emotional stress in autistic people (Williams 1996). Donna Williams compares these additional co-morbid conditions with 'fleas' – 'if you give the dog enough fleas and no flea powder, eventually the stress is going to lead to a breakdown in the dog's health or bring any pre-existing inherited weaknesses to the surface' (Williams Undated, b). If severe, these additional conditions are likely to interfere, distract and disrupt the development and make underlying information processing and communication problems in autism much worse. The majority of these co-morbid conditions may be manageable and treatable either through dietary intervention, nutritional supplementation and/or small doses of medication (appropriate to the co-morbid condition) together with an environmental approach which is *relevant* to not just autism but the additional condition aggravating it. Unfortunately, it is common that when the diagnosis of autism is given, the 'Triad of Impairments' is focused on, and many of the (treatable) underlying conditions are overlooked. Then the idea that someone who is severely autistic will grow up to be just as severely autistic may in many cases depend on whether these compounding co-morbid conditions are recognized and appropriately addressed (Williams Undated, b).

'New disorders' (semantic pragmatic disorder, pathological demand avoidance syndrome and some others) irritate many high-functioning autistic people who see these 'labels' as useless and serving only one purpose – to promote their originators.

Early diagnosis

Paradoxically, it is almost impossible to predict which autistic toddler will become high-functioning. The severity of the symptoms at age two or three is often not correlated with the prognosis (Grandin 1996a).

Now we are witnessing the phenomenon of 'late diagnosis' of autism in adults. At the time they were children autism was not easily recognized. It is quite typical now when so much material on autism is available in books, articles, newspapers and TV programmes that adults with the undiagnosed ASDs become aware that the problems which they have experienced in life (broken relationships, failures at job interviews, inability to hold a job, etc.) actually have a name.

The attitude to the late diagnosis varies among individuals with ASDs. Some actively seek it and become relieved that they can explain their 'oddities' and may look for professional support. Others become angry and frustrated. On the one hand, it is good to finally start to understand what and why they have had so many difficulties, and that it is not their fault that they have experienced these difficulties. On the other hand, they may be angry with the professionals who failed to see their condition and did not help them to cope with it. They may blame the professionals whom they accuse of damaging their lives by punishment for something over which they had no control. They feel frustrated that because of the ignorance and arrogance of some professionals they may be too damaged to reach their full potential (Aston 2000). Is it a surprise that they may feel bitter that 'those responsible' do not take any responsibilities for their own mistakes?

> My health authority became hypocrites for I was soon to learn that the mistakes I had personally made had consequences of punishment, but the mistakes that the professionals of the past had made with me were played down and acceptable. I am so angry now, for most of my life I have been tricked, lied to and used as a scapegoat, this was hurting as I tried to hold onto my growing awareness. (Aston 2000, p.59)

Unfortunately, even now to get the diagnosis depends on…where you live. If there are autism research centres in the area, it is more likely that health and educational authorities are familiar with ASDs, and that there are more provisions and services available there. This fact frustrates many AS individuals who have had to fight to get a diagnosis for many years.

Some autistic and AS individuals do not want to be diagnosed as they do not want to be mistreated, as it is still often the case with anybody who is labelled (different).

Prevalence

Present 'official' calculations of the prevalence of autism may be misleading, especially regarding high-functioning people with autism and AS. There is a possibility that those people who are undiagnosed are just as numerous as those who possess a formal diagnosis, possibly more so. Some do not want to become formally diagnosed because they do not consider themselves to be disordered. Others fear (or suffer from) discrimination, or worse. And what of the statistics for those who are undiagnosed because they are completely unaware of their autism or those who are aware but for whom it is not an issue (Walker Undated)? Andrew Walker, one of those fully-functioning and included autistic people, suggests that the real question about autism and diagnosis should not be *how many*, but rather *how much* autism society is willing or able to afford and tolerate.

For 'horizontal reading':

1.2 – pp.29–38
3.2 – pp.187–190
4.2 – pp.241–255

2.3

Causes

Concerning possible causes of autism, in their articles, books and presentations autistic individuals discuss the same biological factors that we find in the research literature: genetic predisposition, pre-, peri- and postnatal CNS insult, viral infections, structural and/or functional brain abnormalities, abnormal biochemistry of the brain, a dysfunctional immune system. All these (and possibly, some other as yet unknown) factors may cause the development of autism. What is more, different combinations of these factors may be involved, and/or they may be aggravated by environmental variables, such as toxins and complex organic compounds that act to further lower the individual's maximum level of functioning. By the time of birth, the interruption of the brain development (for example, neocerebellum) has already occurred (Hawthorne 2002).

Let us re-examine the theory of the Iceberg of Autism. Any of the factors mentioned above may be placed at the bottom of the iceberg. The middle part of the iceberg (still under the water) will contain factors defined by many autistic individuals as possible explanations of developing 'autistic behaviours' – the Triad of Impairments (which are seen above the water).

So what causes the Triad from the autistic point of view? Many autistic authors suggest that the true deep-rooted cause of all social, communicative and emotional problems is of a sensory-perceptual nature. Bob Morris (1999) calls differently-functioning systems of perception a different set of SPATS – Senses, Perceptions, Abilities and Thinking Systems – that are not in the same spectral range as those of non-autistic individuals.

Let us include SPATS in the 'Autism Iceberg', where 'diagnostic autistic behaviours' can be accounted for by the differences in SPATS. However, I take the liberty of rearranging SPATS into STAPS – a different functioning of

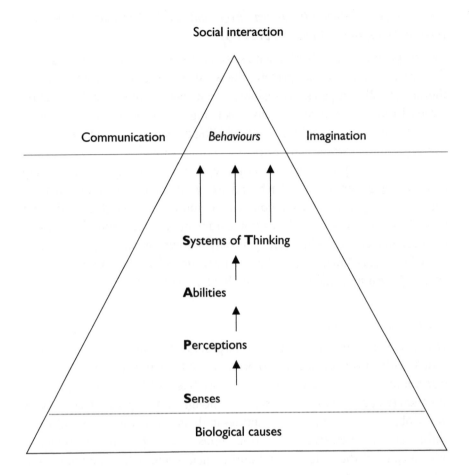

Figure 2.2 The Iceberg of Autism: STAPS

the Senses leads to different Perceptions, that, in turn, bring different Abilities and different Systems of Thinking. We will start with SP (Senses and Perceptions).

Senses and perceptions

'Learning how each individual autistic person's senses function is one crucial key to understanding that person' (O'Neill 1999, p.31). The most common problems reported by autistic people are the following.

*An inability to distinguish between foreground and background information
(Gestalt perception – Bogdashina 2003)*

Autistic people are bombarded with sensory stimuli. They are often unable to filter irrelevant details and perceive the whole scene as a single entity. Hawthorne (2002) compares his inability to adequately filter out information received through each of the senses as being like a freeway crowded with reckless and non-law-abiding drivers, causing massive traffic jams, when mail trucks (thoughts) would have difficulty getting through.

On the conceptual level, gestalt perception leads to rigidity of thinking and lack of generalization. Each and every situation is unique. Even the slightest changes in their environment or routine may confuse and upset them. They may react to all this bombardment and confusion with certain physical movements which are generally known as stereotyped 'autistic behaviours' (Blackman 2001). Their 'ritualistic behaviours' are for reassurance and creating some order in daily life (O'Neill 1999).

Fragmented perception

When too much information needs to be processed simultaneously, very often people with autism are not able to break down the whole picture into meaningful units and so they process only those bits which happen to get their attention (Bogdashina 2003). It seems as though autistic people react to parts of the objects as being complete entities in themselves (VanDalen 1995). As autistic children perceive their surroundings and people they encounter in 'bits and pieces', they interpret and store in their memory their individual (and idiosyncratic – from the non-autistic point of view) impressions of their experiences. They use these unconventional definitions of places, things and people to function in their environment. As these definitions differ from non-autistic ones, the carers find the behaviours of their child incomprehensible. For autistic persons, however, a lot of self-stimulations, including rocking the body, swaying, flapping the hands, rubbing the skin, and countless others, are their attempts to make connections with their senses. They help ground the autistic individual, providing rhythm and order, calm, and simply feel good (O'Neill 1999).

In the context of fragmentation we should discuss a role of attention and how attentional mechanism functions in autism. Impaired attentional functioning may be central to many social and cognitive deficits in persons with autism, as efficient attending is essential to the development of all aspects of functioning. Sensory issues and attentional issues are closely connected and are most likely to be both real and primary. In some cases one may help to cause the other. Both attentional and sensory problems may have developmental consequences which may lead to the full autistic syndrome (Blackburn 1999).

The inability to filter out the information (gestalt perception) and distinguish the relevant from the irrelevant, to distribute different amounts of attention across present stimuli, depending on their significance, and to sustain attention results in increased distraction and overload and impairs cognitive functioning. Involuntary responses to irrelevant stimuli interfere with the processing of relevant information. Without efficient filtering and selectivity of attention the child cannot make sense of the environment. Autistic children are often unable to divide their attention between the object they want and the person from whom they are supposed to ask for it because for many of them shifting attention from one stimulus to the other is a relatively slow process. Another common attentional problem in autism is, the failure of autistic people to establish and maintain joint attention; that is, the ability to attend to the same stimuli as another person. That leads to failure to share experiences. This, in turn, results in the failure to comprehend the meaning of the interaction and hinder social and cultural development. However, overselectivity and narrow attentional focus may be seen not as a deficit but rather one of attentional difference (Lawson 2001).

Distorted perception

Autistic people may experience all sorts of distortions in their perception, especially when they are in a state of nervous overarousal and information overload. No one can guess that their eyes, for example, pick up different signals from the light, shade, colour and movement (Blackman 2001).

Delayed processing

As a consequence of fragmented perception autistic people may experience delayed processing. Perception by parts requires a great amount of time and effort to interpret what is going on with or around them. It may appear as though they do not feel pain, do not want help, do not know what they are saying, do not listen or do not want. However, by the time some of these sensations are processed and understood, they may be several minutes, one day, a week, a month, even a year away from the context in which the experiences happened (Williams 1996).

Hypersensitivities

Hypersensitivities to sensory stimuli are very common in autism. Their senses may be too acute and be disturbed by stimuli that do not bother non-autistic individuals. For example, certain things they touch may hurt their hands (McKean 1999). They may dislike places with many different noises or lights (Grandin 1996a; Lawson 2001; Shore Undated). The fear of certain sounds that hurt their ears may be the cause of many 'challenging behaviours' and tantrums. Many 'bad behaviours' are triggered due to anticipation of being subjected to a painful stimulus (Grandin 1996a).

Hyposensitivities

Sometimes their senses may become dull to the point that they cannot clearly see or hear the world around them, or even feel their own body (Hawthorne 2002; Mukhopadhyay 2000). To stimulate their senses and get at least some meaning of what is going on they may wave their hands around, or rock, or make strange noises.

Inconsistency of perception

Autistic people may be tossed in a sensory maelstrom, so that the sensations may be unbearable one minute and yet completely unfelt the next (Blackman 2001). Fluctuation of the 'volume' of their perception is quite common in autism. The inconsistency of perceiving information, when the sensations (hence, interpretation of what is going on) are changing day to day, hour to hour, sometimes even minute to minute (McKean 1999), does not help the learning of social and emotional cues from people.

These and other 'sensory-perceptual inconsistencies and differences' bring sensory overload in situations that would not bother other people. The vulnerability to information overload is one of the distinctive features of autistic individuals, which often goes unnoticed by their non-autistic communicative partners. If they continue to process all the information coming in, despite their inability to keep up with it, overload sets in. This eventually brings anxiety, confusion, frustration and stress which, in turn, leads to challenging behaviours. Is it surprising that they may lack any interest in being involved in the outside world if the unmodulated, distorted sensory input overwhelms them and the flood of unwanted information continually assaults their senses (Hawthorne 2002)? Stephen Shore (a HF person with autism) calls sensory problems in ASDs (when the senses are turned up too high or turned down too low) 'sensory violations'. Combined with distorted and unreliable sensory information, these sensory differences can make dealing with the environment in an intensive manner, especially when transitions are involved, very difficult. That is why they may stick to the same old routines (it is easier to do what you already know) (Shore 2003).

Consciously or unconsciously, they develop their own perceptual styles, in order to cope with unreliable and often painful perception. These styles may be seen as defensive strategies and voluntary and involuntary adaptations and compensations which the person with autism acquires very early in life. As each individual's perceptual problems and environments in which they are situated are unique, these adaptations and compensations are very individual. The most common perceptual styles in autism are:

- monoprocessing (Williams 1996) or monotropism (Lawson 2001)

- peripheral perception.

MONOPROCESSING

To limit the amount of information and avoid distortions, fragmentation and overload, autistic people may use one sensory channel at a time, while the rest of the senses are on hold. It brings certain restriction in their perception but helps to make sense of information in at least one sensory modality. Later they learn to switch channels and, though not simultaneously through all the senses, they may still get some meaning of an object, event, situation. For example, the child uses his vision and sees every minute detail and that the colours are vibrant and, perhaps radiantly brilliant, but he loses track of his other senses, so he does not make much sense of the sounds in the background, loses the feel of touch and body awareness (O'Neill 1999). People with autism may be unable to process information produced from the outside and the inside at the same time and, for example, while touching something they may feel the texture of the object but have no sense of the hand, and then switch channels and feel the hand but lose the sensation of what the hand is in contact with (Williams 1998).

PERIPHERAL PERCEPTION

Another strategy to avoid overload and get meaning from the outside world is peripheral perception. Autistic individuals can often understand things better if they attend to them indirectly, by looking out of the corner of their eyes (O'Neill 1999) or listening peripherally. In this case it is a kind of indirectly confrontational approach in contrast to a 'normal' directly confrontational one (Williams 1996). The same is true of other senses if they are hypersensitive: the indirect perceptions of smell, taste or touch are often defensive strategies to avoid overload.

System shutdown

Too much sensory overload may result in system shutdown. When the person cannot cope with sensory information, he may shut down some or even all sensory channels. Many autistic children are suspected to be deaf as they do not react to any (even very loud) sounds. Their hearing, however, is often very acute, but they learn to 'switch it off' when they experience overload and cannot cope with the rate of incoming information. To shut down the painful channel(s) they may engage in stereotypic behaviours, or deliberately distract themselves through other channels (for example, touching objects to 'switch off' their vision or hearing) or to withdraw altogether. If this strategy is mastered early in life, they are often reluctant to 'switch the channels back on' again in fear of painful bombardment of unmodulated, unfiltered stimuli. It leads to self-imposed sensory deprivation that, if not addressed, may lead to irreversible hindrance of development.

Many autistic individuals agree that perceptual problems such as feeling deaf, dumb or blind are experienced as very real. They are caused by shutdowns of the sensory systems, that may be, in turn, caused by stress, or brought on by an inability to cope with incoming information (Williams 1999b). In shutting down their sensory systems, they may not receive the stimulation that is required for normal development. Temple Grandin (1996b) hypothesizes that possibly there are secondary central nervous system abnormalities which happen as a result of the autistic child's avoidance of input. The initial sensory processing abnormalities with which the child is born cause the initial avoidance. However, the limbic system which also has abnormalities is not mature until the child is two years old. The possibility of secondary damage to the CNS may account for why young children in early intervention education programmes have better prognosis than children who do not receive special treatment (Grandin 1996b).

Could SPATS explain the 'autistic behaviours' – that is, impairments of social interaction, communication and rigidity of thought? To get the answer to this question, Bob Morris poses another one:

> If you were being FOREVER forced (at times none too patiently) to do upsetting functions or at times acutely painful ones, just because everybody else does it with no discomfort, AND expects you to be the same; would that make you want to be outgoing, and a party personality? *Or,* would you turn away from your tormentors, acting as if you were uncomfortable or afraid or possibly frustrated with them?

> THE DRIVING FORCE (CAUSE), BEHIND AN AUTISTIC'S BEHAVIOR IS, IN MASSIVELY MAJOR PART, THEIR REACTION TO CONSTANT OR OFTEN INVOLUNTARY AND REPEATED EXPOSURE TO ONE OR MORE FORMS OF INESCAPABLE UNPLEASANTNESS, i.e. PAIN, COERCION, and TORTURE (generally UNCOGNIZANTLY applied), INCLUDING THEIR RELATED ANXIETIES, EXACERBATED BY UNUSUAL NEUROLOGICAL WIRING AND THOUGHT PROCESSING, *PLUS* ANY OTHER ASSOCIATED PUNISHMENTS, FOR MERELY HOSTING THIS INFRACTION. (Morris 1999)

Morris develops his argument further, showing the difference between low-functioning and high-functioning autism.

Asperger syndrome and high-functioning autism

> The possession and attempted use of this ab- and extra-normal set of SPATS by an infant, or a very neuroplastic individual, *without* the aid of an appropriately perceptive mentor to help sort out and deal with the subject's SPATS, is a condition powerful enough that autism CAN result. A somewhat more pleasant result of NC [autistic] SPATS, can be a condition named Asperger's Syndrome, that people WITH that condition, perceive as a less-deeply-involved autism. The earlier the appropriate intervention, the better. The more perceptive the mentor and/or the mentoring system, the more likely the subject will become a fully functional, *but significantly different, in talents and thinking,* individual, an NC person, with great value in accomplishing tasks that are difficult for NT humans to perform efficiently. (Morris 1999)

Low-functioning autism

> If the ab- and extra-normal set of SPATS above, happens to include a
> hindrance of normal, for NC [autistic], communication, there is the
> likelihood that deeper autism WILL result, and its depth, will be in near
> direct proportion to the level of 'hindrance'. (Morris 1999)

Then it may well be that finding a way to mitigate the sensory problems will
end LFA, which is a more laudable goal than ending autism in general (Klein
Undated, d).

What could cause the development of different SPATS?

These very real sensory perceptual problems may be connected to (caused by)
genetic predisposition, structural and/or functional brain abnormalities (caused
by viral infections or injuries during pregnancy, delivery or the first days/weeks
after birth), or abnormal biochemistry of the brain, when sensory over-
sensitivity triggers chemical or hormonal responses in the brain. The behaviours (withdrawal, for example) resulting from this may lead to developmental
problems (Williams 1999b). Another possible cause of developing 'autistic
behaviours' may be metabolic problems resulting in multiple food allergies
(leading to an inability to adjust adequately to different foods and resulting in
sensitization and, eventually, food intolerance). If they are left untreated,
severe food intolerance can cause brain damage, arising from both toxicity
and malnutrition due to malabsorption (Williams 1999b).

For 'horizontal reading':

1.3 – pp.39–44
3.3 – pp.191–196
4.3 – pp.256–259

2.4

Development

How we perceive the development of the child depends on our expectations. We know how the child should develop normally. Any deviation from this course, and the child is labelled 'developmentally disabled'. Then we may change our expectations and approach the child differently. However, as autism is not detected before the age of at least 18 months, there is likely to be direct or indirect pressure on the child to develop 'normally' (as expected) (Williams 1998). In the case of babies who would be diagnosed as autistic, there are several things that can happen:

- If the pressure is constructively and informatively utilized in developing a programme for assisting development and this programme is realistically and achievably paced, then the stuck child may dare developmental steps that are always just that bit beyond him or her.

- If the pressure is not realistically and achievably paced then overt or covert war may result. Overt war is outright defiance in the form of attack, active avoidance or withdrawal. Covert war may take the form of compliance without identification with the behaviour one is being taught to perform. The war in this case may remain unseen but fester in the form of emotional or psychological defence that is sometimes (correctly or incorrectly) seen as distractibility, lack of interest, laziness or 'disturbance'. (Williams 1998, pp.92–93)

I have found one of the most logical approaches to non-autistic vs. autistic development in the article *But My Kid is Low-Functioning... You're Not... What You Wrote Does Not Apply!* by Frank Klein (Undated, b), a high-functioning autistic person. Below is the gist of this article. (Though Mr Klein does not like readers to just look for the 'gist'; for the sake of space I am doing just that).

Parents of non-autistic children seem just to follow their instincts (and their own experience with their parents) to look after their offspring. Non-autistic babies (helpless at birth – non-verbal, unable to walk, unable to control their bodily functions, etc.) develop and learn to become more able to do these things over time. Assisting development is merely allowing the genetic blueprint for development to unfold. The child's brain (being stimulated in such a way that the newly-formed neurons are placed in a meaningful way) learns to make sense of its surroundings and respond to the environment. When the tried parenting techniques to assist development of an autistic child do not produce the same results as they do in non-autistic children, the child is labelled disabled, and parents seek special 'intervention' to 'return' the child to the 'normal track' of development. Although parents try their hardest, some of the children never do develop to the point where they can speak, use the toilet, brush their teeth, learn to interact with others, and become self-sufficient. Facilitating development in autistic children is much harder than it is for normal kids, and sometimes parents and professionals just cannot do it. However, a genetic blueprint for development exists in *all* children. As autistic brains are wired differently, by genetics/structural or biochemical differences, to non-autistic brains, we just do not know enough about facilitating development in autistic children to help their 'autistic blueprint for development' unfold. Even the lowest-functioning autistic people have programming for development in their brains. It is just that some barrier, or barriers, have prevented that code from being executed (Klein Undated, b).

Most developmental blocks, however, can be unblocked with the appropriate flexibility, open-mindedness, patience and approach (Williams 1998). If the blueprint of autistic development is faithfully and successfully followed (which is not always possible, considering how little we know about unblocking the development), the autistic baby will develop into a capable, verbal, intelligent, *autistic* adult. Autistic people do have different brain processes than non-autistic people, but if they develop, they can and do learn to speak, to interact, to become self-sufficient. These are signs of development, not of normality (as it is often erroneously assumed that if the person becomes verbal, intelligent and self-sufficient, he has 'recovered' from autism) (Klein Undated, b).

It is important to work *with* autism, instead of against it. Autistic people have ways of learning, ways of remembering, ways of orienting, and ways of working that are different from those of non-autistic people. If an autistic person has the same goal as a non-autistic person, he or she might need to follow a different procedure for getting there, using their natural mechanisms, not trying to do everything the same way as non-autistic people do it (Sinclair 1992). In order to help autistic children to develop in accordance with their genetic blueprints, one needs:

- to know their blueprint (i.e. the programme of their unique development) and the way they make sense of the world (different from the non-autistic one)

- to identify the blocks (or barriers) preventing them from 'programmed development' and to help the child to overcome these barriers

- to know how to facilitate their development considering their individual blueprints.

The majority of cases of autism may be actually compositions of a combination of co-morbid conditions that block and severely disrupt development, communication and information processing. The idea that someone who is severely autistic will grow up to be just as severely autistic may in many cases depend on whether these 'blocks' are recognized and addressed. However, when the child is diagnosed autistic, many of the (treatable) conditions underlying autism may simply be overlooked (Williams Undated, b).

It does not mean that autistic children do not need to be taught and disciplined – *all* children need that:

> Every child needs to be taught to function in the world. Every adult encounters problems and challenges from time to time, and needs to learn new skills or seek help from others. My point is that autistic people should be helped to function in the world as autistic people, not to spend their lives trying to become non-autistic. If an autistic person is engaging in behavior that is dangerous or destructive, or that interferes with the rights of others, then certainly this is a problem that needs to be resolved. If an autistic person lacks a skill that would enhance that person's ability to pursue his or her goals, then every effort should be made to teach the skill. The problem I see is when autistic people are subjected to intensive, stressful, and often very expensive treatments simply for the purpose of making them appear more normal: eliminating harmless behaviors just because non-autistic people think they're weird, or teaching skills and activities that are of no interest to the

autistic person just because non-autistic people enjoy those activities. (Sinclair 1992b, p.2)

Making them normal should never be the goal. Autistic children may need to have both some normal *and* some autistic behaviors extinguished, when they are dangerous or obviously unacceptable. The kind of right to be who and *what* you are...does not mean absolute freedom – the right to play with a ball-bat does not include the right to strike others with it, for example. Normal children might be allowed to play in the yard, but not the freeway; autistic children might be allowed to stim, but not bang their heads. Similarly, certain basic parts of living in society must be learned, like not fighting, not stealing, etc. As with normal children, practical judgement needs to be applied as to what should be tolerated. However, trying to eliminate all autistic behaviour is *not only* cruel and tyrannical, but counter-productive *and* a waste of time that could be used more productively. (Blackburn 1999)

Let us look at how autistic people themselves describe their development and identify the problems they experience. One of the main problems the majority of them identify is differences/disturbances in their sensory perception and information processing. Some hypothesize that sensory problems experienced early in life prevent the brain from getting the stimulation it needs during the critical developmental years. Klein (Undated, a) suggests that if you can get the senses integrated as early as possible in life, the brain will get what it needs, and the child will develop as high-functioning. According to Klein, sensory integration is the single most important factor in deciding how an autistic child will develop. Autistic children are often unable to filter incoming stimuli and are often very sensitive to many of them (that most people ignore/do not notice). Since their parents are usually non-autistic, they are of little help to the autistic child in sorting out sensory information and making sense of their world. This is the first step that begins the loneliness that most autistic individuals feel for much of their life (Joan and Rich 1999). Many autistic children who are considered 'low-functioning' could develop and lead useful and more independent lives if their compensatory strategies were understood, fostered, developed and refined (Williams 1996).

Autistic children learn very early in life to control their environment, and the amount of information coming in. The timing of the beginning of sensory problems can often explain the different routes of their cognitive, language, communication, social and emotional development.

If the capacity to perceive and interpret information is impaired, no verbal conceptualization is achieved spontaneously. In this case the transition from what Donna Williams calls 'sensing' to interpretation and verbal development may be delayed. Developmental blocks (biochemical, metabolic, perceptual, cognitive, emotional, psychological) should be unblocked to free up development. This will bring the beginning of expression through social interaction and communication with others. Without properly making this transition, the child would stay behind and might be staring at a pink billiard ball, resonating with its colour in the absence of any concept of what it is or its use. A lot depends on how consistent and predictable sensory perception and information processing are and how rewarding and comprehensible the new experiences are (Williams 1998).

If the sensory perception is inconsistent, fragmented, distorted and unreliable, the next stages of the process are unlikely to go smoothly. It is hardly surprising that they try to bring predictability and some order in the chaos in which they live by displaying what in mainstream literature is called 'self-stimulatory' ('autistic') behaviours. It is wise to encourage these behaviours (stims) when they do not result in embarrassment for the autistic person, or when they do not prevent them from learning. Engaging the child in more socially acceptable sensory stimulating behaviour such as swinging on swings or spinning on merry-go-rounds can help the child gain sensory stimulating information without engaging in less acceptable behaviours. The parent or teacher can use these early 'sensory' sessions to build rapport with the child (Joan and Rich 1999).

If sensory problems start early and the child learns to shut the systems down (in order to protect himself from painful and scary experiences), he creates a self-imposed sensory deprivation, that leads to complete isolation of the child from the outside world. It prevents him from learning via imitation and social interaction. Those who acquire autism-specific perceptual styles (monoprocessing, peripheral perception) get different experiences from the same stimuli that cannot be shared with non-autistic people whose perceptual styles are 'normal'.

Most, if not all, autistic children may have auditory processing problems, but they vary in severity. Those with minor problems often end up hyper-verbal and above average intelligence, more in the AS pattern than in the classical autism pattern (Klein 2002). There is a group of autistic children (at the so-called low-functioning end of the spectrum) who experience very severe auditory processing problems. They are not only late speakers, but may not speak at all or spend their entire lives with 'dysfunctional' speech. Many of these people have significant problems getting even the literal meaning of receptive speech in any consistent or ongoing way. They can be anywhere from completely functionally 'meaning deaf' to, at best, getting the literal meaning of 50 to 70 per cent of incoming auditory information. Their ability to link auditory information to any 'mental images' is missing – the words fall, meaningless (Williams Undated, a). The ability for a child to automatically learn language cannot proceed if the incoming information is perceived as a confusing jumble of noise, rather than coherent speech, when someone talks to him. The longer this auditory deficiency continues, the longer the neurons will continue to develop in a haphazard (and useless) manner, and the harder it will be to remediate the growing language difficulties (Klein 2002).

Differences in perception lead to development of different abilities and thinking styles, which are often not taken into account by those who live/work with them. 'Autistic thinking' is mostly perceptual in contrast to the 'verbal thinking' of non-autistic individuals. The most common type of perceptual thinking in autism is visual. For visual thinkers, the ideas are expressed as images that provide a concrete basis for understanding (O'Neill 1999). Every thought is represented by a picture (Grandin 1996a). Visual thinkers actually *see* their thoughts. For them, words are like a second language. In order to understand what is being said to them or what they are reading they have to translate it into images. Temple Grandin, probably the most famous 'visual thinker' in the world, describes how she has to translate both spoken and written words into full-colour movies with sound, which run 'like a VCR tape' in her head (Grandin 1996a, b).

Visualized thinking patterns vary from one person to the other. Some 'visualizers' can easily search the memory pictures as if they were searching through slides and are able to control the rate at which pictures 'flash' through their imagination. Others have a great difficulty in controlling the rate and may end up overloaded, with too many images coming all at once. Still others are slow to interpret the information into the 'visual mode', or mentally hold visual images together. Besides, the 'quality' of visual thinking may depend on the state the person is in, and even the time of day. For example, for Temple Grandin (2000), her thought pictures are clearer and with the most detailed images when she is drifting off to sleep.

However, visual thinking is by no means the only possible type of cognitive process in autism. Many people with AS, some people at the higher-functioning end of the autistic spectrum, and a very large percentage of people at the more intellectually disabled autistic end of the spectrum may not think in pictures at all. Many may not actually be able to and may be deprived of what could work for them and their intelligence is then wrongly judged by their inability to link visual images with words (Williams Undated, a). It is important to remember that not all autistic individuals are 'visual' in their thought-production process. Some may think in 'kinaesthetic images', others in 'auditory pictures', etc. Perceptual thinkers have trouble with words that cannot be translated into mental images (whether visual, kinaesthetic, tactile, etc.) and often have problems learning abstract things that cannot easily be imagined via perceptual mode. Social experiences present even greater challenges as they cannot be represented with 'sensory-based mental images' and 'because the social experience itself is not an entity that is there to be sensorily tested out again in any comparable way' (Williams 1996, p.147).

Autistic children are concrete thinkers. And there is a need to understand associative and spatial thought patterns. Being a spatial thinker means that a person represents things in the mind with a multidimensional model. This way of thinking brings both advantages and disadvantages. On the one hand, it is easier to see certain patterns of the world and infer things from those patterns. On the other hand, it is more difficult to do things that are more sequential (one-dimensional and in a line), especially when such a task involves picking a one-dimensional line out of multidimensional possibilities:

> This can look like a slowness or inability about doing certain things, or a learning disability. It can also be puzzling from the outside if you don't understand spatial thought, especially when abilities seem varied (like being able to do complicated geometry but having trouble with arithmetic). To quote myself in a moment of amusement and frustration, 'Infinity not a problem; toothbrushes tie my mind in knots.' (Baggs 1999)

Associative thought patterns may be reflected in the way autistic children use words in an inappropriate matter. Sometimes these uses have a logical associative meaning and other times they do not. For example, an autistic child might say the word 'dog' when he wants to go outside (Grandin 1996a).

The problem for most autistic people is that they do not realize that their sensory perceptual processing is different (for instance, Grandin 1996a; Lawson 2001; McKean 1994; O'Neill 1999; Willey 1999). Temple Grandin, for example, thought that other people were better and stronger than she was

when she could not tolerate scratchy clothes or loud noises (Grandin 1996a).
A typical thought they might have is:

> There is something wrong with me. I can't do things right. Everyone is
> mad at me. No matter how hard I try, something goes wrong. Other
> people can do the things I can't. It must be my fault that I'm having so
> much trouble. (Spicer 1998a)

It is no wonder that they are often unaware that they perceive the world differently from the other 99 per cent of the population because they have nothing
else to compare their perception with (Morris 1999). The first realization of
their differences comes in late teens or even later (Lawson 2001; Willey
1999). It may come as a kind of revelation, as well as a blessed relief, when
they learn that their sensory problems are not the result of their weakness or
lack of character. As more educators, doctors and parents understand these
differences, more children with autism will be helped from their terrible isolation and misunderstanding (which is tantamount to mistreatment) at younger
ages (Grandin 1996a).

However, the problem is that people around them are often unaware of
their different perceptions, and do not make any effort to accommodate and
adjust to these differences:

> Suppose you are colorblind, and cannot distinguish between red and
> green. You are in a room with other people, all of whom have normal
> vision. No one – not even you – knows that you are colorblind.
> Everyone is handed a list of instructions. They are printed in red against
> a green background. Everyone except you knows exactly what to do.
> They cannot understand why you just sit there. The paper looks blank
> to you, and you cannot understand how the others know what to do.
> Think of how you would feel, especially if the others stared at you, or
> whispered, or laughed. (Spicer 1998a)

It *is* possible to help an autistic child develop his or her potential if the carers
work *with* autism, not against it. (However, it does not mean to let the child run
havoc 'because he or she is autistic and this is the way they behave'. All
children need guidance and supervision.) Besides, learning does not end in
childhood. The autistic brain may develop at a much steeper rate than is otherwise expected, even to the point of almost catching up with its non-autistic
counterpart (Hawthorne 2002). The environment may either speed up the
development or hinder it.

Puberty often makes the problem worse. Sometimes 'well-behaved' children may develop unpredictable screaming fits, tantrums and other challenging behaviours at puberty. The hormones of adolescence further sensitize and inflame the nervous system (Grandin 1996a). Many autistic individuals report that fear may become their dominant emotion during puberty (see, for example, Jolliffe, Lakesdown and Robinson 1992; McKean 1994). Tony W, an adult with autism (in Bemporad 1979), recalls how he lived in a world of fear and that he was afraid of everything. About half of high-functioning autistic adults have severe anxiety and panic. Panic attacks seem to come in cycles. For example, for Temple Grandin, they tended to get worse in the spring and autumn (Grandin 1996a). Each individual works out his or her methods for dealing with 'panic attacks' or 'nerves'. For Temple Grandin, for instance, there are two ways to fight the nerves:

> Fixate on an intense activity, or withdraw and try to minimize outside stimulation. Fixating on one thing had a calming effect. When I was livestock editor… I used to write three articles in one night. While I was typing furiously I felt calmer. I was the most nervous when I had nothing to do. (Grandin 2002)

These are just two (out of many) real life experiences that illustrate how understanding carers and professionals can help autistic individuals develop their potential.

Temple Grandin

Temple Grandin is one of the most famous autistic achievers. She received her doctoral degree in animal science and is an inventor of livestock equipment, a lecturer and a writer. Yet she has autism. When she was a small child she had no speech, poor eye contact, tantrums, appearance of deafness, no interest in people, and constant staring off into space (Grandin 1996a). She might throw tantrums that seemed out of the blue. For instance, she used to rip apart her mattress and eat the stuffing, or tear off her clothes and run down the street. Her parents were advised that Temple should be institutionalized. Her mother refused and placed her in a programme for children with speech impairments. The classes there were small and highly structured. By the age of four, Temple began to speak and later was able to attend mainstream school. Once profoundly autistic, Temple Grandin went on to attend university, and eventually earn her PhD in animal science. She was not cured of her autism, but was helped to develop her strengths and to cope with her weaknesses. Temple attributes her success to several people in her life who made it possible – her mother (who did not believe the doctors and kept fighting for her daughter), her therapist (who kept her from withdrawing into her inner world), and her teacher (who encouraged her to develop her interest into a career in animal science).

Ros Blackburn

When asked 'How has a severely autistic child ended up a high-functioning autistic adult?', Ros Blackburn (2000) enumerated several reasons why she had done as well as she had done:

- *early intervention*: Ros says that in some ways autism is a great big gorgeous, cushy habit and the longer you are left to get set in your ways, the harder it is to get out of it.

- *parents*:

  > I had pretty unique parents. I had a mother who was, in many ways, able to turn off some of her natural parental emotions and instincts. She was able to be 'pig horrible' to her child and, in fact, be the cause of her child's distress. Admittedly, I hated it then, but I cannot thank my parents enough now for what they did. I am now able to live on my own (but by no means independently) in my little flat. (Blackburn 2000, p.2)

- *school*: Both primary and secondary schools Ros attended were very small and old-fashioned in style. The classroom setting was fairly ordered, each child having its own desk, rather than shared tables. Teaching materials were out of sight, rather than cluttered around the room. Even the walls were of pastel colours and plain, rather than bright and overstimulating. In many ways, therefore, it helped the easily distracted autistic child to stay focused.

Long-term prognosis of people diagnosed with ASDs is difficult at best. While the effects of autism do not disappear, it is possible through proper early intervention, support and education, leading to self-awareness, to live successful lives. The non-verbal self-abusive tantrumming toddler may develop into an independent, productive adult with merely residual outwardly visible effects of an ASD. Finally, as with all humans, the possible achievement of those on the autism spectrum is unlimited. The challenge is finding the key to unlock the potential (Shore Undated).

Some hints on how to facilitate the development: advice from autistic people to the parents and professionals

What parents and professionals need, more than fluffy 'success' stories of 'autistic' people who have learned to 'act normal', is information about the experiences people have of their particular type of 'autism'-related problems. What parents and professionals need is an understanding of how they might be able to identify different types of underlying problems so that they can work with the causes and not just symptoms. (Williams 1996, p.24)

If you quit looking at them [autistic people] as broken normal people, and start seeing them for the neat whole people that they are, you will begin to see them as I do from my perspective. Throw away your pre-conceived notions of what your child would have/should have/will/won't be, and embrace the child as he is. I know it is hard to do, but for your child's sake, you must. Accept the autism/AS, but don't listen to those that tell you the child is hopeless, or that he will never be able to take care of himself. Low expectations cause low results. Don't expect the unreasonable (like for the autism/AS to go away), but don't go to the other extreme either. Push to make your autistic child the best, most successful autistic he can be, and you may just be surprised by the results. (Klein Undated, a)

If loving parents can try to stand objectively away from their own emotional needs and relate to such children, always in terms of how these children perceive the world, then the children may...find the trust and courage to reach out step by step at their own pace... Gain trust and encourage the child that you accept who and where they are. Through trust they may develop interest in 'the world', and at first this exploration should be on the only terms they know – their own. Only once this is firmly established should you take the safety-net away slowly piece by piece... The way out, in complete contradiction to normal interaction, is *indirect* in nature. In this way it is less all-consuming, suffocating and invasive. The child can then reach out, not as a conforming role-play robot, but as a feeling, albeit extremely shy and evasive, human being... At this point I ought to make it clear that I do not espouse soft options. One must tackle war with war and disarmament with disarmament. I am saying that the war must be thought through, sensitive and well paced. (Williams 1999b, pp.180–181)

No excuses whatsoever were made for autism. Making excuses for autism is so futile, so damaging and above all, so wasteful of learning opportunities. I am inclined to say *'Never, never make excuses for autism, but help the person with autism overcome the problems caused by it.'* (Blackburn 2000, p.2)

Some of what we may be missing, those of us on the autism spectrum, is the ability to adjust to sensory assaults other people accept as normal. We may need to have information presented to us in a different way. Some things may take us longer, or we may accomplish certain kinds of work faster than anyone else but be unable to explain why or how. Our strengths and weaknesses are likely to be unusual when compared to the social norm, and sometimes that will cause us problems in working and living comfortably with those who think the norm should be good enough for everybody. (I'm reminded now of people – and there really are some! – who think a building is wheelchair accessible because there are 'just a few' stairs between the sidewalk and the door.) (Meyerding Undated)

It takes more work to communicate with someone whose native language isn't the same as yours. And autism goes deeper than language and culture; autistic people are 'foreigners' in any society. You're going to have to give up your assumptions about shared meanings. You're going to learn to back up to levels more basic than you've probably thought about before, to translate, and to check to make sure your translations are understood. You're going to have to give up the certainty that comes of being on your own familiar territory, of knowing you're in charge, and let your child teach you a little of her language, guide you a little way into his world… The ways we relate are *different*. Push for the things your expectations tell you are normal, and you'll find frustration, disappointment, resentment, maybe even rage and hatred. Approach respectfully, without preconceptions, and with openness to learning new things, and you'll find a world you could never have imagined. Yes, it takes more work than relating to a non-autistic person. But it *can* be done – unless non-autistic people are far more limited than we are in their capacity to relate. We spend our entire lives doing it. Each of us who does learn to talk to you, each of us who manages to function at all in your society, each of us who manages to reach out and make a connection with you, is operating in alien territory, making contact with alien beings. We spend our entire lives doing this. And then you tell us that we can't relate. (Sinclair 1993)

The parent shouldn't feel his or her child doesn't care or doesn't love, or can't sometimes enjoy the company of others. Autistics will shy away from crowds, and can be very upset by strangers in the house. But they also can feel attached to one or two kind and patient friends. Autistics often are extremely delightful people, with innovative thoughts, who simply have their own way of living and observing things. They are generally very honest and make sane, realistic observations of what they experience. It is highly difficult to hide anything from them. They detect emotions of other people. Often they reflect the emotions of others, so care must be taken to work on keeping the home atmosphere positive, loving and balanced. (O'Neill 1999, p.42)

For 'horizontal reading':

1.4 – pp.45–46
3.4 – pp.197–201
4.4 – pp.260–264

2.5

Theories

So far, all the theories claiming to explain autism that are 'officially recognized as valid' (or, at least, promising) have been originated by non-autistic researchers. The main drawback of these hypotheses is that the views of autistic individuals have not been taken into account (or have been ignored altogether): 'You are denying our reality…you are ignoring us…we are not allowed to exist unless we fit into your theory' (Gerland 1998, p.32).

The original error of many 'theoretical constructs' is that they attempt to describe and account for autism using the methods and perceptions of non-autistics (Morris 1999). That is why:

> Theories to define Autism come and go. Autistic behaviour and living as an autistic does not change when new revolutionary results are published. One doctor or one new trend isn't enough to form a whole picture of this condition, Autism. So many times the human aspect is neglected. (O'Neill 1999, p.24)

ToM

'Theory of Mind' and 'lack of ToM' are useful theoretical constructs that indicate that autistic people find it very difficult to take others' perspectives, to recognize and understand others' feelings, thoughts and intentions. However, yet again, it is used one-sidedly. Do non-autistic people easily recognize feelings and intentions of individuals with ASDs? Considering that autistic and non-autistic people do not *share* perceptual experiences due to sensory and information processing differences, don't non-autistic people find it difficult to take autistic individuals' perspectives? Isn't it more logical to assume that autistic people lack (have a problem with) Theory of Non-Autistic Mind, while non-autistic individuals have trouble interpreting Theory of Autistic

Mind? 'Thus both, the autistic and non-autistic alike, in relation to each other are "mindblind". Independently they are not, together they are... Each is mindblind to the other' (Myers *et al.* 2004, p.57).

> When I am interacting with someone, that person's perspective is as foreign to me as mine is to the other person. But while I am aware of this difference and can make deliberate efforts to figure out how someone else is experiencing a situation, I generally find that other people do not notice the difference in perspectives and simply assume that they understand my experience. When people make assumptions about my perspective without taking the trouble to find out such things as how I receive and process information or what my motives and priorities are, those assumptions are almost certain to be wrong. (Sinclair 1989, p.1)

All people have ToM and it has its validity and makes points of what is noticeable. However, every person has a different kind of ToM. ToM of autistic people is different from people who do not have autism. The way that people with autism think is just as valid as the thoughts of people without autism (Bovee Undated). Because autistic people see most normal people as seeming to assume everyone is like themselves, and would react as they would in the same situation, normal people may often seem as 'ToM-less NTs' to many individuals with autism (Blackburn 1999).

Autistic people cannot be taken for granted, and they cannot be expected to know something just because others know it (O'Neill 1999). Since people usually do not state their assumption explicitly (as they *assume* the other person has the same ToM), many autistic individuals cannot tell what their communicative partners are thinking. As their problems with using 'feeling-words' are quite common, it is difficult for them to find out what the assumptions are and to find a way to communicate discrepancies between what is being assumed and what they are actually experiencing (Sinclair 1989). For example:

> My mind was such that any sensing of fear over what I was to say made it impossible to express directly. The tricks of the mind I would play on myself in order to communicate condemned me to be judged by them. I was convincing my audience of the complete antithesis to what I truly was. What they saw as shallow, I experienced as deep. What they saw as clever, I found simple to reel off without any personal significance. Whilst people around me judged me by their eyes and ears, I was screaming out from beneath the empty façade of my shell to get them to

feel who I was; to close their eyes and their ears, and to try to sense me. (Williams 1999b, p.147)

The extent to which communication is successful depends on how effectively communicative partners are able to identify discrepancies in understanding and to 'translate' their own and the other person's terms to make sure they are both focusing on the same thing at the same time. Many autistic people feel that often it is left up to them to do all this work (and they do not mind this intellectual challenge; they are interested in learning about how people's minds work, and the sense of achievement when they manage to connect meaningfully may be exhilarating). What they *do* mind is when in spite of so much effort they still miss cues and someone who has not bothered to take a closer look at their perspective tells them that their failure to understand is because *they* lack empathy and ToM:

> If I know that I do not understand people and I devote all this energy and effort to figuring them out, do I have more or less empathy than people who not only do not understand me, but who do not even notice that they do not understand me? (Sinclair 1989, p.1)

When they ask for clarification to help them understand, they might be thought of as being stupid, awkward or that they just pretend not to know (Segar Undated).

Let us consider the claim that autistic people 'may not even know that they have minds and may be unable to think about their own thoughts'. Non-autistic children are not born with a 'ready-made' Theory of (Non-Autistic) Mind. They develop it usually by the age of four. As their thought-processes are similar to those around them and develop in accordance with 'normal lines of development', they soon become very successful in 'reading minds'. Autistic individuals may learn to 'read minds' later on in life, and using qualitatively different cognitive mechanisms. As a result, they are not quite successful in applying this theory in everyday life, with rapidly changing social situations, where they have to analyse each change as it comes. Given time they may be able to come to the right conclusion, but may not pick up on certain aspects of an interaction until they are considering it hours or days later (Blackburn 1999). If we remember that their perceptual experiences and thought-processes are qualitatively different from those around them, it is no wonder that it takes them much longer to figure out that other people think differently. For example, it took Donna Williams 13 years to understand that others 'play social games' (saying what they do not mean for the sake of being polite, for instance) for real, and assumed everybody should feel the same:

> When I was about 13, I had already bought into the socially learned game of facades but I'd bought into it late and clumsily, unable to fully integrate it. The database for these facades were picked up mostly from TV characters and I understood mimicry and acting according to stored learned roles. But what had deeply distressed and depressed me around this age was when I tried to get others to stop playing what I saw as a game and to drop their facades. I'd assumed their own facades, like mine, were part of a non-integrated database. I could clearly see straight past the surface and assumed they could too. (Williams 1998, pp.85–86)

Non-autistic people are often unaware of their own oddities, as seen by autistic eyes, but quick to detect the odd in a person with ASD (Meyerding Undated). The illustration of possible misunderstanding caused by lack of ToAM is given in Box 2.4. (Note that this is not a scientifically validated test – it is just an example of how difficult it may be to interpret behaviours if we lack shared experiences and ToAM.)

Box 2.4 ToAM test

1. The mother is crying; her autistic son is standing in front of her, laughing loudly. How would you interpret the child's behaviour?

    A) The child is happy.

    B) The child is upset.

    C) The child is indifferent.

2. The child asks his mother: 'Do you want to go for a walk?' Does it mean that:

    A) the child wants to know if the mother wants to go for a walk?

    B) the child wants to go for a walk?

C) the child is afraid that his mother may go for a walk and leave him at home?

3. The family is invited to a birthday party. The first thing their autistic son does on entering their friends' house is to push everybody out of his way and break the telephone. How would you interpret the child's behaviour?

A) The child hates the hosts and wants to hurt them.

B) The child tries to protect himself.

C) The child is naughty because his parents set him no parameters for his behaviour.

Answers

1–B: The child is frightened because he does not understand what is going on and does not know what to do in this situation. Laughter/giggling is often caused by frustration and confusion.

2–B: The child is echolalic and uses the phrase which he is asked when they go for a walk. It is his attempt to express his desire to go for a walk, using the phrase that always preceded this.

3–B: The child has auditory hypersensitivity, which is worse when the sound is unpredictable (and the telephone might ring at any time). To protect himself, the child breaks the phone.

Weak central coherence theory

What appeals in weak central coherence theory is the metaphor of fragmentation – the 'fragmented world of autism', the 'jigsaw puzzle of autism', etc. Fragmented perception does explain overcategorization (where a single stimulus may bring a reaction that may not be appropriate and is out of the context). However, this theory tries to embrace all aspects of autism and is not necessarily successful. How could this theory explain 'autistic memory' when whole chunks of situations are stored as single entities (as a whole) and may be triggered from outside?

Isn't it the case of a different development of meaning and a difficulty in breaking an unconventional whole (strong central coherence) into smaller units that are typical for the non-autistic mind? These 'non-fragmented' (but very specific) and strongly cohered thoughts unfold in an associative (Grandin 1996a, b) or a serial (Williams 1996) way. These associations may not be conventional but are they necessarily 'unconnected' or are the connections just different? These are just a few examples of the process of associative thinking:

> If I let my mind wander, the video [in her mind] jumps in a kind of free association from fence construction to a particular welding shop where I've seen posts being cut and Old John, the welder, making gates. If I continue thinking about John welding a gate, the video image changes to a series of short scenes of building gates on several projects I've worked on. Each video memory triggers another in this associative fashion. (Grandin 1996a, p.7)

> Touching the doorway to a room may trigger the serial memory of touching the same doorway of the same room another time and the events that happened after this. Serial memory can work for what was heard or seen or through movement but is linked to the same sequence in which events took place or the spaces they occurred in. (Williams 1996, p.148)

People with more severe autism seem to have difficulty stopping endless associations, and find it hard to get the mind back on track (Grandin 1996a). Another interesting argument is provided by Wendy Lawson who, just like non-autistic people, is driven to locate coherence within an understanding of her life, but who, unlike non-autistic people, goes about it differently.

Therefore, in ASD:

- it is not 'weak' coherence but a strong drive for coherence that exists. The problem is based in monotropism, which leads to there being a lack of connections. Therefore, the need to 'order', orchestrate and achieve coherence is very high.

- central coherence is the ability to draw connections together from the 'big picture', which can only occur with least effort, when one has access to the big picture via many different channels (polytropism).

- the need for coherence is extreme in monotropism, where all of the attention is gathered into one place. However, this type of coherence excludes information from outside the attention tunnel. (Lawson 2003, p.7)

Wendy Lawson (2001) defines monotropism or being singly channelled as being able to focus on only one thing at any one time, or only comfortable with using one channel. (Donna Williams names a similar phenomenon 'mono-processing'.) Wendy believes that most individuals with ASD are monotropic; monotropism can account for many difficulties people with ASD experience: for example, difficulties coping with change, processing language, generalizing one's experiences, understanding social situations, etc. (Lawson 2001).

Deficient executive functioning

Being able to use divided attention enables an individual to assess a number of situations and make choices about them far quicker than many autistic people who use single focused attention are able to. Therefore, many individuals with ASDs may have difficulty with executive functioning (organizing, planning, processing, decision making). Sometimes it leads to obsessive ordering, rituals, repetitive behaviour and/or lack of organizational ability outside the attention tunnel (Lawson 2003).

Sensory perceptual theory

One of the main problems autistic people experience is their abnormal perception. They do realize that they perceive the world differently, and many autistic authors consider autism as largely a condition relating to sensory processing (Gerland 1997; Grandin 1996a, b; Hale 1998; Lawson 1998; O'Neill 1999; Willey 1999; Williams 1999b; and others). Their books, articles, presentations are not talking about the Triad of Impairments, they are saying it is all about sensory processing. They are trying to show that the true invisible deep-rooted cause of all social, communicative and emotional problems is of a perceptual nature, and autism, to be really understood, has to be seen above all as a sensory perceptual condition (VanDalen 1995).

> Now I think that the use of speech and of other sensory activities that are normally lumped together as 'communication' are themselves a kind of sensory exploration. One's sense of self as a person is augmented and

developed in the process. The spoken environment is a peculiarly human invention, and like all other environments is learned by experience, both as a receiver and as a speaker. But for me all was distorted and unpredictable. (Blackman 2001, p.11)

However, not all autistic people make sensory perceptual problems the cornerstone of autism. Here we talk about different interpretations of 'sensory problems'. The confusion may be caused by 'official descriptions' of sensory difficulties – hypersensitivities (overresponsiveness) and hyposensitivities (underresponsiveness). In this case, the statement 'Autism is not sensory difficulties' (Klein 2002) is absolutely correct. Autism is about 'sensory differences' which are far more complicated than, for example, 'tactile defensiveness' (another awkward term in occupational therapy literature). Autism is about a different development of sensory perception that brings a different development of cognitive mechanisms. Visual thinking, for example, which is quite common in autism, is the product of this development. While hypersensitivities and 'defensiveness' are by-products that should be addressed as soon as they have been detected. Temple Grandin (1996a, b) puts forward a hypothesis that there is a continuum of sensory processing problems for most autistic people, which goes from fractured disjointed images at one end to a slight abnormality at the other. The routines of life and day-to-day connections which most people take for granted may be painfully overwhelming, non-existent or just confusing (Lawson 1998). When the person cannot cope with sensory information, he may shut down some or all sensory channels. Many autistic children are suspected of being deaf, as they sometimes do not react to sounds and many are taken for hearing tests as early as five or six months of age. Their hearing, however, is often even more acute than average, but they learn to 'switch it off' when they experience information overload. Autistic children develop a profound ability to control awareness of incoming sensory stimuli very early in life. As the child attempts to decipher and 'sort out' sensory information, he or she often engages in somewhat bizarre behaviours aimed at interpreting and integrating the sensory input that they receive. These behaviours include rocking, spinning, flapping arms, tapping fingers, watching things spin, gazing at reflections, etc. Children engaging in these behaviours are attempting to understand the world around them (Joan and Rich 1999). A child with sensory overload learns to avoid overwhelming sensory bombardment early in life. When sensory input becomes too intense and often painful a child learns to shut off his sensory channels and withdraw into his own world. Temple Grandin (1996b, 2000) hypothesizes that by doing this the autistic child creates his or her own self-imposed sensory deprivation that leads to secondary central nervous system (CNS) abnormalities that happen as a result of the autistic child's avoidance of input: 'In pulling away, I may not have received stimulation that was required for normal development' (Grandin 1996b).

> Auditory and tactile input often overwhelmed me. Loud noise hurt my ears. When noise and sensory stimulation became too intense, I was able to shut off my hearing and retreat into my own world. (Grandin 2000, p.16)

> When a baby is unable to keep up with the rate of incoming information, its threshold for involvement or attention is not great before aversion, diversion or retaliation responses step in, or plain and simple systems shutdowns: nobody's home. (Williams 2003, p.50)

To back up her argument Grandin (1996b) cites animal and human studies that show that restriction of sensory input causes the CNS to become overly sensitive to stimulation. Animals placed in an environment that severely restricts sensory input also develop many autistic symptoms such as stereotyped behaviour, hyperactivity and self-mutilation. Grandin (1996b) argues that the possibility of secondary damage of the nervous system may explain why young children receiving early intervention have a better prognosis than children who do not receive special treatment.

The effects of early sensory restriction are often long lasting, and the hypersensitivity caused by sensory deprivation seems to be relatively permanent. One possibility is that (at least most) autism may be a type of developmental deprivation syndrome (Blackburn 1999). Disturbances of attentional mechanism (in combination with sensory difficulties) may also contribute to the condition:

> It could be that multiple initial deficits (such as impaired attention-shifting, sensory issues, etc., or a combination) could cause a type of deprivation. Attending to only a limited number of stimuli could cause the affects of a limited environment. Similarly, failure to attend to social stimuli or to share joint-attention with others could have social deprivation effects. Traumatic sensory experiences may also cause withdrawal or failure to attend, and may cause other effects related to neural over-stimulation, while agnosia-like deficits may prevent learning and association and create its own type of isolation. Also, impaired attention shifting may cause failure to associate stimuli, as may a cortex which has been chronically overloaded and developed accordingly... It should be

remembered that even if causing a child to attend to such stimuli were to prevent some of this syndrome, the core impairments would still be there, and it would be unfair to assume that such a child (or adult) is normal. Just as some talented deaf people may learn to read lips and speak clearly, and yet still be profoundly deaf and unable to hear, it is unrealistic and unfair to assume that an autistic person who learns to function is cured, no longer autistic, or doesn't have disability which requires understanding and accommodation. (Blackburn 1999)

The timing of the advent of sensory processing problems may determine which type of autism develops:

> The exact timing of the sensory problems may determine whether a child has Kanner's syndrome [here: HFA] or is a nonverbal, low-functioning autistic. I hypothesize that oversensitivity to touch and auditory scrambling prior to the age of two may cause the rigidity of thinking and lack of emotional development found in Kanner-type autism. These children partially recover the ability to understand speech between the ages of two-and-a-half and three. [Those] who develop normally up to two years of age, may be more emotionally normal because emotional centres in the brain have had an opportunity to develop before the onset of sensory processing problems. It may be that a simple difference in timing determines which type of autism develops. (Grandin 1996a, p.50)

Autistic people often have difficulty moving from sensory patterns (literal interpretation) to an understanding of functions and forming concepts. With severe sensory processing problems verbal language may be perceived as no more than noise and has nothing to do with either interaction or interpretation of the environment. However, it does not mean that they remain stuck at the early stage of development (before acquiring verbal concepts). They do develop but 'via different routes'. A very interesting (and logical) explanation has been suggested by Donna Williams (1998). She distinguishes between two systems – 'system of sensing' and 'system of interpretation'. In normal development the transition from the system of sensing into the system of interpretation happens in the first days or weeks of life, whereas in autism some operate with a sensory-based system, while others acquire the system of interpretation later in life:

> Those who appear not to seek to make sense of their environment may not necessarily be 'retarded', disturbed, crazy or sensorily impaired, but may, in spite of not using the same system everyone else uses, still have

one of their own. They may, in spite of apparent delayed development, actually continue to use a system that others have left behind very much earlier. (Williams 1998, p.53)

With the system of sensing being dominant, they do not connect verbal labels with sensory impressions. Instead, they have their own words for things, based on sensory patterns. The sensory impressions they store in their memory become templates for recognition and identification of things, people, events. It is at this stage that they develop their cognitive ('non-verbal') languages, as 'the level of literal is enough to be able to use much of the language of interpretation on all levels: the language of touch, visual language and auditory language' (Williams 1998, p.104).

> Both on the level of verbal language, facial expression, body language and signing, the language of the system of sensing does not conform to the rules of the language of interpretation and it would be irrational to expect it to. Yet that is just what most people do expect. Even when it is accepted, it is considered aberrant, useless, pointless. Yet it often conveys experiences many people with interpretation have lost and could grow from knowing. Even understood, it is considered idiosyn-cratic. Yet, language and concepts within the system of sensing are repeated again and again by people devoid of interpretation or in whom interpretation is an inconsistent and secondary system who live on other sides of the earth and have never met each other. (Williams 1998, p.102)

With development and maturation many autistic individuals learn how to move from the system of sensing to the system of interpretation; while persons with low-functioning autism may continue to develop using the system of sensing as the dominant one.

The recognition of sensory perceptual problems is a new field and, unfortunately, many professionals are unaware or unknowledgeable about these problems, how to recognize them or what to do about them (Williams 1996). Isn't it time at last to listen to those who live with autism and consider the problems they identify as the primary ones instead of going in the opposite direction (higher and higher – to the tip of the iceberg)?

An 'experiencing self' theory

Some autistic individuals do have problems with 'experiencing self', when they can easily remember events but not the memory of their own selves participating in these events. There are at least two possible explanations provided by the autistic authors to account for this difficulty:

1. *Lack of body awareness* – Some autistic people lack body awareness (proprioceptive hyposensitivity) and have no concept of their body. For example, Tito, an autistic boy, knew about his body only theoretically – he could recognize himself on the photos, because his mother told him it was him when they looked at the family album, but he did not *experience* his body. To check that he did exist he used…his shadow: he flapped his hands and watched his shadow flapping its hands. It seemed he existed because of his shadow (Mukhopadhyay 2000). Tito got a memory of his mother teaching him the action songs, and a memory of *his shadow* doing the action, but he had no memory of his own self doing it.

2. *Monoprocessing causing 'self–other' problems (Williams 1996)* – One of the versions of monoprocessing is the inability to process simultaneously information of oneself and others, when the person is able:

   > to perceive a whole sense of other but robbed of a simultaneous sense of self; it is as though the approach of other causes the self to disappear. Information continues to be accumulated but as though accumulated not by [the] self but by a computer devoid of self. (Williams 1998, p.29)

An extreme version of the male brain theory

There are many men with ASDs who are good 'sympathizers'. And both male and female autistic individuals have a very strong sense of justice and would passionately fight for the rights of those who have been harmed. Many may be upset for days when they witness injustice. What about women with ASDs (diagnosed and undiagnosed) who are good at 'analysing'? We know examples of HF/AS women who have successfully completed their PhDs. How would we describe their brains – 'female brains with male-brain tendencies'?

For 'horizontal reading':

1.5 – pp.47–53
3.5 – pp.202–207
4.5 – pp.265–283

2.6

Treatments

There is no doubt that autism-appropriate intervention, understanding and mentoring can help autistic individuals enormously, but few, if any, non-autistic people have independent perceptions to be able to do that efficiently, on their own (Morris 1999). When we implement any treatment (medical or otherwise) with non-autistic people we always ask them how they are feeling during the treatment, whether they feel better after that, etc. Below are the answers to such questions by the autistic individuals who have undergone some treatments (but were never asked for their responses during their treatment). We will categorize the experiences in accordance with Donna Williams' subdivision of the most common approaches to treating autism (Williams 1996):

- symptoms and stereotype approaches (that are aimed at taking away the offending or disturbing symptoms/stereotypes to achieve the resemblance of 'normality')

- experience-based approaches (that try to understand autism from not what it looks like but from what it feels like)

- cause-based approaches (that attempt to look at various possible underlying causes of autistic symptoms and other related developmental conditions)

- 'cure' approaches (that seek 'cures' as though there is a 'normal' person within an 'autistic' shell which can be removed with special treatment).

Symptoms and stereotype approaches

Symptoms and stereotype approaches forget that symptoms are not causes. The eradication of symptoms may often be a relief to parents and professionals, and even to some people with ASDs themselves (for whom the achievement of functional ability and some of the (though conditional) acceptance, acknowledgement and inclusion is important). However, these approaches do not consider the idea that so-called 'normal' people should become more tolerant or accommodating and work *with* the condition rather than *against* it. The unspoken implication is to help autistic individuals to get rid of the symptoms and to learn to *act* 'normal' (not to *become* normal). To autistic people who identify with their behaviour and consider it a part of themselves and their personality these treatments may be a demonstration of a non-comprehending world that is lacking in tolerance and empathy. It is like teaching an amputee to walk without artificial limbs, a frame, or a wheelchair, or like 'curing' epilepsy by teaching people how to 'act normal' during a seizure (Williams 1996).

Behaviour Modification / Applied Behaviour Analysis (ABA)

The Behaviour Modification approach is primarily aimed at behaviours rather than the causes of these behaviours. What the ABA treatment does not take into account is that many different causes may produce the same 'behavioural picture'.

Some very young children with autism respond well to gently intrusive programmes in which they are constantly encouraged to look at the teacher/ carer and interact. However, while this programme is wonderful for some children, it is certain to be confusing and possibly painful for children with severe sensory processing problems (Grandin 1996a). Temple Grandin distinguishes two basic patterns of autistic symptoms that can help identify which children will respond well to intensive, gently intrusive teaching methods, and which will not:

> The first kind of child may appear deaf at age two, but by age three he or she can understand speech... The second kind of child appears to develop normally until one and a half or two and then loses speech. As the syndrome progresses, the ability to understand speech deteriorates and autistic symptoms worsen. A child that has been affectionate withdraws into autism as his sensory system becomes more and more scrambled. Eventually he may lose awareness of his surroundings, because his

brain is not able to process and understand sights and sounds around him. There are also children who are mixtures of the two kinds of autism. Children of the first kind will respond well to intensive, structured educational programs that pull them out of the autistic world, because their sensory systems provide a more or less accurate representation of things around them. There may be problems with sound or touch sensitivity, but they still have some realistic awareness of their surroundings. The second kind of child may not respond, because sensory jumbling makes the world incomprehensible. (Grandin 1996a, pp.55–56)

The system of rewards and punishments does not work for many autistic children in the same way as it does with non-autistic children. For example, very typical 'rewards' for good behaviour are hugs and verbal praise. For people with hypertactility (for whom touch may be a very painful experience) or for people with sensory processing problems (delayed processing, vulnerability to sensory overload, etc.) bombardment with 'rewarding' verbal and emotional praise may be seen as punishment for their attempts to 'stay in the world' and lead to undesirable outcomes such as withdrawals and lack of trust in those who are trying very hard to establish interaction and communication with them. On the other hand, such 'punishments' as 'time-out' or (predictable and ritualized) 'telling-off' may be very rewarding for those who find meaning in structure and predictability as tools of coping with fluctuating sensory perceptual and information processing problems.

> Sometimes, the links with rewards or punishments simply aren't made because of problems of connection and the whole behaviour modification program may feel like a senseless ritual of abuse, regardless of its 'good' intentions. What is more, when people display natural responses to 'rewards' that they find disturbing or confusing, or clearly mistake punishments for rewards because they are felt that way, they can infuriate their carers, sometimes resulting in even more confusing, unpredictable or disturbing responses from their carers. (Williams 1996, pp.51–52)

But how can we explain a 'success' of this therapy documented in autism literature? In some cases, 'success' means compliance:

> Compliance is not learning, because you do not connect it with your own thoughts, feelings or intentions. Compliance is mindless. Compliance may appear to achieve things in the short term, but the arrest in the development of connections to thought, feelings and intention may not

only create extreme (generally compliantly repressed) chronic stress, but may ultimately result in physical, emotional or mental breakdown if the effects of pervasive compliance are not properly addressed. (Williams 1996, p.52)

In this case, ABA does not 'cure' (or reduce) autism, it just covers it up (Blackburn 1999). For many people with autism (who have undergone this treatment) the message they got was 'I am not meant to exist as myself' (Williams 1996).

I was able to learn how to laugh at the right times, adopt the 'right' tone of voice, gestures, posture, vocabulary, use of expressions, and (in many cases) social behavior. By the time I was 12 I came across as a quiet, polite, well-behaved child, and if anybody had asked me how I was doing, I would have insisted that I was fine.
    I wasn't fine. (Spicer 1998b, p.2)

In other cases, this therapy may be successful because gentle intrusive teaching started before their senses became totally scrambled:

Catherine Maurice describes her successful use of the Lovaas program with her two children, who lost speech at fifteen and eighteen months of age, in her book, *Let Me Hear Your Voice.* Teaching was started within six months of the onset of the symptoms. The regression into autism was not complete, and her children still had some awareness. If she had waited until they were four or five, it is very likely that the Lovaas method would have caused confusion and sensory overload. (Grandin 1996a, p.56)

So the timing and the nature of underlying autism-related problems should be taken into account to decide whether the ABA is appropriate for each particular individual. For example, if the underlying problems are mostly of sensory perceptual nature, the treatment is sure to fail, and may even hinder the development.

This and similar treatments do not take into consideration that:

- autistic individuals can learn compensatory skills, but not how to be 'normal'

- their perceptions and thought processes are different, and that they cannot change that any more than the blind can learn to see with their eyes

- what is adaptive for normal may be maladaptive for autistic people (and vice versa)

- autistic ways can be better for them and can allow them to function quite well in certain situations and at certain tasks (Blackburn 1999).

If involuntary (autistic) behaviours (aimed to correct problems such as, for example, sensory perceptual distortions and hypersensitivities) are consistently interfering with the ability to interact, communicate or learn, it is more constructive and important to *real* development (as opposed to a well-trained circus act of 'normality') to try to decrease overload. Having people put all their energies into suppressing their involuntary responses (rather than dealing with their causes) makes the perceived necessity for these behaviours even greater: 'People need to be extremely cautious, non-arrogant, non-ignorant and non-assuming when trying to alter a system they do not understand and do not, themselves, use nor need' (Williams 1996, p.173).

It is possible for an autistic person to appear to be pretty much 'like everyone else' in some settings, at least. What is not visible from the outside, however, is the amount of work and stress involved in maintaining this façade (Spicer 1998b).

Speech and language therapy

Traditional approaches to teaching autistic children to speak focusing on eye contact, imitation of sounds, pointing and signing do not work, they are slow and often meaningless to the child as they do not lead to functional communication. Autistic children may have no idea that drills in repeating meaningless (for them) sound patterns may be a way to exchange meaning with other minds (Sinclair 1992a). Jim Sinclair, for example, did not know that language was a tool for communication until he was 12 years of age. The sessions of speech therapy with traditional drills were incomprehensible to him.

PICTURE EXCHANGE COMMUNICATION SYSTEM (PECS)

PECS works with those whose visual perception is reliable. Individuals with visual processing problems may merely see the cards as something to flap, chew or flick. Some can memorize pictures and words but may find it difficult to relate the 2D image to objects because they remember things using other senses (movement, smell, sound or taste). Some with severe visual perceptual fragmentation may not see whole objects. So the development of the ability to think in pictures (as opposed to fragments) is like colour to the blind (Williams Undated, a).

Experience-based approaches

These approaches acknowledge that viewing the condition from its outside appearances is not enough (Williams 1996). The examples of experience-based approaches are options, facilitated communication, sensory integration therapy, auditory integration training and the Irlen method. Let us have a look at some of these approaches from the perspective of people with ASDs.

The options approach

It works almost in antithesis to conventional behaviour modification (Williams 2003) and attempts to relate to the autistic child along any lines which make sense to the child (even if it does not make sense to the child's carer (Williams 1996)). Stephen Shore describes how his mother tried first to get him to imitate her, but failed. Then, changing tack, she tried to imitate her son. In doing so, Stephen became aware of her existence. This imitation had very important educational implications. The educator (parent) meets the child on his or her level, even if it means stimming with the child. When the child becomes aware that the educator is part of his or her environment, the educator can start to pull the child's attention in the desired direction (Shore 2003). However, it may work with some children but be of problematic use for others:

> For example, where the goal of the options approach is to accept, understand and use as a basis for interaction, certain perceptual and sensory 'differences', this does not necessarily mean that understanding will assist people in removing some of these things [sensory or perceptual problems, inability to control movements and behaviours they do not intend] and, thereby, freeing these people to communicate and interact more easily in less 'autistic' ways. Also, where someone is compelled to communicate, interact and behave in ways that they do not intend, so frustrating themselves, the options approach, using any expression as the basis for interaction, may potentially further frustrate and alienate those people who do not identify with or intend these expressions in the first place. (Williams 1996, p.56)

Facilitated communication (FC)

Another technique in the category of experience-based approaches is facilitated communication. It may be useful, for example, for those with impulse-control problems or for those with intense exposure anxiety for whom typing is far less directly confrontational (Williams 1996, 2003). Even if it does not work for all (and no one approach will suit all the individuals), it is important to recognize that FC does give a 'voice' to a group of autistic people who otherwise might never get a chance to be heard:

> I have found so much strength from being able to communicate my thoughts and feelings to people via typing. In fact, being able to communicate has changed my life. Although as you most probably realize communicating via typing is a form of indirect communication, when I communicate via typing I know I can respond. I can ask questions, I can relate my feelings and just in fact be myself with no pressure to speak. (Attfield 1998, p.2)

Some autistic persons (whose communication is indirectly confrontational) may verbally produce what may seem utter nonsense but still be able to type out their felt reality by attributing responsibility for their communication to someone else (facilitator) (Williams 2003). Facilitation in the right hands and with the person for whom it can be of benefit may achieve remarkable results. With an inexperienced facilitator, however, FC can create more problems than it solves:

> A too easy-going approach with someone requiring a firm one, may lead not to the facilitator manipulating the typist, but in the typist intentionally or unintentionally manipulating, confusing or misleading the facilitator... On the other hand, a too firm or too clinical approach used with someone who requires only encouragement and a gentle approach may result in freezing that person out of communication or even blocking their perception of themselves, which is at the basis of an ability to express with intention. (Williams 1996, p.58)

FC works with some people but does not benefit others. 'It is likely that the truth about FC is somewhere between wishful hand-pushing and real communication' (Grandin 1996a, p.57).

Sensory integration therapy (SIT)

There are many techniques used in SIT: some of them are aimed at desensitizing the child to the stimuli they find painful/overwhelming, others to integrate the senses. While recognizing the deficiencies and difficulties many children experience, these approaches still often address the symptoms and not the causes. For example, multi-sensory integration technique seeks to get people to use their senses simultaneously, in an integrated way. Though this approach does acknowledge that some autistic people work in 'mono' (using one sense at a time), it does not take into account what may cause this problem; that is, why sensory integration has not taken place. 'This is a bit like finding someone who can't walk properly and training them to walk without taking account of the fact the person has got broken legs' (Williams 1996, p.59).

There may be several causes leading to 'mono-processing' (in this case, as an adaptation or a compensatory strategy which the person acquires to overcome the difficulties/deficiencies of sensory perception):

- The autistic person is unable to filter background and foreground stimuli, when the brain is unable to filter out enough information on each sensory channel for it to cope efficiently with all that information at once. In this case, using only one channel to process information gives the person an opportunity to process information on one channel rather than getting sensory overload when the person cannot stop the 'flood' of overwhelming and confusing information coming through all the channels:

    If the therapist forces someone like this to look whilst they are listening, one of several things might happen. One is that the person might continue to process what he or she hears but might stare obliviously straight through what he or she is made to look at without registering its meaning or significance. Another is that his or her systems might switch and he or she might process what is seen but might no longer process what is heard. The third, and more disastrous and damaging consequence is that the person might continue to process what he or she hears, also process what he or she is looking at but, after a short amount of time the accumulative effects, or delayed processing caused by too much coming in at once from too many channels, might result in information overload...that...in turn, can result in a sharp attack of sensory hypersensitivity (with its resulting 'tantrums' and 'behaviour problems') or might go further to result in...'total shutdown'. (Williams 1996, p.59)

- Where there is fragmented perception the person may switch off several channels and use one in order to avoid fragmentation and get some meaning from the situation.

Some components of SIT (for instance, application of deep pressure and vestibular stimulation) may be beneficial for some individuals with autism. It is easy to apply comforting deep pressure over large areas of the body to little children by placing them under large pillows or rolling them up in heavy gym mats. Swinging is good for providing stimulation for a deficient vestibular system. These procedures need to be done every day, but not for hours and hours. Depending on the children's anxiety level, some will need access to deep pressure and swinging throughout a day to calm themselves down when they become overstimulated. Touch sensitivity can also be reduced by massaging the body and stroking with soft surgical scrub brushes.

Tom McKean made his pressure suit and used soft brushes to firmly brush his skin to make his body pain go away. Temple Grandin used this therapy method when she invented her squeeze machine. In *Emergence: Labeled Autistic* (Grandin and Scariano 1986) Grandin describes craving pressure stimulation which was an approach-avoiding situation. Temple wanted to feel the sensation of being hugged, but when people hugged her, the stimuli were overwhelming and washed over her like a tidal wave. In the book Grandin describes the squeeze or hug machine she invented to overcome her deficiency. It took her a long time to learn to accept the feeling of being held and not try to pull away from it.

Auditory integration training (AIT)

AIT seeks to reduce auditory hypersensitivity by retraining the ear to tolerate certain frequencies and pitches. In the book *Sound of a Miracle* (1991), Annabel Stehli describes how her autistic daughter's life changed after she received this treatment. As her main sensory problem was auditory hypersensitivity, after the AIT that had greatly reduced this sensitivity, she was no longer terrified of sounds and could participate in the environment. However, while many autistic people do suffer from auditory hypersensitivity (among other sensitivities), the underlying causes of this hypersensitivity may have nothing to do with the perception of pitch or volume but rather with information overload and sensory integration problems (Williams 1996).

The assumption has been put forward recently that the communication difficulties of people with autism may be caused by auditory problems. It is not necessarily true for all people with autism. Those who are echolalic, for example, can repeat back everything that has been said to them. In this case, it is not the problem of hearing per se, but rather the problem of processing auditory information. Retraining the ear, in this case, would not bring understanding or make meaning out of what you hear. Those autistic people who experience pronunciation problems may not be good candidates for AIT either. They may have sensory integration problems (when they cannot hear with meaning and speak at the same time) that have nothing to do with how they perceive sounds; it might be that their brain may not be able adequately to monitor the sound of their own voice at the same time as they are speaking (Williams 1996). Though training a person's hearing to not perceive certain frequencies may bring reduction of stress in the short term for some people, it will not necessarily improve the efficiency of information processing and sensory overload. This could be addressed equally well by using ear plugs in noisy places and reducing the number of simultaneous stimuli (Lawson 2001; Williams 1996). Some people who underwent this treatment report that the benefits were short-lived (McKean 1999), others could see real improvement not only in reducing auditory sensitivities but also improvements in other sensory systems (Blackman 2001).

Irlen method

Some autistic people with visual processing problems have been greatly helped by Irlen tinted glasses, which filter out certain colour frequencies and enable a deficient visual system to tolerate bright light or contrast, to improve depth perception, to stop fragmented visual perception, and to reduce or even eliminate visual distortions. Another reported benefit of tinted glasses is that they may also improve functioning in other systems (when other senses were used to compensate unreliable visual perception) (Williams 1996).

Cause-based approaches

These treatments attempt to take into account the underlying causes of various symptoms of autism. One of the problems of some cause-based approaches is that they assume a single type of 'autism' with a variety of underlying causes when there may be several different types of 'autism' and sometimes more than one type of 'autism' present (Williams 1996).

Biochemical treatments

In some autistic people various diets and vitamin and mineral supplements have brought significant improvements in their processing of information, sensory hypersensitivities, communication, mood and behaviour. Some people have seen these problems as 'causes' when all the signs of their 'autism' have disappeared. Others have seen these problems as 'aggravators', when 'autistic symptoms' have not disappeared but the functioning was significantly improved (Williams 1996).

MEDICATION

Some drug treatments can be helpful to people with autism. Unfortunately, many medical professionals do not know how to use them properly. For instance, there have been cases when the wrong drug was prescribed to an autistic person which caused grand mal seizures; some treatments have made zombies out of autistic individuals who were given enough neuroleptics to put a horse asleep; and some autistic people have experienced serious side effects because of an excessive dose of an antidepressant (Grandin 1996a). It has been reported that doses that are effective for autism are often much lower than the doses used to treat depression in non-autistic people. Too high a dose for somebody with autism may result in agitation, insomnia, aggression and excitement.

Since autism is a spectrum condition, a drug that works for one person may be worthless for somebody else. If a drug has little or no effect, it is not worth taking. Likewise medications that work should be used, but those that do not work should be discontinued. From her own experience, Temple Grandin concludes that some medications (for example, tranquilizers such as diazepam (Valium) and alprazolam (Xanax)) are best avoided; other medications are better for long-term treatment. Each case is different. For instance, though Prozac received some bad publicity, it has been very beneficial for some people, including Temple Grandin. Prozac and Anafanil (clomipramine) seem to be effective for autistic people who have obsessive-compulsive symptoms or obsessive thoughts. The effective doses for Prozac have ranged from two 20 mg doses per week to 40 mg per day. Too high a dose will cause agitation and excitement. If an autistic person becomes agitated the dose should be lowered (Grandin 2002).

Some autistic individuals need medication to control anxiety, panic and obsessions, while others have mild symptoms that can be controlled with exercise and other non-drug treatments. In some cases, sudden outbursts of rage are actually frontal-lobe epilepsy, in which cases anticonvulsant medication might be helpful. However, it is important to remember that 'all medications have some risk. When the decision is being made to use a medication, the risk must be weighted against benefit' (Grandin 1996a, p.123). Besides, autistic individuals may have unusual reactions to drugs – underreactions, overreactions, and a 'paradoxical' (reverse) reaction being the most common (Baggs Undated). During puberty when the problems may worsen due to hormone development, medications such as beta-blockers are often helpful because they can calm an overaroused sympathetic nervous system (Grandin 1996a). Though the proper use of medication (especially when autism co-occurs with epilepsy, or the person experiences severe panic attacks) may be a part of a good autism programme, it is not a substitute for the proper educational programme. 'Medication can reduce anxiety, but it will not inspire a person the way a good teacher can' (Grandin 1996a, p.119).

Psychodynamic therapy

Though the inability of non-autistic people to understand people with autism can create a very high degree of mental and emotional stress in autistic individuals, it does not mean that autism is a mental illness or psychological or emotional disturbance. Psychodynamic therapy often assumes that the person's problems have been caused by the environment. Although the problems of some autistic people are made significantly worse by non-autistic people not understanding their sensory perceptual or processing problems, this is not what the psychotherapist is trained to set right (Williams 1996). Psychodynamic theory denies the reality of autistic people in more ways than one:

> The theory itself allows for the existence of autistic people to be denied – that is, it denies our existence *as autistic people*, by postulating that there we are not who and what we are, but that there is a 'normal' person hidden inside. Secondly, the whole theory actively denies our experience and perspective. The analysts have already defined our thoughts, feelings, desires, and experiences to be false. To the analysts, our differences are not real, and all our hopes, fears, ideas, feelings, and experiences are unconscious fronts of self-deception. Thus, our personal perspectives – what some existential and humanistic therapists would call our 'reality' – is denied as unreal and harmful. This leads to insulting, useless therapy and frustration. (Blackburn 1999)

Many high-functioning autistic people who have been analysed under the psychodynamic model – often by very well-meaning therapists – have not been helped at all, many have been degraded, and some have been harmed (Gerland 1998). What is more, some autistic people believe that psycho-analytical theories have contributed significantly to the common misunder-standing of autism (Blackburn 1999; Gerland 1997, 1998). Many individuals with high-functioning autism still suffer the wound of such treatment (Gerland and Sainsbury 1999).

'Cure' approaches

Contrary to the belief of some parents and professionals that autistic people can grow out of autism, or another extreme, that if 'cures' happen, some pro-fessionals believe that the original diagnosis was incorrect because 'true autis-tics' are incurable, many autistic authors give different interpretations of these issues. First, autistic people display a spectrum of social awareness, communi-cation skills, sensory perceptual and cognitive differences. That is why, depending on the environmental variables, there may be 'success' stories of some autistic individuals *appearing* non-autistic. However, it does not mean that these 'cured' autistics are unlikely to be able to *experience* everything they have learned to perform:

> Like files in a computer, people can mentally store copied performances of emotions, retrieve them, and act them out. But that doesn't mean the performance is connected to a real feeling or that there is any under-standing of a portrayed emotion beyond the pure mechanics of how and possibly when to emulate it... [However,] no matter how much you succeed in distorting the various forms of expression that can be squeezed out if you are working back-to-front, the system remains an autistic one. Any other process of more real growth takes time and nobody advertises slow miracles. (Williams 1999c, pp.210–211)

Treatments based on a 'cure' approach include 'hug therapy' or 'holding therapy' where 'love' is the weapon to break the 'autistic shell' and get through to the autistic person. These treatments assume that all sensory and perceptual systems are intact and integrated and that information processing for the person is basically 'normal', except that issues like 'love' and who is in control have not yet been established for that person (Williams 1996). For those people with autism who experience extreme sensory or emotional sensi-tivity 'hug/holding therapy' may only be seen as 'one more ignorant infliction that further demonstrates people's lack of empathy for their sensitivity' (Williams 1996, p.54). Many autistic people with sensory problems (especially, tactile hypersensitivity) believe that forced holding is not a 'therapy' but a form of abuse, a form of 'sensory rape' (Sainsbury 2000b).

As for 'success stories' of 'holding' to produce the expected or wanted compliance: 'it may only be because it has been incidentally used like an unintentional punishment, teaching people that if they give the desired responses quickly, they are set free' (Williams 1996, p.54).

> My quietness was due to exhaustion and to my being disturbed so much as a result of the experience that I was shocked into a state of terrified quietness, where I could not think of anything much for a while. (Jolliffe *et al.* 1992, p.17)

However, there is perhaps one case where holding therapy may be of some benefit:

> [When self-abuse is caused by] an entirely uncontrollable, instinctive and unwelcome response to information overload…the self-abusive person may develop extreme mistrust of themselves in being unable to stop these unwelcome self-attacks… In this case and this case only, sometimes finding that someone else will protect you from your own uncontrollable self-abuse can be a psychological tool to building trust of oneself and of others and some self-abusive people…have sought this external constraint voluntarily, finding themselves more able to get on with life in between these self-abusive urges. With such people, holding may be one non-violent and effective short-term means of helping some self-abusive people to develop eventually greater self-trust and perhaps also self-management skills in the eventual handling of their own self-abuse. Ultimately, however, these self-abusive urges very often have a biochemical origin much better dealt with, or at least backed up by, a nutritional approach. (Williams 1996, pp.56–57)

Some autistic authors find it very dangerous when 'holding therapy' is seen as the same approach as Temple Grandin's squeeze machine, or desensitization. The main difference is that the latter two do not imply force and allow a person to explore touch and deep pressure in a way which is completely under their control: 'If this [being forcibly held until one stops resisting] had been done to me, I would have found it highly aversive and stressful' (Grandin 1992, p.121).

Similarly, 'holding therapy' should not be confused with 'desen-sitsation'...[the technique] to reduce defensiveness by gradually exposing a child to touch in a way which is safe and enjoyable to them. Obviously, force has no place in such an approach as it would only increase the child's impression that touch is threatening and unpredict-able. It is only possible to learn that touch can be a medium for affection and love if you know that you will be treated with respect, not violence. (Sainsbury 2000b)

Those who strongly advise against 'force holding' do not intend to attack parents for their desire to carry out 'holding therapy' out of love for their child and with the best intentions. The point they are making is that:

the parents' intentions make no difference to the child's experience. It may seem 'loving' to non-autistic people, but to people with autism it seems like torture. Having trusted parents suddenly do horrible things to you and ignore your pleas for help must just make the whole experi-ence even more traumatic and incomprehensible... I want to beg everyone connected with autism to stop this now. (Sainsbury 2000b)

Grandin completely disagrees with the originator of the therapy, Welch (1983), that the child has to become severely distressed for holding to be effective; she insists that the benefits of holding therapy could be obtained through less stressful methods (Grandin 2002).

As autism is a spectrum disorder (or, alternatively, there are several types of underlying problems), all approaches have their time, place and *person*, but none of them is useful all the time, in all the places, with all the people. The question is, how to know when and where that time and place is and for whom these approaches will work to gain the most 'success' and cause the least damage or fewest set-backs. By looking at what is underneath the symptoms, this question might have some answers (Williams 1996). For example:

I have known of people without sensory hypersensitivity who have received 'therapy' meant to aid a condition they didn't suffer from (at great expense). I have known of people with no psychological or emo-tional disturbance or damage being 'treated' for having it (and con-vinced it is in their interests to believe they had it so they could 'get better'). I have known of sensorily and emotionally hypersensitive people who are already suffering from extreme information overload who have been put through the emotional and sensory bombardment of 'hug therapy'. I have known of sensorily hypersensitive people and people with perceptual problems and problems of system integration being put through behaviour modification programs to teach them to behave as though their problems do not exist or even punished for displaying any signs or compensatory adaptations to their problems. What I think was missing in all of these cases was a proper understanding of what these 'autistic' people were dealing with and enough humility for carers and professionals to admit when they weren't sure or didn't know how to help a particular person. What is needed generally are suggestions of how to deal specifically with each of these underlying conditions (types of 'autism'-related problems) so that people get services that don't waste their time, their money or cause further set-backs to a person who has enough to cope with already. (Williams 1996, p.49)

Children in all diagnostic categories of ASDs seem to benefit from placement in a good educational programme. Prognosis is improved if intensive education is started before age three. For example, Temple Grandin finally learned to speak at three and a half, after a year of intensive speech therapy. Children who regress at eighteen to twenty-four months of age respond to intensive educational programmes when speech loss first occurs, but as they become older they may require calmer, quieter teaching methods to prevent sensory overload. If an educational programme is successful, many autistic symptoms become less severe (Grandin 1996a).

The effectiveness of different types of programme is going to vary from case to case. A programme that is effective for one case may be less effective for another (Grandin 2002). Radically different treatments based on different (even conflicting) theories have been found effective in some cases. One of the explanations is that there must be something in the quality of the 'therapeutic relationship' which is important, not specific to the therapy or the theory behind it (Blackburn 1999). For example:

Some of the 'avoidant' (and many 'aloof') children…were put through hours, months or years of psychotherapy or hug therapy to try to get them to release the frustration and pain that therapists assumed they harboured. When any of these 'autistic' people did begin to express themselves, it may have been presumed to be evidence that the original assumptions had been correct and the therapy appropriate. It was probably never questioned whether access to art materials in the therapist's office may have been the real key to their expression; whether it was just quieter in the therapist's office without a TV blaring or any distracting social blah-blah in the background; whether progress may have come down to something [as] simple as the therapist's office not having fluorescent lights in it like home did; or even whether the 'autistic' person (as some do) had spontaneously outgrown their developmental difficulties. (Williams 1996, p.10)

Some improve *despite* the treatment (which amounts to mistreatment) they get.

'To treat or not to treat?' That is the question

There are several opinions on this issue. Some autistic individuals (who have been 'treated' = 'mistreated') are strongly against the interference and suggest that a person should be asked whether he or she wants to be treated or cured of autism. If the person cannot say (or indicate in some way), the most common advice is 'Leave them alone'. It is this approach that infuriates parents and professionals. Many others (who see autism as a separate phenomenon from many autism-related problems) think it would be inhumane and cruel to allow an autistic child to suffer (not from autism but) from extreme sensory perceptual problems (like severe auditory and visual processing problems and hypersensitivities), allergies, digestive or immune system problems, that can and must be treated (Klein Undated, c; Williams Undated, b). The problems caused by these and similar disorders, however, are not corrected with behavioural methods. Rather than attempt to cure autistic individuals, all the energy should be channelled to help those that are destined to become low-functioning to develop into high-functioning (in the early years) (Klein Undated, c).

What about adults with autism? Should they be 'cured' or just helped to function using their 'autistic mechanisms'? One of the opinions on 'cure' for autistic adults is expressed by Jared Blackburn, who compares it with 'curing' blindness in an adult. This person would still have serious visual deficits as his brain had irreversibly adapted to being blind. Blackburn suspects that even if the original cause were removed (or went away on its own – which may happen), the person would still be autistic because it is the developmental results that are important. Even if a person is 'cured' of their autistic 'symptoms' (or behaviours), the person still has an autistic brain, and new (more normal) behaviours may be maladaptive and

> such people are probably worse off because they are no longer performing compensatory behaviors – ie, the 'cured' people have been taught to behave maladaptively. (Blackburn 1999)

The majority of people with autism suggest that in order to provide better services for people with autism, parents and professionals need to be better trained and educated so that they can deal with more than just symptoms. It is vital to differentiate between helping a person to develop and function successfully, and 'curing' the person by eliminating certain behaviours. Attacking symptoms does not get rid of the causes and for many autistic people, if symptoms are suppressed, the causes just create new symptoms to replace the old ones.

> That frustrates everybody. It frustrates parents who put their faith in those working with their children. It frustrates the teachers and professionals who put effort into helping people with 'autism' only to see the same or similar problems recurring. Most of all, it frustrates those adults and children with 'autism' who want REAL help. (Williams 1996, p.24)

Unauthorized but quite common 'treatments' of (diagnosed and undiagnosed) autistic individuals

Bullying

Bullying in schools is a problem not only for autistic children but for non-autistic ones as well. However, children on the autism spectrum are more vulnerable because they often do not know that they may complain to teachers and parents and seek help. They see the problem in themselves. From an early age they are bullied and treated badly because of whom they are. They are often targeted and victimized by other people simply for being different (Aston 2000; Jackson 2002; Newson 2001; Sainsbury 2000a). They know they do not fit in with their school peers but are unable to figure out what they are doing wrong. No matter how hard they try, they are made fun of (Grandin 1996a). They may be called names, spat at, pushed, punched or hit (Carpenter 1992; Jackson 2002; Grandin 1996a). The following is a very typical description of school experiences:

> When I started school I struggled to understand what was going on, but one thing I did understand was that most of the kids were pretty mean to me. I never knew why. (Jackson 2002, p.135)

Even when they are not a target they may still be rejected:

> I remember how desperately I used to wish to be part of other children's games… I may have been unaware that there was anything wrong with me but the feelings of rejection I felt then were to crop up time and time again for years to come. (Segar Undated)

> I was constantly aware that no-one liked me, that whenever we were told to pair up in lessons, for example, I was always the one left over. Even if there were even numbers in the class, the teacher would still have to order someone else to form a pair with me. (Sainsbury 2000a, p.77)

This may bring a fear of even approaching people, as they cannot figure out how others would respond (Sainsbury 2000a; Segar Undated). Unfortunately, bullying is not limited to peers. Sometimes teachers (unintentionally) may bully autistic youngsters without understanding how much they damage their self-esteem and bring confusion in their attempts to understand the world around them. Some teachers may 'misread' and misunderstand the behaviours and see these children as 'manipulative', 'sneaky', 'rude', 'stubborn' and 'disobedient' (Sainsbury 2000a). Many adults with AS describe their school experiences as a range of memories from being best forgotten to impossible to forget because they were so traumatic (Jackson 2002). For example, when asked, 'What would you like teachers of kids with AS to know?' David A. (cited in Sainsbury 2000a, p.76) replied 'That they have the capacity to damage a kid for life'.

Like with any other treatment, better outcomes depend on the people who work with autistic children (both in mainstream and special schools). The failure of many highly educated observers and practitioners to grasp what makes autistics tick is certainly disappointing. There has been much unnecessary damage to autistic individuals *and* their families. The more perceptive the teacher, the more likely an autistic child will become a fully functional, *but significantly different in talents and thinking,* individual (Morris 1999).

Even in special schools that are supposed to help autistic children develop their strengths and cope with their weaknesses, their potential is often overlooked and they may be treated as 'human vegetables' 'with no foreseeable future beyond stuffing plastic cutlery endlessly into bags' (Williams 1999c, p.186). However, some of the most devastating consequences for autistic children may be inflicted by parents, who believe they are acting out of love:

> What message is conveyed by parents who constantly express sadness over their child's differentness from other children? What is communicated by parents who constantly exhort their child to 'act normal', and whose greatest praise and approval are gained by 'not acting autistic'? The unmistakable message is, 'My parents don't want me the way I am.

They're sad that they have me instead of a normal child. The only way they'll like me is if I act like somebody else.' Some autistic children internalize this message and accept 'being normal' as their major goal in life. And it's been my observation that the more deeply invested an autistic person is in being normal, the more likely it is that he or she suffers from anxiety, depression, and low self-esteem. It's a natural consequence of making one's top priority to become something other than oneself. (Sinclair 1992b, p.2)

People with AS are very vulnerable to not only bullying in their childhood, but also being taken advantage of as adults:

Being gifted and having money from work didn't help, in reflection the negative peers around me were jealous and envious, emotions I was unaware of nor understood. These people would take from me and destroy the good I did, telling me I was bad and should give them things because they had nothing. In retrospect each had more than me, for they had socially acceptable minds, but their ignorance was their down-fall. (Aston 2000, p.58)

There are many sad cases of people with autism who have successfully completed high school, college and university but have been unable to make the transition into the world of work. We may find many people on the autistic spectrum in further education (who would prefer to be 'permanent students') as this is the only place where they thrive on the intellectual stimulation (Grandin 1996c). This is another paradox which is quite common in high-functioning autism: the more successful you are intellectually and academically, the fewer chances you have in employment. They often face two main problems: to get a job, and (*if* they get it) to keep it. When they look for a job, they (justifiably?) assess their abilities in accordance with the necessary skills they have to have to do this particular job properly. In practice, however, most jobs have a written job description, which specifies *what* the successful applicant will do, and also an unwritten job description, which specifies *who* the successful applicant has to please, and in what order of importance. People with autism

are more likely to succeed by selling their 'know-how' than selling their 'know-who'. Unfortunately, in a lot of jobs, the 'know-who' is more important than the 'know-how', or is thought to be so by those in charge. (Newson 2001, p.5)

They may develop a reputation for being an expert in their particular field but get into trouble socially. This is just one example:

> I did not understand that people have egos, and that protecting their egos was often more important than loyalty to the company. I naively believed that all...employees would always act in the best interest of their employer. I assumed that if I was loyal and always worked for the good of Swift's [the company Temple worked for], I would be rewarded. The other engineers resented me. They sometimes installed equipment wrong, and they never consulted me. They did not like this 'nerd' telling them how to do it. Technically I was right but socially wrong.
>
> ...I wrote a letter to the President of Swift about a bad equipment installation which caused cattle to suffer. The President was embarrassed that I have found a fault in his operation. I thought he would be pleased if I informed him of the mistake, instead he felt threatened and told Tom [the manager] to get rid of me. (Grandin 1996c)

Getting in trouble over social aspects of work is a problem area for many people with autism. Learning the work part of the job is easy. Many people with autism expect all people to be good. It is a rude awakening to learn that some people are bad and might try to exploit them (Grandin 1996c). AS people often cannot hold down jobs as they are unable (and often unwilling) to 'play social games'. They are straightforward (not rude). They cannot accept that 'know-who (to please)' is more important than 'know-how (to do the job)'.

Employment is very important for high-functioning individuals. And it is about jobs they are able (and qualified) to do, not about jobs they are allowed to do (and which are usually well below their abilities). In practice, it is often a 'catch-22' situation. On the one hand, for many autistic individuals their work may mean the fulfilment of their life; on the other hand, they are often unsuccessful at finding (or holding on to) a job, because the 'outside world' prefers 'sweet-talkers' to specialists who, while being excellent in their field, are often 'uncomfortable' to be with. For example, Anne Carpenter kept losing job after job because despite having excellent verbal and intellectual skills, her social skills were less well-developed. Because of this, most of the time she was working below her potential, outside her training and abilities (Carpenter 1992). We find quite a few autistic individuals with university degrees (MA, PhD, etc.) sitting at home as they have given up trying to find appropriate jobs due to their lack of 'know-who' abilities:

One man has a PhD in math and he sits at home. He needed somebody to steer him into an appropriate job. Teaching math did not work out; he should have obtained a research position that required less interaction with people. The other lady has a degree in history and now works doing a boring telephone-sales job. She needs a job where she can fully utilize her talents, she also needs a mentor to help her find an appropriate job and help open doors for her. Both these people needed support after college, and they did not receive it. The third man did well in high school and he also sits at home. He has a real knack for library research... All these people need jobs where they can make maximum use of their talents and minimize their deficits. (Grandin 2002)

High-functioning people with autism will probably never really fit in with social conventions (Grandin 2002). Those who have eventually succeeded often describe it as 'being lucky'. So what does 'being lucky' mean? It may mean:

- being given an opportunity to develop talents that can later provide an intellectually satisfying career

- having the right people working with them at the right time; people who help most are usually creative, unconventional thinkers who are prepared to accept and respect (and admire) differences (Grandin 1999, 2002; Sainsbury 2000a).

And if they *are* lucky (i.e. being appreciated for their abilities, being treated appropriately and supported by perceptive mentors), they may achieve a fulfilling life, being happy and seeing autism as something positive that has contributed to their achievements:

I know that things are missing in my life, but I have an exciting career that occupies my every waking hour. Keeping myself busy keeps my mind off what I may be missing... My life would not be worth living if I did not have intellectually satisfying work. My career is my life. (Grandin 1999)

In Box 2.5, there are a few scenarios, based on real life stories, of autistic people applying for a job. The readers have the opportunity to imagine if they were their potential employers, whether these particular applicants would be offered the job, and then check their solution with what happened in real life. Another very important issue is lack of services for adults. Adults with ASDs (both 'low-functioning' and 'high-functioning') need as much (if not more) help as children do. However, services are poorly developed. While they are

Box 2.5 Test: will they be lucky?

Situation 1

A (with AS) has been working for the college for two years as a part-time lecturer ('music with children with ASDs'). Recently he has completed his PhD, and is very enthusiastic about this job. He has introduced a new programme for his courses (based on his research) and suggested restructuring of the course which, however, implied some additional workload for the staff. The feedback from the evaluation forms which students fill in at the end of each term is very good (in fact, much better, than that of his full-time colleague and 'boss'). There are some problems, however, that he cannot handle well – he is obsessed with his subject and wants the others at the department to do more to develop it. Once he was even accused of 'harassing his boss' when A told him that he could have done more for the course and showed the boss his ideas of possible improvements. When there was a vacancy for a full-time lecturing job in the college, three people applied: A, K (with no teaching qualifications and with a social service background), and V (with an MA in Education but no experience).

Who got the job: A, K or V?

Situation 2

Two applicants (B – an autistic woman with an MSc in engineering; F – a former lecturer in engineering) for an engineer post at one of the plants are given a guided tour around the place before the interview. In the middle of the introductory tour, B interrupts their guide and points out that the equipment beside which they are standing has not been properly installed and suggests the way to correct the mistake. F insists, however, that it is impossible to know whether the installation is faulty until a test has been run.

Who got the job: B or F?

2. F
1. K
Answers:

children (and their parents are young and fit and able to help) there is some (though still not enough) external support – school, play schemes, clubs and holiday activities. But when they reach adulthood (and become bigger and stronger while their parents become older and less able to help) the external support instead of being increased is actually reduced (Blackburn 2000). More severely affected adults may be placed in residential settings (not necessarily specific to autism), while 'high-functioning' people are left to their own devices. There are little (if any) support systems available. Most people with HFA and AS are denied help by social services and benefits agencies because they have an average or high IQ. So with ASDs the lower your IQ is, the better chance you have of receiving help: 'Would they say to someone who is blind or has cerebral palsy and who has an IQ of 140 that they don't need help?' (Phillips Undated).

With HFA and AS it is often the case.

For 'horizontal reading':

1.6 – pp.54–66
3.6 – pp.208–219
4.6 – pp.284–294

2.7

Miscellany

Thoughts to Share

What's in a name? 'Autistics' or 'people with autism'?

There is a lot of controversy about the (politically correct) term 'people with autism' and (the politically incorrect one) 'autistic people'. NTs prefer the 'person first, then disability' approach, while many autistic people dislike the 'person first' language. Which one is 'right'? Let us look at the arguments from both camps.

Interestingly, the politically correct 'person first' phrasing was started by non-autistic people to show respect for people with autism, because they were seen (and many of them rightly so) as *suffering* from this incurable neurological disorder. 'Person first' language is used to show that it is the person that is important and not the disability.

Recently there has emerged even more politically correct phrasing. 'People with a label of "autism"' (Aylolt 2004) are increasingly being judged not from a medical model of autism (as an impairment or a deficit) but a social one – disabled by social, communication and attitudinal 'barriers'. The idea of changing the attitude of those around autistic people and the ways of communicating with them would be supported by many autistic individuals, but to limit autism to just environmental barriers and ignoring the 'internal ones' (that are likely to be different for different individuals – immune system problems, sensory and motor difficulties, etc.) that may be treated, or to simplify autism as being just a 'label' attached to the person, brings unnecessary confusion. First, if it is a label, can it be easily removed? Second, the language describing non-autistic people may become very complicated –

people without a label of 'autism', and without a label of 'cerebral palsy', and without a label of 'learning difficulties', etc.

This is why many autistic people dislike 'person first' language and see exactly the opposite to what has been intended – the disrespect:

- Autism is not something a person *has*, or a 'shell' that a person is trapped inside. There is no normal child hidden behind the autism. You cannot separate or remove autism from the person; that is why 'person with autism' is not only 'awkward' but, in fact, inaccurate:

  > I can be separated from things that are not part of me, and I am still the same person. I am usually a 'person with a purple shirt,' but I could also be a 'person with a blue shirt' one day, and a 'person with a yellow shirt' the next day, and I would still be the same person. Because my clothing is not part of me. But autism *is* part of me. Autism is hard-wired into the ways my brain works. *I am autistic because I **cannot** be separated from how my brain works.* (Sinclair 1999)

- It gives 'autism' some sort of negative colouring. Autism may be a nightmare at times (for both an autistic person and those who live or work with him), but for many autistic individuals autism is not necessarily a terrible thing and they do not think autism makes them any less a person:

  > If other people have trouble remembering that autism doesn't make me any less a person, then that's *their* problem, not mine. Let them find a way to remind themselves that I'm a person, without trying to define an essential feature of my personhood as something bad. *I am autistic because I **accept and value** myself the way I am.* (Sinclair 1999)

- The 'person first' language may be seen as a prejudice by some people as semantically it makes as little sense as saying 'White Christmas' is racist (Sinclair 1992c).

Those who identify themselves with being autistic (without being negative about it) do not mind even the nouns and refer to themselves as 'autistics'/'autists' (or 'auties') and 'aspies' (a term introduced by Liane Holliday Willey in her book *Pretending to be Normal*, 1999). Some autistic people even suggest capitalizing 'Autistic', like, for example, 'Deaf'. Still others may prefer to separate themselves from autism – 'I am a person with autism.' Whatever term or phrase is used, it is OK so long as the person feels comfortable with it. (After all, it is not about *what* we say, it is about how we feel about it.) If we interact with someone whose preference we know, wouldn't it be more respectful to use the term of his or her preference? *Just a thought.*

Autism: disability, condition or difference?

This is another semantic issue. And again there is no unanimity in this. Those autistic individuals who identify themselves with autism and find pride in it strongly oppose a 'medical' terminology with some 'pathological' colouring. They prefer to interpret D in ASDs as Difference instead of Disorder. Some do not even like 'condition'. Some consider their biggest 'disability' as being in a minority! However, the interpretation depends on the severity of 'D' (whether it is 'difference' or 'disorder'). If a person is high-functioning and lives independently, it is fair enough to emphasize the different ways of thinking and communicating. But if a person needs support 24 hours a day, is it fair to remove 'disorder' and insist that 'there is nothing wrong with him, he's just different'? Will this person get the help, support and treatment he or she needs? *Just a thought.*

Culture of autism?

Some autistic individuals feel that there is something so different about an autistic way of perceiving, thinking, communicating and interacting that it is justifiable to define it as a different culture. Recently there has appeared a movement to be recognized as a minority group, similar to the gay community or the deaf community.

The arguments for being distinguished as a 'cultural minority' are:

- ASDs may be viewed as an alternative form of brain wiring, with its own benefits and drawbacks, and not a disability/disorder in need of curing.

- ASDs are largely genetic and heritable.

- People with ASDs have their own way of perceiving the world, of thinking and using language for communication, which is different from the general population.

- People with ASDs have their own 'cultural' differences reflected in their behaviours regardless of their nationality, such as, for example, stimming and the avoidance of eye contact.

- People with ASDs have their own unique social network (primarily on the Internet).

They emphasize that being autistic does not mean being inhuman, but it does mean being different from the majority (sometimes such descriptions as 'foreigners in any culture' or 'aliens' are used). Because of their different 'brain wiring', they are ill-equipped to survive in the world of NTs (Sinclair 1992). The autistic activists inspire other people on the spectrum to 'come out' and work towards increasing institutional flexibility to the point where their 'special needs' could be accommodated and appreciated. Then the world would be a much more comfortable place for everyone else as well. Such a world would be one where the individual got to decide whether the lighting in the workplace was impairing her ability to function; where bosses would be expected to negotiate with employees about the manner in which information and orders were exchanged; where seeking assistance with certain aspects of daily life was not seen as an admission of incompetence; where it would be as normal for children to have different learning styles as it is to have different colours and textures of hair (Meyerding Undated). They oppose the idea of a 'cure' for autism, and insist that curing autism is like curing left-handedness.

Autistic people are not different from non-autistic people

There is another extreme view expressed by some individuals with ASDs – 'We, autistic individuals, are not different from non-autistic ones. We all are human and have a lot in common. We do nothing that you do not do. We stim a lot? But you also display stims – tapping things or pacing to and fro, when you are bored or anxious.' Yes, we are all human, but there is a danger in this interpretation of 'we-are-not-different' approach. If autistic people are no different from non-autistic ones, what is this fuss about? If I can stop these behaviours, you can. Pull yourself together, mate, and get on with your life, like everybody else does.

Some do-gooders urge autistic people to overlook the differences and concentrate instead on 'how alike we are'. Will it help both autistic and non-autistic people to be ignorant about differences? Perhaps, instead of dwelling on similarities, people should be asking themselves, 'What is wrong with being different?' *Just a thought.*

Aren't we all a bit 'autistic'?

This is an idea that many autistic people find quite offensive. There is a very big difference between a non-autistic person who insists 'But I'm just like that too' (meaning 'I also exhibit that behaviour') and an autistic individual (Spicer 1998a). That is true, that we all have times when we do not feel our bodies, or are hardly aware of what is going on around us, or when we cannot tolerate loud noises, or we ask the same question all over again to get some reassurance and so on. These behaviours may look similar to 'autistic behaviours', but they are far from the same. Non-autistic people display these behaviours in specific situations, they know what the world is like 'normally'. For autistic people, these behaviours *are* normality (they do not know any different), so the perception of self and the world around them is very different to those who 'are a bit autistic from time to time'.

Attitudes to autism

There are autistic people who would not choose to become NTs. They identify themselves with their condition and are happy about it. Temple Grandin, for example, says if she could snap her fingers and become non-autistic, she would not do it, because autism is a part of what she is. She has found her place along the great continuum and celebrates the assets of her autism (for example, her ability to think visually) (Grandin 1996a). There are also autistic people who feel distorted or imprisoned by their condition who fight the constraints or discomforts of their autism and seek ways to push out its constricting boundaries. They may be both proud to be an autistic person and determined not to allow their autism to dictate the terms of their lives (Williams 1996). There are those who would like to change some things about their experiences but maintain others, or to feel free from autism for some time and then get it back; for example: 'If I'm ever asked if I would like to get rid of my Asperger's Syndrome, I say "I would like it if I could get rid of 40 per cent of it, and keep 60 per cent of it"' (Phillips Undated). Gunilla Gerland, when asked whether she wanted to be 'normal', said that she might, for a week or two – but then she would want her autism back again.

There are those who are motivated to change their autism under the pressure 'from outside'. Sean Barron (Barron and Barron 1993) describes how the pain of feeling different motivated him to acquire more social skills. Others, on the contrary, do not see anything wrong with being different:

> [Some] autistic people say that they wish they weren't so different from other people…[because] they don't like being mistreated, and they know the reason for the mistreatment is that they're different and don't fit in. I never reached this conclusion myself (why should I be unhappy with the way *I* am just because the way some *other* people are is obnoxious?), but I can understand the reasoning… The idea of wanting to fit in for its own sake, of being different as a misfortune in and of itself, is not an idea I've heard expressed by autistic people. If an autistic person is unhappy about being different, it's because non-autistic people have taught the autistic person that bad things will happen to you if you're different… Feeling sad about the mere fact of being different is a handicap that non-autistic people have. It's not *our* problem. (Sinclair 1992b, p.1)

'Pretending to be normal'

The goal of many treatments for a variety of disabilities (autism included) is to teach people to look and act 'as normal as possible'. However, is it wise to do so? For example, if we teach somebody who is blind to look and act as if the person could see, we actually disable this person. 'Pretending to be normal' comes with a price. If the treatment (which is merely training to 'act normally') is even partially successful, for the person it is achieved at the expense of being able to *function as well as possible* with one's disability. Adapting, accommodating and coping with a disability often requires learning to do things *differently* from the ways non-disabled people do them (Sinclair 1998).

Some people with autism (who have been taught that autism is their enemy, and to be included they have to learn how to act 'normally') are motivated to mimic others and act as if they were non-autistic, others are forced to 'act normal':

> It was this fear of having 'my own world' taken away that resulted in behaviour which forced me to deny 'my own world' in place of a more presentable, well-mannered, sociable, though emotionless, shell. 'They' never got to lay a hand on the real me, but more and more, to their elation, I began to stop visiting myself. I began to stop looking at the spots and losing myself in the colours. I began to lose a grip on my love

of the things around me and, in doing so, was left with 'their' shallow securities and complete lack of guarantees. My hatred became my only realness and, when I was not angry, I said sorry for breathing, for taking up space, and even began to say sorry for saying sorry. The total denial of a right to live was a consequence of learning to act normal. Everything outside of me told me that my survival was to rest on my refining the act of acting normal. On the inside I knew that by definition this meant that whatever and whoever I was naturally was unworthy of acceptance, belonging or even life. (Williams 1999b, pp.70–71)

The issue of the cure for autism

Another very important issue to be addressed is: do autistic people themselves want to be cured of autism? As the severity of autism varies considerably, and the attitude to the condition differs depending on individual circumstances, we have a wide range of opinions on the 'cure' for autism:

- The majority of HF and AS individuals see autism as a part of who they are and do not want to be 'cured':

  > I find great value and meaning in my life, and I have no wish to be cured of being myself. If you would help me, don't try to change me to fit your world. Don't try to confine me to some tiny part of the world that you can change to fit me. Grant me the dignity of meeting me on my own terms – recognize that we are equally alien to each other, that my ways of being are not merely damaged versions of yours. Question your assumptions. Define your terms. Work with me to build more bridges between us. (Sinclair 1992a, p.302)

  > The catch is, if I was going to be 'cured' into a completely different way of thinking, acting, feeling, and being – into a whole new person – I would never, could never, accept it. Not only would that not be me, but I think that normalcy is overrated anyway, and that to become normal would be a 'de-provement' rather than an improvement. To be cured of autism would be to become someone else; the person I am now would cease to exist. Thus, for me, *curing* my self would be equivalent to *killing* myself. I value my existence, and don't want to end it by turning into someone and something totally different. (Blackburn 1999)

- Some wanted to be 'cured' but of certain things; for example:

I would like to be able to *look* normal selectively. Actually, if I really try, I can *sometimes* do it for a short time in certain situations. A more efficient, effective, reliable, and durable system would be better. What I do is called '*acting*'... I don't know how convincing I am, but it takes forethought and effort and can't be done continuously. Some might call it 'fake', but it can help get what I want – and besides, I'm honest with it, and don't use it to deceive others, per se. I suspect that some 'strangeness' still shows through. (Blackburn 1999)

- Some people do want to be cured, to become 'indistinguishable' from non-autistic peers. (However, they seem to be in a minority.)

Many autistic individuals have united their efforts in Autism advocacy, Autism Liberation and Aspies For Freedom movements. They strongly oppose such groups and institutions as Cure Autism Now (CAN) and Defeat Autism Now (DAN). Are they enemies of those parents who want to help their autistic children? Far from it! There is again some sort of misunderstanding caused by misinterpretation of the word 'cure'. HF and AS people are against the idea of 'cure' as eradication of people with ASDs, against a possible genetic test to prevent autistic children being born, against treatments that seek to change the *behaviours* and eventually bring more harm than good to autistic children. But it does not mean that they deny the necessity for help and treatment for any *underlying causes* of LFA (such as sensory processing difficulties, immune or toxicity problems) in order to facilitate the development and move to the HF end of the autistic spectrum:

Those of us living on the [HF] end of the autistic spectrum would never suggest our more affected autistic peers be left on their own, kept from intervention, encouraged to twist in the wind and turn like a top. Not at all. In fact, we would be the first among all to suggest those with autism need strong support systems, solid language intervention, sensory integration therapy, occupational therapy, social skills training, and anything else that might be deemed appropriate for growth and development. (Willey Undated)

If both ('pro-cure' and 'anti-cure') sides re-defined the term 'cure' and re-consider their positions, wouldn't they find that they, in fact, have more views in common than different? *Just a thought.*

'Autistic bullies' and 'token autistics'

Recently we have witnessed the phenomenon of 'autistic bullies' (for the lack of a better term). These are newly diagnosed individuals who suddenly discover that all their past problems can be explained by somebody else's fault. They do not seek the understanding of what is different about them and how they can compensate their weaknesses and use these differences for their advantage, but rather blame NTs (both parents and professionals) for all their misfortune. The fact is, these individuals, being unaware of their condition in the past, have developed a very low self-esteem. The diagnosis for them has provided the explanations of others' fault in all their past and present problems. Because of their (negative) experiences they still operate with the concepts they used in the past when being bullied. Whatever is said to them (even if you agree with some of their views but use different words), they would misinterpret and twist the message. And don't you dare to correct them! ('Sorry, you have misunderstood me.') If you do you may find yourself on the receiving end of their rage – 'He/she called *me* an idiot, stupid and cognitively ill!' Rather than understanding and addressing their difficulties, they criticize everything and everybody.

After many years of having been bullied, they become bullies themselves. As a young AS lady put it – 'sometimes former victims make the most efficient perpetrators'. They may bully and insult others in order to compensate for their low self-esteem. They project their own failings and insecurities on other people, and attack and criticize in others the very problems they themselves experience. And it is not only the parents and professionals who would be hurt by their attacks. Other autistic individuals, who have different views and are prepared to address their difficulties, become perfect targets for these autistic bullies. Those who cooperate with parents and professionals are labelled 'token autistics'. This is very unfortunate, because these very few individuals may alienate others (who accept and appreciate their autism but do not idealize it) from advocacy for the understanding and acceptance of differences. This 'aggressive advocacy' is more of a hindrance than promotion of acceptance. It is not surprising, therefore, that many HF and AS people want nothing to do with this sort of advocacy. They find the tactics 'autistic bullies' use questionable at best, because they try to advocate in the midst of hatred for others, and for people claiming to fight for the rights of others it is both demoralizing and frightening (Smith 2005). In his article 'Why I don't want to be an autistic advocate anymore' (2005), Joel Smith enumerates several reasons why negative traits brought into the autistic advocacy community by a few individuals, in fact, interferes with true advocacy:

- Too many who claim to be autistic advocates believe the autistics should get rights because they have intelligence that the rest of the world lacks.

- Too many who claim to be autistic advocates believe that their subgroup of autistics is more able to be the voice of autism than other subgroups.

- Too many who claim to be autistic advocates look at themselves and their own personal needs above all other autistics.

- Those who shout about how horrible those awful NTs are, are themselves engaged in exactly the same negative acts they accuse NTs of doing, e.g. bullying, favouritism, hero-worship.

The author concludes that maybe when autistic communities figure out a way to represent the cause without fighting each other, and without trying to exalt themselves above other groups of non-autistics, then it will be worthwhile to promote a true advocacy for the rights of all people, including autistics (Smith 2005).

Is recovery possible?

Most HF autistic people state that recovery from autism is impossible. And it is not necessarily that those who have claimed to recover were not autistic in the first place. Probably they were. And they still are. They are indistinguishable from their peers and have been lucky to have found their 'niche' (usually, in the field of autism). They are HF/AS persons, hardly 'sufferers' any more. A very good example is Raun Kaufman who is said to have completely recovered and is successfully employed to promote the very programme that helped him. Raun says he is not autistic any more. And there are even more 'Rauns' out there who still do not know that they are on the spectrum.

Here we have the problem of semantics again. People who were diagnosed as severely autistic often *are not expected* to live independently, or even talk. Thus, when a 'hopeless' child does learn to talk, to interact and show average or above average intelligence, he is proclaimed 'recovered' by parents, professionals and himself (Klein 2002). Others are aware that they have 'closed the gap' with non-autistic people but advanced along a kind of parallel path, and are still on the spectrum. They do live independently, have no problem with interaction, but their cognitive systems function differently (Shull 2003).

Donna Williams describes many 'waking up' stories when, with particular intervention (addressing the underlying problems of each particular person), individuals with autism make great progress. Every case is different (there is no one type of autism, and no one treatment that can fit all). For some, it may be the effect of dietary intervention or supplementation in decreasing major sensory perceptual and information processing problems; for others, it may be speech therapy in overcoming dysfunctional language; for still others, it may be addressing sensory (especially auditory) processing problems; for some, progress may be brought by the desperate desire to be like and copy others; and for the most unfortunate, by an extreme environment which makes it dangerous to remain in an 'autistic state' (Williams Undated, c).

Famous aspies

Many famous people (geniuses) of the past are said to be on the autistic spectrum. They include great names such as Albert Einstein, Isaac Newton and Thomas Jefferson, to name but three. The irony is that many researchers are looking for 'autistic genes' and working out a genetic test, in order to warn the parents that their baby may be autistic, and yet the father of modern genetics, Gregor Mendel, was possibly HF autistic or a person with AS (Grandin 1996a). How would he feel about it now?

There are many books and articles on the subject available, written both by believers and sceptics. Autistic authors have done their own research into the lives and families of the geniuses of the past, recognizing their own traits in these aspies-achievers. Some identify signs of AS in famous contemporaries as well – scientists, actors and writers. Bill Gates is possibly the most famous present 'candidate' for AS. In her book *Thinking in Pictures* (1996a) Temple Grandin devoted an entire chapter under the title 'Genius is an abnormality' to the link between intellectual giftedness and creativity and abnormality.

Some sceptics, however, are not convinced. They say that attempting to diagnose using only biographical information is extremely unreliable, and emphasize that any behaviour can have various causes. Fair enough. But an ASD is diagnosed on the basis of behaviours; we do not know the causes of many behavioural manifestations of autism. How is it possible to diagnose now using descriptions of behaviours but reject this principle when we study people of the past? Besides, the 'behavioural diagnosis' of Victor, a wild boy of Aveyron (described by Itard in the eighteenth century), and other cases of possible autistic people who lived in the twelfth to the nineteenth centuries (Frith 1989, 2003), surprisingly have not aroused much scepticism. Is it because some people do not want even to consider the possibility that ASDs may be associated with great achievers? *Just a thought.*

NTs pay for the skills autistic people are taught to change

Professor Edward de Bono (1971) has developed 'lateral thinking' programmes that help improve creativity. The process involves looking at problems from unconventional angles. Many company executives are prepared to pay a lot of money to learn these techniques to boost their ability to make management decisions. Shall we laugh or cry, when we pay money to learn how to think AS/autism style, while we work really hard to change HF/AS individuals (who naturally develop this ability) to NTs (Handley 2003; Thompson 2003)? *Just a thought.*

For 'horizontal reading':

1.7 – pp.67–71
3.7 – pp.220–226
4.7 – pp.295–300

Further Reading

Books written by autistic individuals themselves are an invaluable source of information on autism. Whether they are autobiographies or books on specific aspects of the condition, these books describe first hand the reality of autism, the ToAM, their experiences, abilities and problems. Each author writes about very personal and individual experiences, but one cannot help but notice common themes. In their accounts the reader will find answers to many questions, and will get the idea of Theory of Autistic Mind, which is significantly different from Theories of (Parent's or Professional's) Mind.

Autobiographies

Grandin, T. and Scariano, M. (1986) *Emergence: Labeled Autistic.* Novato, CA: Arena Press.
An autobiography of possibly one of the most famous of contemporary achievers with autism from the time when her parents were advised to institutionalize her as nearly hopeless to developing into a high-functioning autistic person with a doctorate degree in animal science and the reputation for being an expert in her field.

Williams, D. (1999) *Nobody Nowhere: The Remarkable Autobiography of an Autistic Girl.* London: Jessica Kingsley Publishers.
Williams, D. (1999) *Somebody Somewhere: Breaking Free from the World of Autism.* London: Jessica Kingsley Publishers.
A remarkable autobiography of an autistic woman from her childhood to the age of 25, and its sequel which describes the four years after the diagnosis and her attempts to leave 'her world'.

Williams, D. (1999) *Like Colour to the Blind: Soul Searching and Soul Finding.* London: Jessica Kingsley Publishers.
This is a story of Donna's relationship with an AS person, revealing how they learn to build a 'specialship' and to 're-discover' themselves by removing barriers imposed by autism.

Lawson, W. (1998) *Life Behind Glass: A Personal Account of Autism Spectrum Disorder.* London: Jessica Kingsley Publishers.
Wendy Lawson, a woman with Asperger syndrome (who was once considered to be intellectually disabled and schizophrenic), shares her understanding of autism and gives the reader a fantastic insight into the world how she sees it.

Willey, L. H. (1999) *Pretending to be Normal: Living with Asperger's Syndrome.* London: Jessica Kingsley Publishers.
Willey, L.H. (2001) *Asperger Syndrome in the Family: Redefining Normal.* London: Jessica Kingsley Publishers.
These two books detail the life of a woman with AS and her family (one of her daughters has AS, as well).

There are many other autobiographies written by people on the spectrum. Here are just a few:

Blackman, L. (2001) *Lucy's Story: Autism and Other Adventures.* London: Jessica Kingsley Publishers.

Hale, A. (1998) *My World Is Not Your World.* Tadcaster, N. Yorkshire: Archimedes Press.

Fleisher, M. (2003) *Making Sense of the Unfeasible: My Life Journey with Asperger Syndrome.* London: Jessica Kingsley Publishers.

Schneider, E. (1999) *Discovering My Autism: Apologia Pro Vita Sua (with Apologies to Cardinal Newman),* and *Living the Good Life with Autism* (2003). London: Jessica Kingsley Publishers.

Gerland, G. (1997) *A Real Person – Life on the Outside.* London: Souvenir Press.

Shore, S. (2001) *Beyond the Wall: Personal Experiences with Autism and Asperger Syndrome.* Shawnee Mission, KS: Autism Asperger Publishing Company.

Hadcroft, W. (2004) *The Feeling's Unmutual: Growing up with Asperger Syndrome (Undiagnosed).* London: Jessica Kingsley Publishers.

'Autism textbooks'

There are some books by autistic authors that offer valuable and fascinating insights into what it is like to be autistic and which also suggest strategies to address underlying deficits and problems.

Williams, D. (1996) *Autism: An Inside-Out Approach.* London: Jessica Kingsley Publishers.
The subtitle of the book says it all: 'An Innovative Look at the "Mechanics" of "Autism" and its Developmental "Cousins".'

Williams, D. (1998) *Autism and Sensing: The Unlost Instinct.* London: Jessica Kingsley Publishers.
The book explains how the senses of autistic people work and shows the different developmental routes of autistic and non-autistic individuals.

Williams, D. (2003) *Exposure Anxiety – The Invisible Cage: An Exploration of Self-Protection Responses in the Autism Spectrum and Beyond.* London: Jessica Kingsley Publishers.
The book describes the condition 'Exposure Anxiety' that is quite common in autism, its underlying physiological causes, and approaches and strategies to overcome it.

Grandin, T. (1996) *Thinking in Pictures: And Other Reports from My Life with Autism.* New York: Vintage Books.
The book describes autistic experiences and thought processes by someone who 'experiences and thinks' them. Supported by research, it is a very detailed account of what it is like to be autistic. Temple Grandin's book is one of the best descriptions of autism from the inside. The only caution to be made is not all autistic people think in pictures.

Lawson, W. (2001) *Understanding and Working with the Spectrum of Autism: An Insider's View.* London: Jessica Kingsley Publishers.
The book provides both explanations of how autistic people make sense of the world, and ways to deal with difficulties which they experience.

Lawson, W. (2003) *Build Your Own Life: A Self-help Guide for Individuals with Asperger Syndrome.* London: Jessica Kingsley Publishers.

Newport, J. (2001) *Your Life Is Not a Label.* Arlington, TX: Future Horizons, Inc.

Jackson, L. (2002) *Freaks, Geeks and Asperger Syndrome: A User Guide to Adolescence.* London: Jessica Kingsley Publishers.
The book is written by a boy with AS (who was 13 at the time). It is an honest and witty account covering a lot of issues, including difficult topics such as bullying, school problems, friendships and relationships.

Sainsbury, C. (2000) *The Martian in the Playground: Understanding the Schoolchild with Asperger's Syndrome.* Bristol: Lucky Duck Publishing.

O'Neill, J. (1999) *Through the Eyes of Aliens: A Book about Autistic People.* London: Jessica Kingsley Publishers.

McKean, T. (1994) *Soon Will Come the Light: A View from Inside the Autism Puzzle.* Arlington, TX: Future Horizons, Inc.

PART 3

Autism

Parents' Perspective

Definitions and Classifications

Let us look at autism through the eyes of parents who have been there.

Autism knows no geographical boundaries...it affects parents in the same way the world over. Autism is, probably, the most difficult of all disabilities to cope with. Of course, it would be wrong to define disabilities as 'better' or 'worse', but it is justifiable to assume that autism does create a great strain on families, incomparable to other disorders. There are several reasons for this. First, very often autism is difficult to identify; it is in a way 'invisible'. There is no evidence of any disability in the child's appearance, in contrast to, say, children with cerebral palsy, Down syndrome, or physical impairments. Hence, the child's often 'bizarre' behaviour is misunderstood and mis-interpreted ('spoilt, naughty child!') and parents are under constant stress for being blamed for their inability to discipline their offspring. Sometimes autism is called a 'hidden disability'. (Unfortunately, it does not remain hidden for long. These so-called 'bizarre' behaviours may be sudden and shocking.) Second, in addition to the negative attitude from the outside, parents often feel rejected by their own child, creating a feeling of uselessness and unreturned love on the inside. And third, it is a great physical and emotional strain raising a child who can live without any sleep for more than 20 hours, who does not eat food prepared for him, who might be aggressive and get into tantrums out of the blue – in short, a child who needs 24-hour supervision, each day, every day.

Autism is a spectrum disorder. However, the autistic spectrum is not just a continuum of one colour from mild to intense, but rather a range of colours, all different and all of varying intensity. For example, a person with AS does not have mild autism. Their social impairment can make AS just as difficult to cope with as more classical manifestations of autistic disorder (Stanton 2001).

The parents' definition of autism may range from very negative comparison of the condition with the 'death' of their child to a 'gift' that has changed their lives and themselves as parents. The definition depends on the severity of the symptoms displayed by the child and the amount of knowledge, attitude and acceptance which the parents have. The same parents may define autism differently at different stages of their lives. Some descriptions of autism by the parents (both those whose children have just been diagnosed with ASDs and those who have educated themselves about autism) are given in Box 3.1.

Box 3.1 Definitions of autism

Positive descriptions

> Autism…can teach a person, a family, a community, and even the world so much about people, life, and humanity. In its own special way, autism is a gift… Autism is acceptance of an individual for the special person that they are and will become. It's truly unconditional love. (Flanagan 2001)

> My [autistic] son is the best thing that has happened in my life. He's changed not only my life but my personality (for the better, I hope). I can't imagine my life without him. He's given me so much that I'm afraid I won't be able to repay him. (A mother of a 14-year-old autistic boy. Personal communication)

Negative descriptions

> Autism has stolen my child. It's like a death in the family. I hate autism. (Mrs N. Personal communication)

Another negative comparison is: 'Autism is a medical disability like a cancer/AIDS, etc.'

The difficulties an autistic child brings to a family are enormous, especially for the mother. And no matter how much she gives, the child still needs more.

Siblings often feel abandoned by a mother given over to the care of an autistic child (Elizabeth Stanley in Sperry 2001). However, despite many challenges autism brings, it also offers a great opportunity for personal growth. Morton Ann Gernsbacher (2004), a psychology professor at a major research university, confesses that her autistic son has taught her far more than she ever learned in her lab:

> Every time he walks by a poster avowing that autism must be eradicated, he teaches me grace. Every time he ignores one of the countless scholarly articles that tower above my desk, asserting he is disordered, he teaches me tolerance. Every time he embraces a world that so frequently rebuffs him, he teaches me unconditional love. (Gernsbacher 2004)

Paradoxically, autism may make parents re-evaluate their lives and develop into different (better) personalities, who can, for example, take little for granted and see triumphs in the tiniest achievements, be delighted with such trivial things as watching their offspring buttoning his shirt or answering their question not with an echolalic phrase but with a simple 'yes, I do'. With time, parents may re-define autism from a tragedy to something of a blessing:

> Autism teaches us to help others at all costs. It shows us how to improve on their lives and on our own lives without invasion and judgement. It helps us to understand that changing the person is not the goal of our endeavors. Autism also teaches us to find both the beauty and the humour in the 'quirky' little behaviors that we all have. (Flanagan 2001)

What is interesting is that, as difficult a disability as autism can be, difficult children often produce difficult parents. Atypical parenting is often a coping reaction to the child's behaviour rather than the cause of the behaviour. Perhaps it comes from our deep desire to improve our child's quality of life. (As the mother of an autistic boy I have to confess…I am difficult.) I have met hundreds of parents of children with autism over the years and I would like to give you my classification of the parents of autistic children. It is conventional to classify autistic children according to the impairments of social interaction and describe their characteristics by grouping them into four main types: the aloof group, the passive group, the active but odd group, and the over-formal, stilted group (Wing 1996) (see Chapter 1.1). I will try to do the same with the parents, using almost the same headings, though the subdivision the parents fall under does not necessarily coincide with that of their child. Besides, like their children, with time, the parents can shift from one subgroup to another.

The aloof group

This is a very common type of parent in the countries where autism is not recognized. These parents believe the 'specialists' when they say that their child is hopeless. They may or may not institutionalize their child, as advised. If the child is kept at home, the family tries to 'hide' him or her from people, feeling ashamed of having such a disabled child but still loving him. They feel helpless to change anything in their life. They are typically very sensitive to the stares of people while out with the child in public and often end up with tears of shame and bitterness. They avoid social contact and live in their small isolated world, and the child is cut off from the world not only mentally but also physically.

The passive group

These parents are not completely cut off from other parents. This group may be subdivided into two categories. (1) The parents are sure there must be a pill or a treatment that would solve all their problems and, sooner or later, it will be offered to them. They accept all the offers they are given, they are very obedient, never question specialists, and often the child is traumatized when the parents agree to place him into hospital and treat him with medications prescribed by the 'specialists'. These parents have no doubt that 'the specialists know best' and they do what they are told in regard to treatment. (2) These parents may attend different courses, support group meetings, participate in on-line forums, but their main concern is, 'Tell me what to do, not why.' They avoid reading theoretical books on autism because they find them depressing and feel overwhelmed by the information. The only books they find useful are the 'books with bullet points' – 'Do this; Don't do that.' What they want is practical solutions to *their* child's problems, but without figuring it out themselves when the information is provided. Unfortunately, there is no (and will never be) single book that will give the solutions for Alex/ John/Sarah.

The active but odd group

The 'active' but sometimes 'misdirected' group looks for any information in their attempt to find a 'cure' for their child's autism. They travel to different cities or even to different countries just to consult the specialist they have heard of or to try the treatment they have read about, irrespective of the effects (or ill-effects) (for example, holding therapy is often tried despite the child's hypertactility). They are sure they are doing their best for their child (who 'suffers from autism'), and are ready to spend all their money on the most expensive treatments. Their love is great, but perhaps 'blind' as well. Sometimes the children benefit from it, sometimes they are harmed.

Other parents may accept that there is no cure for their child's autism and look for the best treatment they can provide to make the life of the child and the whole family easier. They become zealous advocates of a single approach that seems beneficial for their child and believe will benefit other children with autism. They are very enthusiastic and keen to talk about one particular approach (which they use with their own child) at conferences, seminars, etc. They learn 'how to talk' but, unfortunately, not 'how to listen'. When someone disagrees with their point of view they become offended and refuse to discuss any other methods or issues that are outside the scope of their interest.

The professional group

Fortunately, this is a numerous group, and growing. These parents decide to change their focus and become 'professional parents' for their child (and 'difficult parents' for professionals). They start with the assumptions that specialists might be wrong, they cannot know everything; that research is being carried out, and what is considered to be 'right' today may turn out to be 'wrong' tomorrow; and that nobody knows their child better than they do. Like the third group, these parents actively seek information, but are reluctant to try everything. They are akin to permanent students, with a desire to learn about all the theories and approaches to find the right ones for their own child. They are very critical and express doubts about everything. They question and want explanations, rather than accepting information at 'face value'. Eventually they become better educated in autism than are many professionals (and, hence, become even more 'difficult'). Because they know it is impossible to help their child without helping others, they unite their efforts and work together. It is these parents who establish organizations and societies aimed at building a brighter future for their children. They seek cooperation with open-minded specialists and HF autistic individuals, and fight against ignorance and the incompetence of bureaucrats. Their efforts and activities give us hope and keep us moving forward. I have to admit – I do admire the difficult parents who make the lives of their children easier.

What Ruth Sullivan, a mother and an advocate for autistic people, wrote about parents of autistic children in 1984 is relevant today (with the addition of a very powerful source of information – the Internet):

> Parents of autistic children learn early in their child's life how little professionals know about autism. Trained by their culture to trust the experts, they are soon dismayed and unsettled to learn that the 'experts' know as little as they do, or less. Alone, especially at first, and faced with an extremely atypical child, many exhaust themselves in finding information that might help. They soon realize that the service providers will not provide unless there is a better understanding of autistic children and the urgency of their needs. With the fervor of desperation they read articles, study references, write to authors, call authorities in the field, exchange information with more knowledgeable parents. They will often deluge a professional with material from their latest research... It is this growing number of well-informed, activist parents who have been and continue to be instrumental in raising the level of knowledge and awareness of autism. They are largely self-taught, and some dedicate their energies and long segments of their lives to the job of getting services for their own and other autistic children. (Sullivan 1984, p.233)

Autism affects not only the child with the condition but the whole family. The news that the child is autistic is sometimes described as 'an autism bomb'; the devastation is considerable. The family may experience 'living in the war zone' not only because they do not know much (yet) about what is wrong with their child but also because of 'environmental factors' – that can cause the Triad of Difficulties for the family (see Figure 3.1). This Triad consists of:

- difficulties in social interaction: friends and relatives may try to be supportive and offer (unhelpful) comments, 'He seems to look normal. He will be all right. He will grow out of it.' Others will distance themselves because of the child's 'bizarre' behaviours. The general public will offer nothing but stares and contempt for 'poor parenting'

- difficulties in communication: when parents try to find some answers or ask for help, professionals may find them 'overprotective', and 'difficult'. Their attitude is described as 'biased' ('of course, you cannot be objective: it is your child'). Trying to 'break the wall of misunderstanding', parents suddenly may find themselves to be 'communication impaired' as their explanations may be 'too emotional', or 'too angry' (and hence dismissed by the professionals)

- difficulties in imagination: as parents' experiences are so different from others', it is very difficult (if not impossible) for the parents to express their views and needs – those to whom they talk have a different 'set of concepts' of family life and are unable to change their attitudes (which displays a rigidity of thought and behaviour).

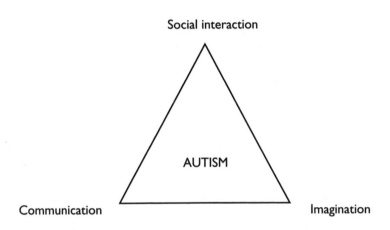

Figure 3.1 The Triad of Family Difficulties

HFA, LFA, 'mild autism', 'severe autism', etc.

Some parents who have learned to accept their child for what he or she is and want society to change their attitudes to the condition (and accept their child the way they do) find the term 'low-functioning' offending. One mother was furious when her son was called low-functioning. Interestingly, she had no problem calling him 'autistic' (although some parents do not want to recognize that autism is part of their son or daughter), but despised the terms 'HFA and LFA': 'My son is not low-functioning, you are!' (Personal communication.) In fact, these parents are very vulnerable. They feel offended when no offence is intended. One should be very careful choosing the words to describe their child, as it is very individual and nearly impossible to predict which terms will have negative implications for these people. In contrast, other parents do not mind the term LFA and (what is more important) do not see negative implications in it. For them, 'low-functioning' simply means that the person cannot live independently and needs more support, whereas 'high-functioning' refers to an individual who may attend mainstream school (with support) and go on to live semi-independently. As one parent (being on the spectrum herself) says: 'Call my kid (and me) purple if I can get what we need with that label' (cited in Schafer Report 2004).

Some parents do not like the term HFA (or, 'more able' person with autism) because it does not show the difficulties their child faces despite the abilities. For example:

> This term able is a real red herring in my mind. Able to do what? Speak on any given subject and tell you every fact known to man about aircraft, engines, flight paths, crash statistics, then yes, he's able. To hold you in conversation which only interests him and no one else, then yes, he's able. However, to be able to wait in line, or tie his shoe laces, see to his own personal hygiene needs, sit around the table and have a meal with a group of friends, or just play with the children in the street... then no, the plain fact is that Brian has evolved from a child with severe behavioural difficulties caused by his autism into a young man who is steadily going into a state of depression because of his autism. He realizes there is something wrong with him and this is heartbreaking, he knows he's different, he keeps asking why he's different, if something goes wrong he always thinks it's because of him. (Riva 1999)

For many parents there is no such thing as 'mild autism'. Both HF and AS children experience tremendous problems in their lives. The fact that autism is not easily 'seen' in them makes it even more difficult. People do not make any adaptations to their 'idiosyncratic' behaviours and assume that they are not trying hard enough or are deliberately being awkward. Because they are 'indistinguishable' from their peers, uninformed (or ill-informed) educational and social services deny any support and put the pressure on these children to 'behave properly'.

For 'horizontal reading':

1.1– pp.21–28
2.1 – pp.77–96
4.1 – pp.233–240

3.2

Diagnosis

Some parents try to ignore the problems and do not seek a diagnosis until their child reaches school age. Their beliefs are often confirmed by friends or some doctors unfamiliar with autism – 'Every child is different', 'Boys are lazy', 'She can talk but she doesn't want to', etc. Other parents actively seek for diagnosis as they want the answers to their child's behaviour. However, unfortunately, parents can wait a long time for a referral to a qualified person to diagnose autism. For example, the average delay for parents in the UK from the time they first seek professional help to the diagnosis is estimated to be 3.81 years (Howlin and Moore 1997). Some parents view the diagnosis as a confirmation of their suspicions that something is wrong with their child and experience relief when they finally know the 'name'. For others, the diagnosis is a blow that they find very difficult to come to terms with.

There may be some 'side-effects' of diagnosis:

- broken marriages (unfortunately, divorce is quite common in families with autistic children)

- strained relationships with relatives: some relatives deny the problem and encourage parents to 'discipline' their child, others feel pity for parents (and see their child as 'a tragic event'), and that is even worse than anything else

- loss of friends, leading to social isolation

- ill-judgement of 'do-gooders' – staring, blaming parents for the child's behaviour ('lack of discipline', etc.).

Early diagnosis

Much depends on early diagnosis and early intervention. The 'profound aloneness' described by Kanner is not for life if the child is 'picked up' early. Without early diagnosis there is no early education. Without early education the chances of the child moving from 'profound aloneness' to participation in life are considerably reduced. The average age of diagnosis in the UK is now over six years. Only half of the children receive a diagnosis before the age of five. By that time a child has lost precious years of early intervention. This is very unfortunate, especially when parents feel that something is 'not quite right' in their baby and seek help as soon as possible. But due to inexperience and the lack of knowledge of many physicians, the first signs of the disorder may be easily missed, and instead of diagnosis for their child the parents may get the diagnosis for...themselves – Munchhausen's Syndrome by Proxy.

In 1977 Professor Sir Roy Meadow described what he called 'Munchhausen's Syndrome by Proxy' – where parents are said to have harmed their children in order to draw attention to themselves. It is named after Baron Munchhausen, a fictional figure who is famous for telling tall tales. Originally this new 'syndrome' was 'diagnosed' in parents with children who died in infancy. The 'Meadow Law' was used in many court cases when the parents were jailed for the 'murder' of their babies – 'one cot death is a tragedy, two is suspicious and three is murder'. Unfortunately, this 'diagnosis' was very popular and resulted in many innocent parents being jailed. This most ill-founded theory flourished in childcare and social services for more than 15 years until it was proved wrong, harmful and damaging. Now the Meadow Law and Munchhausen's Syndrome by Proxy have been discredited and rejected in court cases on cot deaths. However, this 'diagnosis' has not gone away. Parents who blame the MMR vaccine for their children's autism (whether they are right or wrong) have been accused of abusing (!) their offspring – deliberately harming their children to draw attention to themselves. Some parents say they have been threatened by either health or social services with Munchhausen's Syndrome by Proxy if they continue to complain about vaccine damage.

It is not only in the context of MMR that some parents have been accused of having this infamous syndrome. Some professionals always blame parents when they see a child with behaviour problems who looks physically normal. If parents come to doctors or teachers again and again seeking help with their child's problems, the professionals may accuse them of 'imagining things' or 'fabricating the child's symptoms', and eventually blame parents (usually mothers) for their children's behaviours. In this case, Munchhausen's Syndrome by Proxy turns to 'neobettelheimism' which, unfortunately, is still happening today. They do not understand that it is not about 'fabricating educational disabilities and demanding "unnecessary" special school services', it is about the help and support the child needs. I'd like to see a mother who really *wanted* her child to be labelled as disabled just for the sake of it! If the parents seek help they know their child has problems and the sooner he or she is diagnosed and provided with specialist support, the better the prognosis we may expect. Another application of Munchhausen's Syndrome by Proxy which is still in place at present is (false) accusation of parents with AS children of child abuse. Some local authorities, schools and social services misread the 'bizarre' behaviours of the children and suspect parents of psychological (and/or physical) abuse. Several cases have been reported in the British newspapers when social services tried to take AS children from their families into care because of bruises and wounds on the bodies of the children. As it turned out, these children were severely bullied at school and self-harmed to suppress the frustration. Fortunately, the children were articulate enough to defend their parents in court and explained their apparent signs of abuse. (What is not widely known is that there is violence in some families with an autistic child. However, often it is not the parents abusing the children but rather their autistic children who 'abuse' the parents. These physical outrages are often the results of panic attacks, when the child cannot control his behaviour and may hit, kick, scratch or bite the parents. In most cases, parents keep quiet about these incidents for fear that their child would be taken from them into care. They suffer silently as they have no trust in the existing system that cannot understand and address these issues.)

Prevalence of ASD in parents

At present, many cases of late diagnosis of autism (especially AS) are of parents whose children have been diagnosed. The more they learn about the condition, the more they recognize certain traits in themselves. With a real possibility of a genetic link, this is often the case. Tony Attwood (2000) commented on a research study on the genetics of AS conducted at Yale University. The researchers examined the profile of abilities of 99 families that had a child with AS. In 46 per cent of the families there was a positive family history of AS or something very similar in first-degree relatives. This shows that what Attwood calls 'the broader autism phenotype' is probably more common in families than we first thought. At present we do not have any clear guidelines as to whether such individuals should have a diagnosis of AS, residual AS, the genetic term of broader autism phenotype or (Attwood's preference) the Asperger's personality type. The research on the siblings of a child with AS has revealed that they may have 'fragments' of AS in the profile of abilities. The individual characteristics may not be sufficient in number or severity for a clear diagnosis but if we are unsure where the boundaries are between the normal range and AS, then such children could be considered by some clinicians as having a diagnosis of AS, especially if this created a better understanding of the person and access to educational programmes and services (Attwood 2000).

For 'horizontal reading':

1.2 – pp.29–38
2.2 – pp.97–103
4.2 – pp.241–255

3.3

Causes

Genetic

Some parents strongly oppose the idea of genetic causes of autism and quote, for example, the statistics from the California Department of Education that show that autism in that state has increased 273 per cent over the decade. They argue that the same diagnostic criteria were used as in previous years, so a 'wider' definition of autism cannot be to blame, and people cannot genetically mutate in half a generation (Moynahan 1999). Others may recognize the traits of their children's reactions in themselves or their relatives and find that a genetic cause is quite plausible. Both Kanner (1943) and Asperger (1944) believed that the syndrome they described might be genetically transmitted. Asperger reported that the features tended to occur in the families, especially the fathers of these children. Now we know that it is not necessarily a 'father-related' link. Quite a few AS mothers have been officially diagnosed, to say nothing of hundreds (if not thousands) of undiagnosed 'female relatives', who may seem not to be on the spectrum as their social skills are better than men's and they can 'pass for normal'. Many family histories of those with autism show at least some genetic connection. For example:

> Family histories of high-functioning autistics often contain giftedness, anxiety or panic disorder, depression, food allergies, and learning disabilities. In many of the families I have interviewed the disorders were never formally diagnosed, but careful questioning revealed them... My own family history contains nervousness and anxiety on both sides. My grandmother has mild depression... She is also very sensitive to loud noise... My sister is bothered by confusing noise from several sources. On my father's side there is explosive temper, perseveration on one topic, extreme nervousness, and food allergies. Both sides of my family

contain artists. There are also signs of immune system abnormalities in myself and my siblings. (Grandin 2002)

Many parents with AS are keen to be 'proper parents' for their children and are eager to do everything they can to help their child. There seem to be both advantages and disadvantages of being an AS parent of an autistic child.

Advantages:

- they have better understanding of their child's problems and often may have shared experiences.

Disadvantages:

- sensory problems (hypersensitivities, overload, monotropism, etc.)

- attentional problems.

Some researchers, however, have issued a warning:

> The fact that some parents of children with HFA and AS themselves have autism-associated features begs the question of parenting skills in such individuals. It would not be unreasonable to assume that poor empathy in the parent might contribute to some behaviour/psychological problem to the child, quite apart from any genetic influence. (Gillberg 1998, p.207)

These views have been developed further (see, for example, Jennings Linehan 2004). Jennings Linehan coined the term 'parenting-disability' to describe the problems AS parents face while parenting their children. However, this approach is based on misconceptions resulting from a literal understanding of 'textbook definitions' of autism – lack of empathy, lack of ToM, weak central coherence, etc. To back up her point, Jennings Linehan quoted Dr Willey (who has AS) about difficulties she experiences because of AS.

As for 'parenting-disability', one does not have to have AS to be classified for it. Fortunately, it is rare, but there are cases when parents neglect (or even abuse) their children. For example, one mother left her two young children at home alone while she went on holiday to Spain with her boyfriend. The story was covered in the British newspapers. And the mother was neurotypical. Is it useful to diagnose 'parenting-disability' in AS parents on the basis of a literal interpretation of ASDs? Then we would have to generalize that any parent with a disability (cerebral palsy, blindness, deafness, etc.) is not fit to look after their children. Parents with visual impairments, for instance, also cannot 'read' the facial expressions of their kids. Does it mean they will fail to support them emotionally and psychologically?

Such well-known AS authors as Dr Willey and Wendy Lawson have children. Yes, they have experienced difficulties (what parents don't?), but are they 'parenting-disabled'? On the contrary, sometimes motherhood 'unlocks' a side in an AS parent that has been hidden from view. AS mothers may feel 'connected' with another human being and feel closer to their babies than anyone else can. Sometimes it is the baby's arrival that may help undiagnosed AS mothers to start making sense of their lives for the first time. That is exactly what happened with Dr Willey and Gaynor Barrett (a young woman with AS whose baby daughter has brought her happiness and connection with the world outside the world of her own).

Metabolic problems

Some parents believe that their child was born normal and then slides into autism because of metabolic disturbances that may be caused by the inability to prevent toxins leaking into the bloodstream, with the result that the brain is being bombarded by chemicals which interfere with neurological transmission. And it is here where MMR as a cause of 'regression into autism' may fit in.

MMR

Some parents feel sure that the cause of the child's slipping into autism was the MMR vaccine. They go to court to claim that their children were permanently damaged by the MMR jab. Having heard these 'horror stories', many other parents reject it fearing that their children may develop autism and demand three separate jabs instead of the MMR. However, officials insist this would be no safer than the triple vaccine and would expose children to an extra risk of catching the diseases between the jabs. This controversy is unlikely to be resolved till more is known about the effects of MMR. Till then, parents do have the right to know possible risks and side-effects of the vaccination or being unprotected by it.

Let us put the Triad of Difficulties we discussed in Chapter 3.1 into the context of the Iceberg theory. There is no doubt that having an autistic child in the family may bring a lot of mental and emotional problems for the family to cope with. One of the reasons might be because it is very hard for (non-autistic) parents to imagine what it is like to be 'autistic' and the differences between a non-autistic brain and an 'autistic' brain (that does not make sense of things in the same way) mean confusion for both sides. Understanding, compassionate and supportive carers may not be informed enough from an 'autistic' perspective and that is why they may not know how to show this understanding, compassion and support in a way that will make sense to their autistic child (Williams 1996). If they *want* to understand but probably do not know how to, the logical solution would be to learn from each other. 'The person with "autism" is, however, so often put in the role of learner and so rarely in the role of teacher that someone like this may never realise they can inform people and help them to understand' (Williams 1996, pp.289–290). Besides, the difficulties the families face can be aggravated by environmental ignorance, which can be broken down into Lack Of Tolerance, Understanding and Support (LOTUS) (see Figure 3.2).

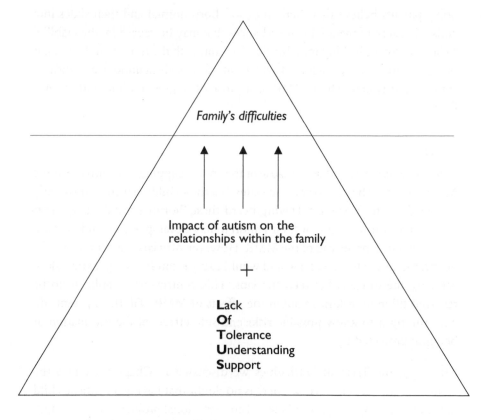

Figure 3.2 The Iceberg of Family's Difficulties

This is just one example of the frustration parents feel that are caused by this 'environmental ignorance':

> Every trip out is an unknown adventure and a potential disaster. Comments overheard or reported back can humiliate if they come from a stranger, and damage relationships if they originate closer to home. When you think about it, no parent wants their child to behave in an 'odd' way, antisocially or dangerously. If there existed a normalisation technique we would go for it. There isn't, so perhaps it is other people who need to work on their attitudes and their behaviour; and non-disabled grown-ups really have no excuse for making a difficult situation worse. (Evans 1999, p.12)

I doubt if there is a family with an autistic child (especially but not necessarily at the lower end of the spectrum) who do not experience frustration from time to time, when they may lose their temper out of a pure inability to deal with the problems and yell, cry and throw things. Sometimes they may come close to hurting their children or themselves. Some mothers have confessed there were times when they wanted to end their lives as they had no strength to deal with the immense pressure which autism puts on family life. And it is often their autistic child who indirectly prevents them from committing suicide (just the thought of what would happen to him, who would love him the way the mother does, may bring new strength in this never-ending battle for their child). Some parents are unable to cope with the challenging behaviours of their child (especially aggression and self-injury) and may consider out-of-home placement for him. Some parents cannot tolerate the thought of what would happen to their child when they are no longer there to protect him.

The lack of understanding, tolerance and support may bring tragic results. Some stories shook the world. An Australian mother killed her ten-year-old autistic son and tried to commit suicide. The boy did not die because he had autism but because of the lack of help his family received. A man in California shot and killed his 27-year-old autistic son and then shot himself. A British couple driven to despair and financial ruin by their AS daughter's obsession with shopping flew to Tenerife to carry out a suicide pact. They had felt let down by the lack of support from the authorities and their daughter was let down by the professionals.

In some cases, AS, and the problems caused by it (if no appropriate educational programme is in place), are recognized when it is too late; for instance, when a person with AS ends up in court for manslaughter or other criminal offence. Then specialists are there to explain the behaviours. Wouldn't it be better to work with these people and families as soon as the person is diagnosed and avoid such tragic events?

For 'horizontal reading':

1.3 – pp.39–44
2.3 – pp.104–112
4.3 – pp.256–259

3.4

Development

Autism is rarely (if ever) detected from birth. Seemingly normal babies are said to regress into autism as they grow older. In the parents' accounts we may find several possible scenarios when autism becomes 'visible':

- Something may be wrong from the start.

- A perfect baby:

    o may sleep through the night and take 'scheduled' naps during the day

    o rarely cries, seeming content with everything

    o coos, smiles

    o reaches milestones in time

    o typically evokes this response from relatives and friends – 'You are so lucky. He or she is a perfect baby.'

- A 'handful' baby:

    o does not sleep much

    o has feeding problems

    o has ear infection after ear infection

    o cannot be left alone for a minute

    o screams without any apparent reason

    o is always 'on the go'.

- A combination of these, for example, a child may start as a 'perfect' baby and develop into a 'handful' one.

In any of these scenarios the early signs of autism may be easily overlooked (see Box 3.2).

Box 3.2 Signs of autism that may be easily missed

- A fascination with lights, sounds, body movements
- Happy when left alone
- Does not like to be held
- Rocking, spinning, tapping objects, flapping arms
- Playing with parts of toys (e.g. a wheel of a car)
- Lining up objects
- Does not like it when his toys have been touched or rearranged
- Screaming when his hair is washed, or his nails are cut
- Perimeter hugging
- Unusual food preferences
- Hair, once soft, may become wiry and coarse
- No recognition of familiar adults when they change their clothes, hair style
- No reaction to loud sounds/his name (suspected deafness, but may be alert when the slightest noise is heard, e.g. opening the box of biscuits)
- May start talking and then:
  - loses the words
  - idiosyncratic language development

The first concerns may be caused by delayed speech development. However, there are always friends/relatives or even doctors who are ready (with good intentions) to reassure you that there is nothing to worry about: 'He is a boy – all boys are lazy', 'He is so clever: look at his eyes', etc. At first, parents may often believe that if the child could just start talking, then everything would be OK. However, they realize very soon that they are wrong.

This desire to have a happy, healthy baby who is not different from the norm may silence the first unconscious concerns. Any parent wants the child to easily fit in and follow their dreams of his or her development; for example:

> When Tariq starts 'stimming'…or flapping, especially now that he is full grown, I automatically want him to stop and act 'normal'. Internally, my reaction can be rather desperate because I don't want him *and* me to be noticed as different. I also still find myself trying to avoid taking photographs when he is not behaving 'normally'. There is a certain image that I prefer of him in my head, as much as I hate to admit that. (Naseef 2001, p.198)

There are several possible scenarios of development of parents – from the time they learn that their child has problems to the time they get used to the idea and accept it. The period between diagnosis and acceptance can be very long and very painful, a period during which parents may go through several stages.

Stage 1: Denial

They do not want to believe that their beautiful, beloved son or daughter is disabled. Sometimes they do feel that something is wrong with their child (especially, when they compare him with his peers). At other times, however, they persuade themselves that all is well, that their child is developing normally. (He passed his major milestones at the usual ages, didn't he? She is so good at switching on the TV or finding the video she wants, isn't she? His eyes are very deep and wise, aren't they?) They find their situation hard to accept, and very often get offended when friends or relatives mention some strange features in the child's behaviour and suggest they consult a doctor. To stay at this stage too long is very dangerous, as the sooner the diagnosis is made and the intervention is started, the better chances the child has for the future. There are some parents (fortunately, very few) who refuse to accept the truth and deny the necessity to meet their child's special needs: 'He is normal. His father was also slow in acquiring speech, but now he is an engineer', etc. Very often it is the child who is harmed by this attitude.

Stage 2: Shock

Shock follows. The reality of having a child with autism often causes shock. No matter how well the parents are prepared to 'learn the worst', the fact that 'the worst' has happened brings shock which is followed by…

Stage 3: Helplessness

At this stage, parents are emotionally paralysed, unable to do anything. At first, they feel helpless because they do not know what autism means and what they are to do. Paradoxically, the more the parents learn about it, the more confused and helpless they sometimes feel. Very often, they think that they are the only family in the world to have a child like this, that nobody can understand their problems. (To know that there are many others in the same situation brings a great relief and desire to seek help.) The feeling of helplessness is often followed by that of…

Stage 4: Guilt

Parents may feel guilt, and question if they are to blame for their child's disability. This is the stage when families either get stronger, uniting their efforts to help the child, or split up because the parents blame each other or each other's relatives in having 'the wrong gene'. Along with guilt often comes shame. Some parents become ashamed of their child, not wanting to take him out in public, or reluctant to talk about him with their friends as if he did not exist, etc. They view the pain as punishment for something they have done in the past. Fortunately, most parents move through this issue, but are met with an equally challenging set of feelings.

Stage 5: Anger

Parents question, 'Why our child? What did we do wrong? Why do other parents drink, smoke and have normal children and we don't?' Sometimes, subconsciously, the parents feel pity for themselves. In the cycle of acceptance, this is another dangerous stage to get stuck in, as parents tend to put their energy into blaming everybody and everything for their misfortune, rather than seeking help.

It is necessary to note that some parents miss one or two stages, some stop on certain stages longer than others. After having gone through all these emotional swings the parents approach the point with several paths to follow. The choice is very individual and depends on personal factors. Whatever road they choose, the most important thing to arrive at is acceptance.

Stage 6: Acceptance

The parents love the child for who he is and for the very differences that make him unique. Another important step is to stop feeling pity for themselves and to enjoy the company of the child. As a result, the family is happy and united in their efforts to improve the quality of the child's and the whole family's life. They become proud of their child's progress. Even the smallest signs of improvement (he buttoned his shirt, she managed to put on her socks, he answered 'yes' to the question) are seen as a triumph and victory for the whole family in their continual battle for their child. The parents do not feel ashamed of their child and take him out everywhere, trying to involve him in all their activities as much as possible, ignoring the stares of ill-informed people. They learn to love their child not despite the child's differences but because of them. A very good tool to help, I think, is a good sense of humour! It can often transform a seemingly devastating situation into an amusing story to share with friends and relatives. As an example, a few years ago there was a reception for some Ukrainian officials at the Town Hall in Barnsley where I was interpreting. My autistic son was in the same room sitting near the door with one of my friends. After the official part of the reception, an invitation to have a drink followed. At that briefest moment of complete silence when everybody turned to go to the tables, my boy said very loudly: 'But first, everybody to the loo!' The Russian-speaking attendees roared with laughter. Yes, I was embarrassed, but so what? It happened, and now I cannot help smiling when I remember this episode!

For 'horizontal reading':

1.4 – pp.45–46
2.4 – pp.113–125
4.4 – pp.260–264

Theories

The parents' attitude to theories of autism is not homogeneous. Parents who are also professionals and not only live with an autistic child, but also work with autistic people, are very much interested in theoretical explanations. Typically such parents-professionals are very sceptical about theories 'originated in the office' by those who are not in constant contact with autistic people. They often question 'office-made' theories and hypotheses and are very flexible in their attitude to new ones. For these parents, if the data (they receive from their everyday experiences) do not fit the theory, they easily let the theory go, in contrast to professionals for whom their 'creation' is like a baby, and they try to accommodate the data to it. Other parents are not interested in theoretical constructs at all; they do not need theories but want help from 'enlightened professionals' – those who are knowledgeable and experienced in the field of autism. Still others create their own theories which, they think, can explain the development of autism in their own child; for example, they name as the main 'suspects' of the cause of their child's autism immune system problems, mercury poisoning, gut problems, severe allergies or MMR.

ToM

Whether some parents are interested in theories or not, the lack of ToM (here ToPM – Theory of Parents' Mind) displayed by both some autistic people and some professionals has very significant implications. Teachers, psychologists and other professionals will not always see things the same way that a parent does. This can be very frustrating, as the parents have actually to fight for their children against ignorance of others (Lawson 2001). What is more, there are different 'theories of parents' mind', depending on the parents' views on treatments and what they want their child to achieve.

Lack of ToM among different groups of parents

It originates from the different views on the ways to help the child and the desired outcomes. Those parents who are desperate for a 'normal' child, and want to do everything they can to make their autistic child to look as normal as possible, and support the activities of such organizations as Cure Autism Now! (CAN) and Defeat Autism Now (DAN), would not understand those parents who try to help the child to function (but do not mind him remaining autistic) and support the views of HF autistic individuals who are against a 'cure' for autism (Don't Cure Autism Now). Paradoxically, both groups have a lot in common, but do not realize it because of mind-blindness, leading to misreading the intentions and feelings of their 'opponents'. These are examples of misunderstanding among different groups of people, which have resulted from lack of ToM.

What supporters of the 'anti-cure movement' say: 'We don't need cure, we want acceptance'

WHAT THEIR OPPONENTS HEAR

'Leave autistic children alone (that is, let them suffer). Don't do anything to help them. Change the attitude of society.'

THE INTENDED MESSAGE OF THE 'ANTI-CURE MOVEMENT'

'Address your children's (treatable) problems (such as sensory processing difficulties, lack of self-help skills, gut problems, etc.), help them develop into self-sufficient successful adults (who are people with HFA), but don't train them to look normal at any cost. It is necessary to differentiate between autism (that is not a bad thing) and autism-related problems that disable the child (and can be treated). Let them be different, but educate those who cannot tolerate any diversion from the "norm".'

LACK OF TOM

Both groups have the same aims but different interpretations.

What supporters of the 'cure concept' say: 'We want a cure for autism for our children'

WHAT THEIR OPPONENTS HEAR

'They want to kill/defeat/destroy us and replace us with somebody else (who is normal).'

THE INTENDED MESSAGE OF SUPPORTERS OF THE 'CURE CONCEPT'

'We don't want our children to suffer, never to be able to live independently, be outcasts. We won't be always there to protect them.'

LACK OF TOM

Both groups want their children to be happy and as independent as possible, but use different approaches to achieve it.

As we have developed different strategies to teach autistic children 'mind-reading' (see, for example, Baron-Cohen 2003b), we have to do the same for their parents ('mind-reading' of other parents who disagree with our views) and for professionals ('mind-reading' of parents). Unfortunately, it is quite common for professionals to be mind-blind when dealing with the parents of autistic children. In Box 3.3 there is an example of an exercise for professionals who lack Theory of Parents' Mind.

Box 3.3 An example of an exercise for lack of ToPM

You are a SEN administrator who is responsible for evaluating suitability of provision for SEN children. In your area there is one provision for autistic children, but, unfortunately, parents are not happy with it and try to persuade you to send their children outside of the area where there are schools for children with autism that have good reputations. You have limited financial resources and cannot afford sending all the autistic children in your area to these good schools. Parents do not understand that it is not easy to find good specialists, and you considered yourself lucky to find someone to appoint as a teacher who has got some knowledge of autism. You are aware that parents do not like the approach used in the school – being mostly a baby-sitting provision. However, what else do they want – their children are looked after. Other parents are not so lucky and stay at home with their autistic kids.

Now do this test

Your child is seriously ill, and he needs an urgent surgical operation. Unfortunately, the hospital is far away. Will you hire a taxi (which will be very expensive) to take him there, or will you take him to the dentist round the corner (after all, he knows something about the anatomy of the body, and should be able to operate, shouldn't he?)? If the nurse would insist on the latter option (it is cheaper), how would you feel?

That is how parents whose children are stuck in inappropriate provisions feel about their situation. And it is not wrong to compare physical emergency with a mental one. Yes, these children will not die, but wasted time when they have a chance to develop may result in lifelong suffering; that is, inability to communicate, lack of self-skills and complete dependence on the carers. It *is* urgent to help them *now* with proper educational treatment, instead of being satisfied with a 'tick' in your report from your boss – 'the child attends the provision locally, the demands of the parents are unreasonable'.

What hurts the parents most is that such specialists lack not only understanding (ToPM) but also empathy – after all, it is not their child.

It is the parents who have to cope with broken nights, violent outbursts, bizarre behaviours and tantrums. And it is doubly hard to know that you have not got much time to change things (as one day you will not be there to provide the care for your child). When the parents experience a lack of understanding and empathy, their frustration is difficult to imagine. Educating professionals and autistic people in ToPM is a necessity.

However, parents need to learn the theory of autistic mind as well (at least, be aware that autistic people have feelings and interpretations of what is going on around them, that may be very different from the perspective of others). This is an exercise for parents: Think what autistic people would hear when parents say:

- Autism is worse than cancer, because people with autism have normal life spans.

- Autism is worse than September 11 and AIDS combined.

- When we were told that our son was autistic, it was like experiencing a death in our family.

Can parents understand the feelings of their autistic child when they hear these statements?

One may argue that these may hurt HF and AS people with autism but they are different from low-functioning autistic children who *suffer* from autism. However, aren't non-verbal low-functioning children hurt by this attitude? Unintentionally we may hurt some children when we think they do not understand what is going on. This is how Tito, a non-verbal autistic boy, describes it:

> One day, father came home from the club and dropped a magazine on the table. He looked so depressed. 'Read it.' He told mother. She read it and then she argued about my ability to communicate with him. I knew at once that the magazine contained some article which has something to do with me. But what could be written about me in it? Obviously something hopeless about autism.
>
> I got the message.
>
> My father did not believe in my communication any more.
>
> I got the message.
>
> Autism was something which made the people close to you doubt you.
>
> I got the message.
>
> I need not be proud about my communication. Because I would not be believed. (Mukhopadhyay 1999)

Fortunately for Tito, his mother took a 'having nothing to do with any literature on autism' stance because she felt she did not need to learn about autism from any doctor when she could learn it from her son. She believed in him and in her own self. She continued teaching Tito with increased determination. Her motto became, 'Find a way or make a way' (Mukhopadhyay 1999).

Autism as an extreme version of the male brain

This is the theory that has both infuriated some parents and has been enthusiastically welcomed by others. Parents who want the world to embrace differences and accept that there is no such thing as 'normality' see this hypothesis as a matter of celebration of their children's uniqueness and worthiness. Typically, these are parents of children with HFA or AS. They witness the suffering of their offspring from bullying by their peers and misunderstanding from their teachers. Others (usually, but not necessarily, with LF autistic children) felt insulted and met the 'maleness theory' with open hostility. It is little wonder that after 'night-shifts' watching their child wandering around the house, keeping all the doors locked in case he might escape, coping with violent outbursts, head banging, seizures, uncontrollable screaming, sensitivity to light, touch and sound, lack of verbal abilities and other numerous challenges the parents face every day, they cannot accept that autism may be seen as a 'gift' or just a 'different way of thinking'. These parents consider this theory of ASD misleading, damaging and dangerous as it may be misinterpreted by the general public (who have no first-hand experience with autism) as merely an inconvenience to the person and the family and it may be addressed by educating the society and adjusting the environments to this unique cognitive style. These parents do make an erroneous assumption about the theory that is aimed to explain the universal features of autism (present in *all* autistic individuals, both with LFA and HFA/AS). However, they are right that the consequences may be devastating if the general public viewed autism as something 'cute' without being aware of the many autism-related problems (that accompany the condition in many, though not all, cases).

For 'horizontal reading':

1.5 – pp.47–53
2.5 – pp.126–137
4.5 – pp.265–283

3.6

Treatments

There are many therapies available at the 'autism treatment market'. None is proven to be successful for all children, but some produce remarkable results. Many parents are prepared to try everything, from faith healers to psychiatric treatments, in order to find the right treatment for their child. In the countries where autism is still not recognized and is therefore misunderstood and mistreated, the parents may go to any healers or spiritualists who claim they can exorcise 'an evil spirit' living in an otherwise healthy child. Sometimes, the 'treatment' may end tragically.

Some parents want to 'free' their child from this 'evil' (autism). Others see their goal to make their children as functional and independent as possible and use any tools (which may be seen as not acceptable) to achieve this goal. Others aim to ensure the happiness of their child and, at the same time, never change who he is (Flanagan 2001). It is a challenge to balance accepting who the child is and appreciating his different abilities with giving him the skills to function in the real world:

> We want our children to be happy, to achieve and to cope as adults without hurting themselves or anyone else. Accepting this as a realistic set of goals is not easy – particularly if more than one child is affected... Sleepless nights result from the knowledge that there may be nobody to care for our disabled children when we die, that they may never find love from anyone outside their immediate family. (Evans 1999, p.12)

> I now spend every day trying to make life easier for him [Brian, her son], developing strategies for him to cope. Making sure he has the right education and developing his life skills, although I have to say I don't think Brian will ever be able to live independently. I will try to give him all the help I can to make him as independent as possible, he is

my life, I totally love and cherish him – unconditionally – which in my mind means total acceptance, not trying to change him or cure him. (Riva 1999)

Diets

Some parents have reported considerable improvements when they put their autistic children on gluten-free/casein-free diets, even to the extent of 'full recovery from autism' (Moynahan 1999). Some parents see the changes in a few days:

> The effect was dramatic. After five days without milk products, Louis began looking at us, laughing and babbling again. Eight weeks later, at his assessment, he didn't test autistic…by noon that Sunday [Amanda, a mother, had] put Edward on a casein- and gluten-free diet. By Wednesday his behaviour was better than it had been for months, and he seemed to be coming out of his shell. By Friday of the same week, when he had a doctor's appointment, Edward was acting more like a normal child of his age… The doctor was amazed and told me that she would now have trouble labelling him autistic. (Moynahan 1999, pp.35, 36)

In *Fighting for Tony* (1987), Mary Callahan tells how taking her son Tony off milk transformed him from an autistic child to a normal teenager. The danger of reports of this kind is that many parents who are inspired to follow suit may become bitterly disappointed if these 'miraculous' results do not happen not only after a few days, but after many months.

Other parents report some positive changes in a few months. Two possible scenarios of 'getting out of autism' when on casein- and gluten-free diets have been reported:

- 'more normal' behaviours are noticeable almost immediately

- the child goes through the phase of withdrawal and seems to be in pain like a drug addict for a few hours or days, then improvements can be seen.

A parent-run charity 'Allergy-Induced Autism' has been founded in the UK. It provides parents with information about the diet (www.kessick.demon.co. uk/aia.htm).

Psychodynamic therapy

As autism causes a lot of mental and emotional problems for the carers, they and their children may be referred to psychoanalysts for psychodynamic therapy. Many parents have low self-esteem and may blame themselves for the cause of their children's behaviours and their inability to change them. This has been exploited by some psychotherapists. The same goal may be achieved by counselling and training that would provide explanations of 'why the child does this', for how they can assist their child's development and address challenging behaviours, and ideas for how to cope with the stress of dealing with an autistic child in the context of each particular family. The counsellor/therapist should be knowledgeable in autism and be prepared to listen to the parents' concerns.

Auditory integration training (AIT)

The publication of Annabel Stehli's book *Sound of a Miracle: A Child's Triumph over Autism* (1991) brought AIT great attention and interest. Stehli described the remarkable results of AIT on her autistic daughter Georgiana who had spent the first 11 years of her life in special schools and institutions, but speedily recovered from her autism after treatment with AIT. Hundreds of parents, inspired by this story, took their children to AIT centres, but so far no more 'miraculous' results have been reported. AIT does bring improvements in many autistic individuals who suffer from auditory hypersensitivities but it is not a cure for autism. In those cases where hypersensitive hearing is a result of compensating for other primarily affected sensory channels (for example, vision) the treatment is short-lived.

Options (Son-Rise)

Some parents do not like the 'options' approach as they do not feel in control. Others report very positive changes in their children who had been 'unreachable' before treatment. Imitating their child, creating a common language, encouraging the child to imitate them may bring immediate and remarkable results. However, soon after the beginning of the therapy, the question arises – 'Now we have established communication – what next?' So many parents move on to other therapies that enable them to teach children necessary skills and do things they may not want to do.

Floor time

The success of 'floor time' therapy (if started very early) is documented by Patricia Stacey (2004a), the mother of an autistic boy, in her book *The Boy Who Loved Windows*. Walker was just nine months old when the symptoms of autism became noticeable. Stacey movingly describes their family's efforts to reach the child, her meeting with Dr Greenspan and floor-time sessions (20- to 30-minute sessions eight to ten times per day). The author is very honest describing the problems this demanding intervention brought to the family:

> There seemed no way out: floor time was a challenge, a game, a vocation, a prison sentence. How on earth could I do eight to ten sessions a day, take care of my five-year-old daughter Elizabeth, myself and a house? Suddenly the problem wasn't Walker any more and what he could and couldn't do. It was me, my limitations, human limitations. (Stacey 2004a, p.262)

Stacey describes some of the triumphs and turmoil of Walker's early life and the impact of Walker's problems and the amount of time and effort to help him had on her marriage. As he was picked up very early, by the age of four Walker is reported to have recovered from autism, and now 'is a warm, intelligent, engaged schoolboy, who occasionally has his unruly moments' (Stacey 2004b, p.99).

TEACCH

Some parents like the idea of TEACCH but see the flaws of it as well, for example workstations – they prefer to teach their children in different surroundings and situations to help them generalize. They are realistic and know they have to prepare their children to live in an outside world where it is not always possible to adapt the environment for each and every individual. They want to equip their children to live in the community and see their goal as adapting the child to the world, instead of having unrealistic expectations of the world adapting to their child.

Applied Behavioural Analysis (ABA)

Some organizations (for example the Association for Science in Autism Treatment – ASAT) claim that ABA is the only scientifically valid treatment for autism. Dr Rimland (who is a supporter of ABA) defines this position as indefensible because it gives a distorted view of what science is all about, as well as a willingness to ignore all relevant evidence (Rimland 1999). Some parents who lack the knowledge of research on the validity of other interventions follow the 'ABA is the only way' specialists and, as a result, do not consider other possible treatments which can bring considerable improvements with less effort and fewer negative consequences for a child.

The 'pro-ABA as the only treatment for autism' parents are not in the majority, but as they are very 'loud' in their campaign, their views are widely known. However, the 'volume of the voice' does not necessarily add to the credibility of such statements as 'ABA is the only one *scientifically-proven* and *medically necessary* approach'. They base their philosophy on the assumption that autism is a medical condition that can be compared to cancer, and ABA is the equivalent of chemotherapy. The conclusion drawn from this is that either autistic children are successfully treated with the only one scientifically-proven and medically necessary therapy – ABA (like chemotherapy is medic-ally necessary for treatment of cancer) – or they are doomed to a life in institutions. (However, if autism is a 'serious medical illness' that can be compared to cancer, why treat it with behavioural methods? No one suggests treating cancer with ABA.)

Those autistic people who oppose ABA are 'diagnosed' by the parent-supporters of the treatment as 'non-autistic', or 'not autistic enough' and their arguments are rejected without any considerations. The problem arises when other parents of autistic children give their voices to the 'anti-ABA movement' and whose children (both with LFA and HFA) improve via treatments which are different from ABA. Does it mean that their children as well are not 'truly autistic', or that these parents do not love their children enough to apply 'the only scientifically-proven and medically necessary' treatment?

And let us not forget that among those 53 per cent of 'unsuccessful' children, some children were harmed by the therapy. Families whose autistic children were severely traumatized in the ABA programmes have founded an organization called CIBRA (2004), with the mission to provide a national and international support network for parents whose children (including adult children) have been traumatized, injured or even killed by ABA. They want to raise public awareness of the risks involved in the treatment. On their website parents share their experiences and give support and advice to those who need it. There are numerous stories of children who regressed during the treatment. They describe their youngsters whose basic trust has been destroyed and they end up avoiding people. One boy cannot even go near any educational materials without severe panic attacks, since these were used in his behavioural programme. In their *Open Letter to Families Considering Intensive Behavioural Therapy for Their Child with Autism* (CIBRA 2004), they warn other families about possible risks and give personal stories to illustrate their concerns. For example:

> We found that the most dangerous outcome of the philosophical directives of behaviorism is violence to the sanctity of an individual's right to protect himself. That is what destroyed our child: he was denied the basic right to defend himself against unbearable anxiety. When he needed to get out of a situation he could neither understand nor bear, he was forcibly restrained and we were told, 'All we're asking him to do is sit in a chair.' His world was denied validation and treated as if it did not exist. His cries for help were ignored; 'extinction' is the term. What was 'extinguished' was not an isolated 'tantrum' behavior but our son's basic sense of security and safety, his ability to regulate his emotional system, and his understanding of moral behavior (i.e. that 'when I'm hurting, adults will help me'). (CIBRA 2004)

Other parents consider ABA to be particularly destructive of their child's emotional development, when hugs and kisses (gestures normally used to express affection and love) are used instrumentally, when the child is required to give and receive these gestures as part of the training, without regard to his or her actual feelings. As for eliminating a targeted 'behaviour' by responding to it in a discouraging way (or not responding at all), the child may learn that he should hide pain and not seek comfort when he hurts, because for the child the 'targeted behaviour' may be his way to communicate distress. The CIBRA group share their concerns and experiences with the treatment in the hope that others can be spared the pain these families have been through. Are their views valid? Or were they just unlucky? Or are their children not autistic? Or do they not love their children enough? It is so easy to dismiss other views and insist that only yours are valid.

We all use behavioural methods with our children, both autistic and non-autistic ones. There is nothing wrong with this. But insisting rigidly that ABA is the *only* treatment is wrong. The sound approach to ABA should be as a complementary treatment to other approaches that address each particular child's problems, such as, for example, diets for food intolerance, or sensory diets for sensory processing problems.

The teachers report that some children (who are on the ABA programme) are enrolled into mainstream schools, bringing impressive lists of skills in their files. However, sometimes, these skills 'disappear' at school, and teachers do not believe that the child is capable of doing what his parents say he can. The teachers have to start teaching the same skills again 'from scratch'. When children return from a therapy room (with one-to-one training) to the real world at some point, surprise, surprise, they are autistic again (Riva 1999).

Some parents (fortunately, very few) sometimes use very tough measures to achieve good results. Unsurprisingly, these methods (withholding food, hitting, etc.) do work, and the child may be forced to 'leave the autism shell' and participate in the real world and eventually even believe that the treatment has done him good (Baggs Undated). The ends justify the means. Or do they?

Others try to 'modernize' ABA and make it more 'their child's autism-friendly'. These parents refuse to follow strict 'prescriptions' of the therapy if they see it frustrates their child. (One mother literally pointed to the door, when an ABA consultant insisted on following the 'ABA procedure' to the letter.)

All parents use behavioural methods with all children (both autistic and non-autistic ones). All parents see their responsibility to teach their child certain skills to function in life. But to put the ABA on a pedestal as being the *only* way to teach autistic children does not seem to be reasonable. Some mothers insist that all the skills their autistic children have developed could not be acquired without this treatment. From this statement arises the question, how do they know that other treatments would not bring the same (or better) results, possibly with less effort? One mother did admit that when they hospitalized their daughter and used a behavioural approach in an attempt to get her to eat, 'it was tough going, but it worked'. Why use behavioural methods to treat sensory or gustatory or any of the other treatable problems which are quite typical in autistic children?

Cure

There are parents who believe that it is possible to cure autism and those who accept that it is impossible. Some parents raise money to try to get the treatment they have heard about as 'a miraculous cure for autism'. Others hate the whole idea of 'miraculous cures'. They know that it is possible to help their child to improve (and even become 'indistinguishable' from his peers), but do not see it as 'recovery from autism':

> Brian is not recovering – he is not ill, he doesn't have cancer, he is not going to be cured, and most of all he does not have to be cured. He is totally and unconditionally loved for who he is. Brian is a young man

with autism. Yes it's difficult for him, yes it's a struggle for us every day, but that's the way it is. So I stopped years ago trying to either blame someone or something for him being autistic, or waiting for the next miracle cure... We just live day by day, accepting, developing and working on helping Brian. He's really progressing well at school, learning living skills, learning how to live and cope with autism. (Riva 1999)

Some parents (already under enormous pressure trying to cope with their child and maintain their marriage) feel they have to raise money for a treatment promising a cure. And in the beginning of any treatment they may see their child improving that confirms their belief in this particular approach. However, it may be said about *any* treatment. The reasons are:

- With one-to-one supervision and intensive treatment (five to six hours a day), *any* child may improve, whatever approach is used. It would be surprising if consistent and systematic work with a child did not produce at least some beneficial results, whatever the approach (Jordan *et al.* 1998).

- When parents are actively involved in the treatment of their child, they are likely to see beneficial effects. This is the 'halo' effect: because of their expectations, parents may notice positive results where they otherwise would not notice them.

- A very important factor is the personality of the therapist or the teacher. Temple Grandin, for example,

> cannot emphasize enough the importance of a good teacher. A good teacher is worth his or her weight in gold. Some teachers just have a knack for working with autistic children. Other teachers do not have it. (Grandin 1996b)

Considerable improvements (or even 'complete recovery') have been reported about all the approaches. Though these cases are anecdotal, it is no wonder that parents find them inspirational and are eager to try them ('What if it works for my child?'). The real question is, which approach is best for this particular child? Timing when the treatment starts is also important. The earlier the intervention starts, the better the outcome. However, the brain continues to grow and change throughout life. That is why there is hope not only for children but also for adults with autism, using different approaches (suitable for each individual) to improve functioning. Unfortunately, sometimes it is very difficult for parents to find a school/provision suitable for their child. How can parents leave their child in the provision if they do not trust the professionals who will work with him?

I fully agree with Mike Stanton, the father of an AS boy, when he says 'With autism, the more we understand the less there is to cure' (Stanton 2001). If we know why the child behaves the way he or she does and we can either adjust the environment or help the child to cope (through diets, sensory aids, exercises, desensitization, etc.), there will be less of a problem with the so-called 'bizarre autistic behaviours' or they may even disappear altogether. Another very important point is that while it is natural for parents to hope that their child will 'become normal', they should take pride in whatever achievements their child makes.

Sometimes we may witness progress without intervention or even despite it.

Without intervention

The child continues to develop, whether the treatment is in place or not. Some autistic children unconsciously learn how to protect themselves from painful experiences and how to use the mechanisms available to them to get meaning about the world around them:

> Jake [her grandson, who had not received early intervention due to family circumstances] continued to make progress despite the lack of formal intervention. We learned later that the games, the bouncing and swinging, the songs and play routines were all working their magic on the 'neuroplasticity' of a three-year-old brain. As one therapist said, 'Jake is learning despite us all'. Jake was, by himself, creating new pathways as we watched barely aware of the heroic struggle of this remarkable three-year-old. (Schulman 1999, p.3)

Kanner (1971) observed that there was usually some natural progress in autistic children as they grew. A certain number of his patients became very high-functioning as adults, even though they had not been given any special treatment at all. There have been (rare) reports of mysterious spontaneous recovery when children continued to improve so greatly that they could no longer be considered autistic (with parents unable to explain this 'miracle') (Rimland 1994).

Despite intervention

There are cases when autistic children improve *despite* intervention; for example, having been abused through painful treatments that do not look abusive to the carers or therapists. (Some of them describe the 'tortures' they were put through later in life.)

Whatever treatment programme or therapy is used, it does not make the person 'less autistic'. The successful treatment will give the person the ability for self-management and the self-knowledge to develop better compensations for their difficulties. That, in turn, will decrease symptoms and make autism less disabling (Gerland 1998).

The ways parents are treated

It is not only the way the child is treated that is important, but the way the parents are treated by those who are involved professionally with their child.

> My problem, like that of many parents and autistic people, is that we have first hand knowledge of autism and a fair degree of expertise in applying that knowledge. But we have no way of validating our knowledge, skills and understanding other than by going on courses where lecturers tell us things we already know and do not want to hear from us the things they do not know. (Stanton 2001)

Unfortunately, mistrust between parents and some 'know-all' professionals does exist. Many parents educate themselves about autism and check any recommendations given by professionals. But instead of becoming partners in determining their child's future and choosing the appropriate treatment, they are often treated by professionals as the 'main problem', and their views are dismissed as biased and unreliable. It is worth remembering, though, that it was the parents who initiated some of the most outstanding programmes for autistic children and founded the first schools and provisions for children and then for adults with autism (while the professionals' only recommendation was to institutionalize them). For example, the first day-school for autistic children in the USA was established in 1952, initiated by Harriet Mandelbaum of Brooklyn, the mother of an autistic boy. In 1964 the first autism society in the world was formed in England (the National Autistic Society) by a group of dedicated parents. In November 1965 the National Society for Autistic Children (now the Autism Society of America) was founded by parents and interested professionals. Benhaven in New Heaven, Connecticut, was founded by Amy Ladin Lettick when no school would take her son Ben. Jay Nolan Center in Newhall, California, was named after the autistic son of actor Lloyd Nolan and his wife Nell, and was started by a group of Los Angeles parents. In 1970 two fathers of autistic sons – Victor Winston, a publisher, and Herman Preiser, a naval engineer – founded the *Journal of Autism and Childhood Schizophrenia* (now the *Journal of Autism and Developmental Disorders*), which has become an invaluable source of information on autism and research in the field. TEACCH in North Carolina, the first state-wide educational programme for autistic children, was founded by Eric Schopler with tremendous support from parents. At present, we see similar developments in countries where autism is not widely recognized yet. For example, a small group of parents founded the first Autism Society in Ukraine in 1994, and in a year, after having failed to persuade professionals that their autistic children need educational programmes and not institutionalization, opened a small school for autistic children in Gorlovka, Ukraine. Some professionals forget that all these provisions and organizations (where they work now) and many treatments were initiated by parents.

Instead of dismissing parents' views as subjective and irrelevant, it is important to provide training for parents. A lot of research is geared toward helping autistic children to learn, but not much going into helping parents understand what is going on inside their children (Schneider 1999). A parent training programme is essential for several reasons:

- the parents are with their child for life (unlike professionals who may quit at any time)

- the parents need to understand their child and develop ways to communicate and teach him

- if the parents have training and have similar views on autism and treatments, they will know what is going on at the child's school and they will be able to cooperate successfully, creating consistent approaches

- if the parents have not only practical experience but also knowledge of autism, they will be able to ask the right questions to be sure that the programme is suitable for their child.

And last but not least, one should mention the treatment (or mistreatment) the parents experience in the hands of 'autistic bullies'. Those autistic individuals who have 'found their destiny to fight for the rights of *all* autistic children' (and who have no children of their own) seem to know how to raise someone else's children much better than their parents. Yes, some parents may make mistakes and be misled in their attempts to help their offspring. But instead of educating them, sharing the experience of what it is like to live with autism, and sharing personal stories of what worked and what did not work in their cases, some autistic individuals accuse parents of mistreating the children.

For 'horizontal reading':

1.6 – pp.54–66
2.6 – pp.138–161
4.6 – pp.284–294

Miscellany

Thoughts to Share

'Professional parents' and 'unprofessional professionals'

The experience of many parents shows that, the more you know about autism, the more you suffer at the hands of professionals who know less. The parents who try to give their views on the way their child is treated may be dismissed or ridiculed. For example, a mother was made a laughing stock by a teacher of her autistic son, when she said that milk was not good for him and possibly also not for some other autistic children. The teacher could not believe his ears and roared with laughter, 'Milk is good for *all*. It's a pity I must tell you this obvious fact.' The mother left the meeting feeling very distraught and powerless. How could she explain to this 'professional' about milk intolerance, to say nothing about other issues which may contradict his 'obvious beliefs'? How could she trust this person to take proper care of her son? If you have an ill-educated professional, there is no hope your child will be supported properly. And the scariest thing about it is – you can do nothing to change it.

Shall we shout? (An unintended experiment)

When dealing with service providers, and education and SEN administration, many parents use a 'shout loud policy' – 'those who shout the loudest will get what they want'. Being a professional, I was very uncomfortable with this idea. There is a system in place, isn't there? Every child deserves and will be provided with the services they need. However, recently I had to reconsider my position on this issue. I found myself in the position of 'just a mum' trying to follow (obediently) the rules of the system. This is the story that turned into an unintentional experiment not to 'shout loud' when you want something for your child. The only regrettable factor was that it was my son who was a 'guinea pig'.

As soon as my son turned 15, it was time to think about his transition to a post-16 education. So in November 2003 a case conference regarding his placement the next September was held in his school. All the right people were attending. We discussed possible options and I was given leaflets about those available, and asked to visit them and consider their suitability for my son. That became my priority, and by the January I had provided my son's Education Officer (whom we never met as she was very busy) with all the necessary information, including the provision of our choice. Then...nothing happened. Feeling very uncomfortable, in February I sent another letter asking about the progress. The letter was acknowledged and we were told that the Local Education Authority (LEA) was currently considering it and would be in contact with me 'in the near future'. It made us all feel happy for a time, but nothing happened again, and another letter with the same query was sent in March. And again it was acknowledged, and again nothing happened. By April 2004, I was losing it. A few months to go, and still no transition plan was in action, and no decision had been taken about the placement. Surely they know how important it is to prepare the autistic person for all these changes? June came and went. Nothing from the LEA. Another letter to the person in charge, and this time there was a difference – no reply, no acknowledgement, nothing. In July (with a couple of weeks to go before the summer holidays), it was not only my son who had regular panic attacks, I had them as well. These were aggravated by the feeling of guilt – why hadn't I listened to my friends and why hadn't I 'shouted loudly'? How could I have waited for so long? Even if these 'specialists' did not know that when services are not provided it results in weeks or months of lost opportunities for autistic individuals, I did. And I let it happen. I could not forgive myself.

In August 2004 I contacted the service we had decided on in November 2003, and was told that, yes, they had a placement for my son; and no, nobody from our LEA had contacted them about it. To make a long story short, my son stayed at home in September. After many phone-calls and letters the LEA started the process in September (ten months later). There was no transition period, no proper preparation for this big change in the life of my son, and...no apology. Just a letter that his file had been transferred to the provision. To add to the insult, the letter was stamped with 'Our Audit Commission CPA score EXCELLENT and improving!' If this is the best, I don't dare to think about the worst. After this 'unintended experiment', I am very careful when I talk about the necessity of being 'loud' with parents. Sometimes, we do have to shout, if we want our children to get the services they deserve and are entitled to.

So who is disabled?

Dealing with disabled people is never easy. You want to do your best, for example, for an autistic individual, and then you get hit or kicked. It often ends up with an exclusion of the student from the provision. When parents want some explanations, the decision is accounted for 'safety of the staff' – 'They are not paid to be hit.' Of course they are not. They are paid to work with these people, i.e. to understand their behaviour and to apply the appropriate strategies to manage it, while building on their strengths. For example, the child could be disturbed (in pain?) by anything from a change in classroom routine to background sounds (that are intolerable for him). As the child has problems communicating what is wrong, his only way to express his frustration is by screaming, hitting, running away. As if it was not already hard enough for him, we might then blame him for his behaviour and punish him by excluding him from school. Do those professionals who choose this option to 'protect their staff' think about the parents of the child? Their options are very limited – keep the child at home because he is 'unmanageable'. If the staff cannot cope with the job, or are not qualified or trained to work with autistic individuals, is it the right job for them? There is a very big difference which professionals often overlook. If the professionals cannot do their work, they can always quit and find employment somewhere else. Parents, however, cannot go away. They have to deal with these problems on an everyday basis. If people who are supposed to help them and their children cannot help, then who can? Kevin Phillips, a young adult with AS, feels very angry with those professionals who have let him down and brought many years of suffering for him and his family:

> If people employed in these positions think it is acceptable to carry on as they are, then I suggest they should either move on with the times or seek alternative employment. (Phillips Undated)

One mother suggested a strategy to cope with 'unprofessional professionals': 'Consider them disabled. Then you will feel pity for them.' But this strategy will help only to fight your anger for a few days, then the question will come:

Why don't they stay at home on disability allowances, and let people who are capable do their job? Does society need to pay people for damaging the lives of our children and the whole families?

On 'autisticism': how much autistic should be autistic?

Recently, an undeclared war has started between the parents of those with 'real autism' and those whom they call 'so-called, self-proclaimed "autistics" (who are not autistic at all)'.

So how 'autistic' should you be in order to be considered 'autistic'? To prove that these NTs 'masquerading as autistics' are in fact non-autistic, the parents refer to 'respected diagnosticians' who confirm that those who are as articulate as the 'don't-cure-us bunch' clearly show abilities whose absence are the defining characteristics of autism. Full stop. So, to be logical, if our children (my son included) eventually learn how to express their views, will they automatically become 'non-autistic' and will they lose their ability to understand what it feels like? And some more questions (just out of curiosity): How shall we refer to autistic authors (for example, Temple Grandin, Donna Williams, Wendy Lawson, Liane Holliday Willey, to name just a few)? Shall we exclude them from the autism spectrum as well?

Here we deal with 'one-sidedness' again. A very important implication in this matter is not that high-functioning people with ASDs should be listened to because they are always right. No, they may be wrong. But the reaction from some parents is disproportional. Is it wise to create a precedent for future parents to shut up *our* children when they have grown up and are able to express their views? Is it wise to (unintentionally) teach future parents how to hurt our (grown-up) children (when we won't be there to protect them)? I definitely don't want it to happen to *my* son (diagnosed as a low-functioning, severely mentally retarded autistic toddler) who didn't talk till he was seven, whose behavioural 'outbursts' (caused by panic attacks and sensory overload) and suspected epilepsy resulted in three cases of hospitalization (not for him, but for me – broken nose, dislocated shoulder, and the last one – concussion). It took me many years to address his sensory hypersensitivities, gut problems, stress and anxiety. Now he is a *very* articulate 16-year-old young man who *dares* (good boy!) *to disagree with me* on some issues. I don't want anybody to shut him up and insult him in the future because they feel he has no right to express his views (which are likely to be different from mine). The solution is simple – no, not to agree with everything uttered by people with ASDs. Let us agree, disagree, argue, discuss, but respect and listen to each other, and hope that our grown-up children will be respected and listened to. *Just a thought.*

Autistic societies

When their children were refused any rights and any help, and were labelled hopeless and not worth effort or money, many parents decided not to give up on their children and, as there was no support from the authorities, they established organizations and schools that would work with their 'hopeless' kids and provide the much-needed support and encouragement to the families. These parents found strength in uniting their efforts and sharing financial, psychological and emotional burdens. It was the parents who established autistic societies that give hope for a brighter future for their children. These societies were born from the anger and frustration of parents in their desperate attempt to help their children. Started by small groups of parents, autistic societies have developed in strong influential organizations comprising parents and professionals whose activities have brought a considerable change in the well-being of families affected by autism. Originally, these societies were founded for families with autistic children. But as the children grow up, the organizations include the development of services for autistic adults into their objectives. However, now we are witnessing a strange and not very positive trend in the development of some autistic societies. They are parents- and professionals-centred. Those autistic children who developed into high-functioning autistic adults are, unfortunately, not always welcomed into these organizations. There are, however, a number of high-functioning and AS people who are interested in working with people on the lower end of the autistic spectrum as much as improving their own lot (Arnold 2002). Why do some autistic societies reject their help? Is it about validity of opinions and lack of Theory of Different Minds? Some autistic advocates *are* difficult because they are likely to discuss or fight against the ideas that do not coincide with their own. Still, it is important to work with them – both teaching and learning from them. Instead of rejecting their views without any consideration, it would be beneficial to introduce 'the rules of fair play' – 'If you want to be heard, be prepared to listen. If you want to be respected, learn to respect others', etc. If there are no contradictions and attempts to resolve them, there is no development. If there is no development, there is stagnation. Isn't it time to re-think the policies, and reconsider future plans? Parents and professionals need all the help available to bring real and speedy changes in the attitudes of the authorities and general public to the needs of autistic children. There is still a long way to go. *Just a thought.*

A few messages to the parents from autistic people

We need you. We need your help and your understanding. Your world is not very open to us, and we won't make it without your support. Yes, there is tragedy that comes with autism: not because of what we are, but because of the things that happen to us. Be sad about it, if you want to be sad about something. Better than being sad, though, get mad about it – and then *do* something about it. The tragedy is not that we're here, but that your world has no place for us to be. How can it be otherwise, as long as our own parents are still grieving over having brought us into the world. (Sinclair 1993, p.4)

On our behalf, we wish you strong voices and much courage. And in return, we will offer you our strong voices and our courage. Together, we can find creative and moral ways to make autism find the best of both worlds – yours and ours. With you on our side, we with autism will learn how to reach the sky. All we need is a boost by you. (Willey Undated)

What is autism?

If someone asked you what it meant,
What would you say?
'A disability,' one said,
'Not able to dance, sing and play.'

Is that true?
I'd say to you.
Or have you just forgot
Autism is not as simple as you thought.

If someone asked you what it meant,
What would you say?
'It's the brain,' somebody said
'It doesn't function well at day.'

Now that's not true,
I'd say to you.
Though their brain is not like ours
It still works well,
And makes them special,
They can do anything with their powers.

We've got a routine for life
They take it by the day
If someone asked you what it meant,
What would *you* say?

Olesya Bath, age 12, sister of an autistic boy

For 'horizontal reading':

1.7 – pp.67–71
2.7 – pp.162–173
4.7 – pp.295–300

Further Reading

Some sources of information are more reliable than others. It is good to start with general books (such as 'complete guides') and then to move on. Parents need to be well-informed and prepared to deal with all sorts of problems. Many parents are willing to share their stories. For many others it is good to recognize themselves in these stories and be reassured.

Stanton, M. (2000) *Learning to Live with High-Functioning Autism: A Parent's Guide for Professionals*. London: Jessica Kingsley Publishers.
It is a very reassuring book. The author's knowledge and experience as a father of a HF autistic boy can help other parents to realize that they are not alone – many parents have been there, done that and survived.

Cutler, E. (2004) *A Thorn in My Pocket*. Arlington, TX: Future Horizons, Inc.
This is a book by Eustacia Cutler (Temple Grandin's mother) about raising her daughter. It is a story of the development of the non-verbal, often violent child into a high achiever.

Boyd, B. (2003) *Parenting a Child with Asperger Syndrome: 200 Tips and Strategies.* London: Jessica Kingsley Publishers.
The book is written by a mother of an AS boy, Kenneth Hall (an author himself – *Asperger Syndrome, the Universe and Everything: Kenneth's Book*, 2000), and helps parents to respond positively to the challenge of AS and find the 'treasure' in their child's way of being.

Holland, O. (2002) *The Dragons of Autism: Autism as a Source of Wisdom.* London: Jessica Kingsley Publishers.
The book contains plenty of strategies that may make the child better able to cope with life, reducing his meltdowns and helping him to accept change.

There are books written by mothers with their children contributing their chapters. These books show different perspectives and give real insights into the life of the family:

Barron, J. and Barron, S. (1993) *There's a Boy in Here.* London: Chapmans.
Mother and son share their experiences on their struggle with autism. Judy describes the events and Sean provides commentary on these events from his point of view. When a child, Sean had extreme behavioural problems, putting his family through horrible trials.

McDonnell, J. (1993) *News From the Border.* Boston, MA: Ticknor and Fields.
The book includes an afterword by Jane McDonnell's son Paul, who has made great progress but is still autistic.

(Some books are written by mothers from their child's perspective. These may be fascinating stories, but they are better classified as fiction, where authors put their words into the child's mouth.)

There are novels with autistic individuals as the main characters. One example is:

Haddon, M. (2003) *The Curious Incident of the Dog in the Night-Time.* London: Vintage.
This book is a fascinating read that increases the awareness of the condition.

There are many films, magazine and newspaper articles about treatments and 'miraculous cures' that may be misleading. However, it does not mean that a 'happy ending' is impossible. Children do develop and, with proper support and treatment, they do improve considerably. Practical, realistic information (based on research) is much more useful than popularized 'happily-ever-after' stories. It is good to consider different approaches (and not to 'be stuck in one gear'). The more information we get, the more flexible in our approaches we become.

Biomedical treatments and diets

Lewis, L. (1999) *Special Diets for Special Kids: Understanding and Implementing Special Diets to Aid in the Treatment of Autism and Related Developmental Disorders.* London: Jessica Kingsley Publishers.
An easy-to-read book about how and why to implement a dietary intervention strategy for children and adults with autism.

Floor time

Stacey, P. (2004) *The Boy Who Loved Windows: Opening the Heart and Mind of a Child Threatened with Autism.* London: John Wiley and Sons.
The mother of an autistic boy who was diagnosed very early describes her efforts to reach her son using the 'floor time' therapy.

AIT

Stehli, A. (1991) *Sound of a Miracle: A Child's Triumph over Autism.* New York: Avon Books.
Annabel Stehli tells of her daughter Georgie's recovery after AIT treatment.

ABA

Maurice, C. (1993) *Let Me Hear Your Voice.* New York: Fawcett Columbine.
The author describes how her two autistic children were brought to what appeared to be complete recovery by the very intensive application of the Lovaas behavioural programme.

Sinclair, J. (1993) 'Don't mourn for us.' *Our Voice*, 3. Syracuse, NY: Autism Network International.
An excellent article by a HF person with autism that must be read by any parent. You may agree or disagree with its author, but it gives an autistic perspective on what it is like to live with autism among non-autistic parents. It suggests possible solutions for creating mutual understanding and acceptance:

PART 4

Autism

Professionals' Perspective

Definitions and Classifications

The group of professionals includes all the specialists working (directly and indirectly) with autistic individuals and their families: researchers (biomedical, psychological and educational), doctors, consultants, clinical and educational psychologists, teachers, support staff, speech therapists, occupational therapists, social service workers, counsellors, Special Educational Needs (SEN) teams, administrators, policy makers and any other specialists that may be in contact with autistic individuals or their families. Each of these professionals may have different views on different aspects of autism, and different levels of experience, as well as different backgrounds and environments. It is difficult to believe but, even now, in the countries where specialists are not familiar with autism, you may hear all sorts of definitions, depending on the knowledge (or lack of it) of each particular specialist. Here are just two examples of these 'definitions':

> 'Autism is a symptom' (Chief Speech Therapist, Gorlovka, Ukraine, personal communication).

> 'If a child can talk, he is not autistic' (Professor of Psychiatry, Donetsk, Ukraine, personal communication).

Apart from these ill-informed descriptions, professionals define the condition in accordance with the diagnostic criteria (the Triad of Impairments). However, each researcher (or a group of researchers) may introduce into the definition some features which they consider to be core ones (for instance, cognitive impairments, metabolic problems, or difficulties in forming affective bonding with the mother) with the Triad in the background (see Figure 4.1). Some researchers 'rearrange' the primary and secondary characteristics of autism and include as major features such 'secondary' symptoms as abnormal (unusual) responses to sensory stimuli, anxiety and stress.

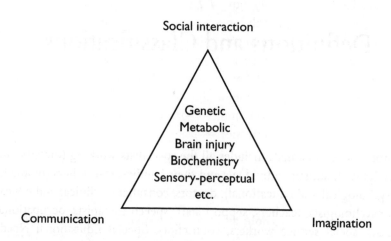

Figure 4.1 The Triad of Impairments with additional 'highlights'

A spectrum characteristic of autism is widely recognized. However, some professionals prefer to distinguish between different 'autisms', or several different categories of autism/AS. For example Stella Waterhouse (1999) suggests the following categories of autistic disorder, each of which is defined by its possible problems:

- *perceptual autism* (linked to a damaged limbic system)

- *perceptual Asperger syndrome* (linked to frontal lobe problems)

- *reactive autism* (limbic system)

- *reactive Asperger syndrome* (frontal lobe)

- *induced autism* (limbic system)

- *induced Asperger syndrome* (frontal lobe)

- *secondary autism* (caused by accident or illness).

Most professionals are honest in their attempts to help autistic people. They try to be open-minded, acknowledge their own limitations without blaming their clients when the help they have to offer is not enough; they describe problems autistic people *have*, not the problems autistic people *are*; they are unwilling to jump to conclusions and are open to questioning their own beliefs (Sinclair 1992a). Sadly, however, some professionals, like dinosaurs, believe their ideas are the only ones which are right; they are resistant to change and are unable to see beyond non-autistic theories and the artificial categorization which these theories created (Williams 1996): 'Some professionals are the dinosaurs of today and some are the dinosaurs of tomorrow and some try hard not to become dinosaurs at all' (Williams 1996, p.8). As there are so many classifications and categorizations of autistic people, let us try to do the same with the professionals, using the same framework we find in the Triad.

The aloof group

These professionals 'sit in a hole' and cannot see anything outside it. They try to blame autism on parents. Their attitude reflects a dangerously outdated view of autism (neobettelheimism) and places more burdens on already desperate families. For example, one professor of Childhood Studies claimed that unruly behaviour by many children (including autistic ones) was being falsely attributed to medical conditions when better parenting was needed. A senior manager of a provision for autistic teenagers complained that he had had problems with the parents, not their children (forgetting to add that he actually provided baby-sitting, not educational treatment, and parents were not happy about it). Their typical favourite announcement (that they use to start any conversation with the colleagues or parents) is 'My understanding of autism is...' Unfortunately, parents are not interested in *their* understanding of autism but are concerned about the manifestation of autism in their child and the ways to help him; while the colleagues soon discover (usually after the first five to seven minutes) that this understanding is very limited and incoherent.

The passive group

These professionals see their job as a place of employment. They come to the office/school/provision, go through the daily routine and return home. They know what they learned at college or university (...years ago) and truthfully follow their 'manual'. What is beyond it is of no concern to them. Some have had no training in autism at all, but have attended a conference or a training seminar and feel they are fully qualified to work with autistic children/adults or make decisions concerning their families. They are quite confident in their 'knowledge' and offer their 'expertise' to anybody who will listen. It is quite typical for them to say, for example,

> He cannot be autistic because he is too interested in people/shows emotions (for instance, cries when upset, smiles a lot, or wants to please people, or gives eye contact/talks well).

The active but odd group

These professionals are very active and their knowledge is very wide...in a very narrow field. They devote all their energy to the development of one single theory (that they try to stretch beyond the limits to cover every single aspect of autism) or suggest a single therapy to cure autism. They dismiss anyone (a researcher, a parent or an autistic person) who dares disagree with them. They never admit that they might make a mistake. A subgroup of 'active but odd' professionals includes those who have just started to work in the field but very quickly consider themselves 'experts'. They are very ambitious and see their achievements through a magnifying glass. For example, if they manage to co-author an article for a journal (along with ten other contributors), the next day they would add 'published author' to their name. A semi-humorous term introduced by Morris (1999) brilliantly describes such 'experts':

> **Bafflegas**: What you use, when you are representing yourself to any audience as knowing what you're doing, and you aren't exactly... 'If you can't Dazzle 'em with Brilliance, then Baffle 'em with Bafflegas.'

The professional group

They never stop learning (and with autism one has to learn every day, or you will be left behind). Their motto is 'With autism the more you know the more you understand how little you know'. They are not afraid to admit that they do not know something (it is impossible to know everything), lack specialist knowledge and refer the child to a specialist. They are humble enough to admit to a parent 'Sorry, I don't know. Let us think together what is best for your child.' Theo Peeters describes such professionals as 'professionals bitten by the bug of autism', who choose to work with autistic people not 'in spite of

Box 4.1 What makes a good autism professional? (Adapted and modified from Peeters 1999)

1. To be attracted by differences.

2. To have a vivid imagination, not restricted by rigid conventional 'mindsets'.

3. To be able to give without getting (ordinary) thank yous.

4. To be willing and able to adapt one's natural style of communication and social interaction.

5. To have the courage 'to work alone in the desert' and, possibly, to be criticized instead of being applauded for one's enormous efforts.

6. Never to be satisfied with how much one knows. Learning about autism and educational strategies is continuous. 'The professional who thinks he has found it has lost it.' Training in autism is never 'finished'.

7. Accept that each bit of progress brings a new problem. Once you start you know that the 'detective' work is never over.

8. Be prepared to change one's views if they turn out to be wrong. Not to be ashamed of saying, 'Sorry, I was wrong. Let's do it otherwise.'.

9. One needs to be prepared to work in a team. Because the approach needs to be coherent and consistent, all professionals need to be informed about the efforts of others and the levels of help they provide.

10. One needs to be humble. We may be experts in autism in general, but parents are the experts about their own children and we need to take into account their wisdom. The professional who wants to stay 'on his pedestal' is not needed in autism. When collaborating with parents it is important to talk about successes, but also admit failures ('please help me').

autism', but 'because of autism' (Peeters 1999). To become a 'professional professional' one has to possess certain personal characteristics. Box 4.1 (p.237) outlines the profile of a good autism professional.

HFA and LFA

There has not yet been developed a professional consensus on the boundary of HFA: where LFA ends and HFA starts. However, cognitive level and verbal functioning have been chosen as the main criteria for distinguishing HFA from LFA or 'severe autism' (see Box 4.2).

Box 4.2 The proposed boundaries of HFA

It has been reported that autistic children with certain scores of IQs exhibit different behaviours and patterns of skills on cognitive tests. The following criteria for HFA have been suggested:

Performance IQ above 70 (Bartak and Rutter 1976)

Full Scale IQs:

- above 80 (Rumsey, Rapoport and Sceery 1985)

- above 70 (Asarnow *et al.* 1987)

- above 65 (Gillberg, Steffenburg and Jakobson 1987)

- above 60 (Gaffney and Tsai 1987)

Non-verbal IQ of 70 or above and/or global IQ above 55 (Cohen, Paul and Volkmar 1986).

AS and autism

Some researchers believe that the definition of autism (or ASDs) should be inclusive of AS as they have not found significant qualitative differences in clinical features, developmental course and neurocognitive profiles between HFA and AS. Wing (1991) suggests that both autism and AS are best regarded as falling within the continuum of social impairment, which may differ in their clinical manifestation due to the degree of deficit in the cognitive, language and motor areas. This view is supported by recent studies.

With regard to neurocognitive profiles, mixed findings have been reported. Prior *et al.* (1998) used cluster analysis techniques to empirically examine the existence of diagnostically homogeneous subgroups such as classic autism and AS. Three clusters emerged: an autism group, an Asperger group, and a mild (HF) group. Comparisons of symptom profiles showed that the Asperger group was differentiated on the basis of the presence of joint attention skills, limited friendship capacities, pedantic speech and circumscribed interests. The researchers did not find any differences between the groups in early language history. They identified higher verbal ability and mentalizing capacity in the Asperger group in comparison with autism and the mild groups. The researchers conclude that, although there were symptom differences between the groups, the results are best explained on the basis of differing degrees of developmental compromise, and support a spectrum concept of autistic disorders (Prior *et al.* 1998). The slight superiority of AS people with regard to their language skills in adulthood may be explained by the fact that because individuals with autism are so much delayed in their language acquisition in childhood they are unable to catch up with the linguistic development of the AS group (Eisenmajer, Prior and Leekam 1996; Szatmari 2000). People with AS are believed to make better efforts to adapt socially than people with autism. They have a genuine desire to make social contact and friendships. A comparison of neuropsychological characteristics of children with AS and those with HFA (Manjiviona and Prior 1995) also supports the spectrum notion of autism rather than distinct diagnostic categories and the current clinical diagnostic differentiation may be primarily influenced by the child's perceived IQ level.

The other findings, however, indicate that AS and autism may have some clinical similarities but different neuropsychological profiles (Pomeroy, Friedman and Stephens 1991): autistic children in the study did well on tests of visual–spatial skills and immediate recall, but did poorly on tests of abstract verbal skills, whereas children with AS did not show the same cognitive weaknesses, and actually scored higher than both autistic children and controls on one test of abstract thinking (the 'Trial' task, which required them to shift rules used in solving problems). Pomeroy *et al.* (1991) reported that autistic children's deficits were related to an 'executive function' disorder (i.e. deficits in cognitive operations controlled by the frontal cortex, including planning and inhibition), whereas children with AS were not. These findings are consistent with earlier findings by Ozonoff *et al.* (1991), who found that individuals with AS had different cognitive profiles than those with autism. Frith (1991) insists that, for the time being, a distinct diagnostic category for AS is very useful for two clinical reasons. First, many parents of AS children will find this particular diagnosis more acceptable (in contrast to severe classic autism). Second, many children with milder forms of ASDs would be left undiagnosed and therefore without the services and understanding they need (Frith 1991).

For 'horizontal reading':

1.1 – pp.21–28
2.1 – pp.77–96
3.1 – pp.179–186

4.2

Diagnosis

It has never been easy to diagnose autism. There are some problems that may complicate the process:

It is easy to diagnose 'pure' autism, but such *cases of classic autism are very rare*. So the diagnostician needs to be very experienced in order to detect ASD symptoms in 'unclassic' cases. As autism is a spectrum disorder, the manifestations of its characteristics vary greatly. ICD-10 and DSM-IV provide only *some* examples of the behaviours because it is impossible to enumerate *all* possible manifestations of ASDs. That is why, if clinicians are inexperienced in diagnosing autism, they may often miss the pertinent features because 'they are not in the book'. They may not recognize the condition, especially when it is not 'classic' and occupies far from the central position on the spectrum.

The social impairment in autism is not defined by the quantity of interactions or the desire for social interaction. It is the quality of interaction that must be examined. The social impairment may be confusing to teachers because often they may observe the student interacting with peers in the classroom. However, the same student may have difficulties learning social interaction in unstructured situations, initiating social behaviour without supports, and sustaining social interactions in a reciprocal manner (Lord 1984; Smith 1990; Walters, Barrett and Feinstein 1990). One cannot diagnose ASDs from a checklist of symptoms or from reading a diagnostic manual. A checklist can alert us to the possibility of autism but it cannot eliminate autism. One needs training in the use of diagnostic tools and experience with people with autism (Stanton 2001).

Different clinicians use different criteria and diagnostic instruments. Some may use DSM-IV or ICD-10, others may use the criteria identified by Kanner

(1943) or Asperger (Gillberg and Gillberg 1989), still others may distinguish between high-functioning and low-functioning, or between mild, moderate and severe autism, etc. There have been developed numerous assessment tools (see Box 4.3) to help detect autism. In the hands of experienced professionals they may reveal a lot about the child's condition, whereas they are sure to bring confusion if used by someone unfamiliar with autism. What complicates the matter even more is that the results of 'screening' may be different in different checklists.

There is even more confusion with the diagnosis of AS. Some researchers consider the diagnostic criteria of AS in DSM-IV as 'inadequate' and 'unworkable' because they do not coincide with the cases in the original study by Hans Asperger. Several studies suggest that if strict DSM-IV/ICD-10 criteria are applied, a diagnosis of AS becomes impossible (Ghaziuddin, Tsai and Ghaziuddin 1992; Manjiviona and Prior 1995). To resolve the problem, in addition to the two official classification systems, a few more have been developed; for example, Gillberg and Gillberg (1989) and Gillberg (1991). Unfortunately, instead of clarifying the matter, these numerous descriptions may add to the diagnostic confusion.

Box 4.3 Most commonly used assessment tools

For assessment of autistic children, specific assessment tools – rating scales and evaluation checklists – have been developed. The most commonly used standardized tools are:

- *The Autism Diagnostic Observation Schedule (ADOS)* (Lord et al. 1989). This is a developmental test which involves the examiner interacting with the child for 20 to 30 minutes. Eight tasks are carried out to ascertain certain behaviours in the areas of social interaction, imagination, play skills, and the ability to explain feelings. A diagnostic algorithm is used and professional training is required.

- *The Autism Diagnostic Interview (ADI)* (Le Couteur et al. 1989). This is a standardized interview developed as a supplement to the ADOS. It takes about one to two hours to complete. The areas of the triad are given detailed coverage. Specialized training at the Rutter

Institute is required. An algorithm is provided to aid diagnosis.

- *Form E2* (Rimland 1964). This is a diagnostic checklist containing 109 questions about the child's early developmental history, social responsiveness, speech development, etc. The completed form is sent to the Autism Research Institute in San Diego, CA, where it is entered into a large research database and compared to previously collected data. The scores range from -45 (lowest) to +45 (highest). The average score on Form E2 for a child diagnosed as 'autistic' by professionals around the world is -2. Children who score +20 or higher are considered to be cases of *classical early infantile autism (Kanner syndrome)*. Children who score from -15 to +19 are regarded as autistic, while children who score -16 or lower are described as *autistic-like*.

- *The Autism Behavior Checklist (ABC)* (Krug, Arlick and Almond 1980) is a scale of 57 behaviours grouped into five areas: sensory, relating, body and object use, social and self-help. It also includes components to obtain samples of vocalizations, an interaction assessment, and a prognosis of learning rate.

- *The Childhood Autism Rating Scale (CARS)* (Schopler, Reichler and Renner 1980). This rating scale, devised in North Carolina for use in the TEACCH clinic, relies on a comprehensive set of observations. The scores range from 15 to 60: 15–30 for 'non-autistic', 31–36 for 'mildly–moderately autistic', 37–60 for 'severely autistic'.

- *The Gilliam Autistic Rating Scale* (Gilliam 1995) contains 56 behaviours grouped into four areas: stereotyped behaviours, communication, social interaction, developmental disturbances. It takes about five to ten minutes to complete. A total raw score is computed for each of the four subtests and then converted into Standard Scores (range from 1 to 19), Autism Quotient (from <69 to 131+) and its percentile. The data are meant to indicate probability and degree of severity of autism: very low, low, below average, average, above average, high, very high.

- *The Psychoeducational Profile (PEP)* was developed by
  Schopler and Reichler (1979) and revised (PEP-R) by
  Schopler, Reichler and Lansing (1980). This assessment
  involves the child undertaking a series of activities
  covering an inventory of behaviours and skills relevant to
  autism, and is designed to identify uneven and idiosyncratic
  learning patterns. The PEP-R assesses the child's behaviour
  in seven function areas (imitation, perception, fine motor
  skills, gross motor skills, eye–hand integration, cognitive
  performance, cognitive verbal) and in four main areas of
  behaviour relevant to the diagnosis of autism (relating,
  play and interest in materials, sensory modalities and
  language). Each behavioural item is scored in one of three
  ways: absent, mild, severe. For function areas three
  different scores are: pass (indicates that the child clearly
  understands and performs the task), emerge (indicates
  that the child has some understanding but cannot yet
  complete the task), and fail (indicates that the task is
  clearly above the child's level of understanding or ability to
  perform). This assessment of developmental functioning
  allows for specific identification of the child's strengths and
  weaknesses and is useful in the selection of skills which
  are emerging for the Individual Educational Plan. The
  number of 'emerge' scores shows the areas in which the
  child is likely to improve his skills and they should be
  taken into consideration in planning his IEP.
- *The Diagnostic Interview for Social and Communication
  Disorders (DISCO)* (Wing and Gould 1991) is a
  semi-structured interview schedule that collects
  information on 300 features of development and
  behaviour and records developmental changes. It uses six
  diagnostic systems and can be used with individuals of any
  age and ability. Answers can be coded for computer entry.
- *The Checklist for Autism in Toddlers (CHAT)* (Baron-Cohen et
  al. 1992) was designed to identify autism at 18 months of
  age. The CHAT assesses pretend play, protodeclarative
  pointing and gaze monitoring by parental report and
  health practitioner observation through direct testing.

Some clinicians might use *descriptions* such as 'Kanner syndrome/Kanner autism'. However, sometimes it may be misleading because Kanner syndrome may mean 'severe autism' to some, while to the others it is 'HFA' as Kanner (1943) originally described 11 children whom he identified as intellectually unimpaired.

Another problem is defining disorders that comprise some autistic symptoms but do not meet the full criteria for autism or AS. As there is no general consensus regarding their status and naming, different clinicians may give different descriptions which do not represent officially recognized labels, but may show the possibility of autism. These descriptions are 'autistic-like conditions', 'autistic tendencies/features', 'autistic behaviours', 'autistic-like features/traits'. Sometimes these conditions are distinguished by quantitative measures. For instance, Peeters and Gillberg (1999) suggest that any individual with five or more of the symptoms listed by DSM-IV or ICD-10, but not meeting the full criteria for autism, AS or childhood disintegrative disorder, should be diagnosed as suffering from other autistic-like conditions; and the individual showing three or more characteristics, but not meeting the full criteria, should be diagnosed as having 'autistic traits'.

Because of the complexity of ASDs, *misdiagnosis is still quite common.* It is especially true for people with HFA and AS born in the 1960s and earlier, who were labelled as mentally ill, emotionally disturbed, or having mood or personality disorders. Even now some clinicians often adhere to past practices and misdiagnose autism as mental retardation (intellectual disabilities) or schizophrenia.

Sometimes professionals focus on some impairments while ignoring other aspects of development. The result is that ASDs may be overlooked. This is especially true for adults who have not been diagnosed as autistic during childhood and is most likely to happen with those who are most able (Wing 1998). Autism can be confused with such conditions (characterized by similar symptoms) as mental retardation (intellectual difficulties), schizophrenia, Landau-Kleffner syndrome, Rett's syndrome, Tourette's syndrome, disintegrative disorder, obsessive-compulsive disorder, specific language disorders and some other conditions (see Box 4.4).

It often happens that parents take their child to see *a range of practitioners who view the child through the narrow lens of their own speciality* and the child gets a different diagnosis from each and a different course of treatment: semantic pragmatic disorder from the speech and language therapist; obsessive-compulsive

Box 4.4 Conditions which can be misdiagnosed for autism

Mental retardation/intellectual disabilities

Though a child with autism can have some degree of mental retardation (intellectual disabilities), the diagnosis of autism – not mental retardation – is appropriate if a child fits the diagnostic criteria for autism, because autistic children need an educational approach and treatment which differs in certain important respects from those required by other mentally retarded children (Wing 1979). To differentiate autism and intellectual disabilities professionals should evaluate the 'unevenness' of the child's profile of development. Children whose primary disability is mental retardation will show a more generalized development delay than a child with autism. While autistic children have uneven development – delays in some areas and not in others – non-autistic children with intellectual disabilities tend to be slower in all areas. One should also observe the development of social, communicative and symbolic play skills. The social development in mental retardation/intellectual disabilities without autism is just delayed not impaired.

Schizophrenia

In the past (and still even today in some countries) some researchers argued that autism was a type of schizophrenia, and that childhood schizophrenia and autism were essentially the same syndrome, or that autism in childhood developed into schizophrenia in adulthood (Bender 1947; Bashina 1980). Most researchers and professionals in the field of autism now assume that autism is a distinctive and valid diagnostic category, clearly different from schizophrenia and other mental illnesses.

There are some similarities between autism and schizophrenia as they both occur along spectrums. The extreme social withdrawal and emotional flattening that is characteristic of severe schizophrenia may be misdiagnosed for autism. However, there are a number of differences between these two conditions, which can help experienced clinicians to distinguish autism from schizophrenia:

- The onset of autism is in infancy or early childhood whereas schizophrenia tends to appear later in childhood or in adolescence. In those rare cases when schizophrenia does occur in childhood, the young child with this disorder has delusions or hallucinations, and uses speech to communicate irrational thoughts. In contrast, the young child with autism does not use speech to communicate (Powers 1989). (NB: If a teenager or an adult with autism talks to themselves it does not necessarily mean that they are schizophrenic!)

- People with schizophrenia often experience delusions and hallucinations while autistic people usually do not.

- In most cases of schizophrenia there are periods of remission and normal functioning, while autistic people do not usually fluctuate in this manner (Wing and Attwood 1987).

Language disorders (elective mutism, developmental receptive language disorders, etc.)

Autism may appear similar to different specific language disorders, as one of the main symptoms of autism (and usually the first symptom the parents worry about) is delayed acquisition or lack of speech. Very often children, later diagnosed as autistic, are referred in the first place to speech therapists/speech pathologists who have to decide whether the child has autism or some other language disorder. To understand the nature of the child's speech difficulties, one should know first of all the child's developmental history and evaluate his interests, relationships and style of his play. If the child is mute, the problem to define is whether it is elective mutism or autism. Children with mutism exhibit some joint-attention behaviours (pointing at objects in order to ask for them; showing and giving objects to other people in order to share their interest in them, etc.). Children with autism have difficulty establishing joint-attention and seldom use any gestures to communicate. If a child has speech, though its acquisition is delayed, to differentiate autism from any other specific language disorders one should analyse whether it is used to communicate and interact with people and one should evaluate the deviant aspects of speech and language of the child. The abnormalities of the language and speech of autistic children (echolalia, metaphoric language, neologisms, play with words, pronoun reversal, abnormal intonation, etc.) reflect the cognitive, social and communicative impairments, whereas the difficulties with understanding and expression of the language of non-autistic children with a special language disorder show, though immature and slow, relatively normal social development. They can use other means to express their interests and communicate their needs. Sometimes it is very difficult to eliminate a language disorder in diagnosing autism in high-functioning autistic children. Special charts have been worked out (for example, Aarons and Gittens 1993) to help professionals clarify the differences.

Tourette's syndrome (TS)

Symptoms of TS include tics such as grunting and twitching, obsessions and compulsions, attention deficit disorder, anxiety and depression, and coprolalia (uncontrollable cursing). A clinician should be very careful not to misdiagnose autism for TS as treatments for these conditions are rather different. (However, TS may co-occur with autism.)

Landau-Kleffner syndrome (LKS)

Some children diagnosed as having autism or PDD actually suffer from LKS. Identifying such children is very important because early treatment of LKS can often partially or even completely correct the language and behaviour of children with this condition. LKS generally strikes formally normal children between the ages of one and eight. Children with LKS first lose their receptive language skills – either gradually or suddenly – while retaining some expressive language. In addition, symptoms may fluctuate, with periods of remission followed by deterioration (Stefanatos, Grover and Geller 1995). Children with LKS also develop seizures – either overt or subtle. While the children's non-verbal IQs remain at or above normal, many of them (about 70 per cent) develop such symptoms as withdrawal, aggression, hyperactivity, failure to make eye contact, insensitivity to pain, resistance to change, monotonic voice, echolalia or lack of speech, problems with gross and fine motor skills, unusual gait, habits such as licking or smelling food before eating it, rituals, unusual responses to sound, and irregular sleeping patterns. Morrell, Whisler and Smith (1995) identify the defining characteristic of LKS as a severe epileptiform EEG abnormality, most commonly a bilateral spike-wave disturbance, maximal in the posterior temporal regions of each hemisphere and virtually continuous during slow wave stages of sleep. Dr B. Rimland (1995) considers that a major problem with LKS is that most specialists who see children with late onset receptive aphasia are not experienced with LKS. Rimland (1995) offers the following set of criteria to recognize LKS:

- normal development and age-appropriate language for the first three to seven years (in autistic children problems may appear before age three)

- loss of receptive language while retaining some expressive language

- 'telegraphic' speech; that is, with few verbs

- suspicion of deafness

- child frustrated, puzzled by change in himself

- sleep disturbance

- specific sleep EEG patterns, characteristic of LKS.

Rett's syndrome (RS)

In the mid-1960s, paediatrician Andreas Rett noticed that several retarded girls in his practice made peculiar continuous 'hand-washing', hand-wringing or clapping movements. He eventually identified an unusual constellation of symptoms in these patients, and observed 31 girls and women with similar symptoms. Additional symptoms included hyperventilation or breath-holding; air-swallowing; bizarre night-time laughing spells; screaming spells; unusual responses to pain; scoliosis; small, cold, blue feet; and some others. This condition was named after Dr Rett – Rett's syndrome. Children with RS are often misdiagnosed with autism because during an early stage of development many children become aloof and lose eye contact. The two disorders, however, have strikingly different prognoses. While autistic children with an appropriate treatment develop skills over time, children with RS lose the skills they once had. As these two conditions may have different causes it is important not to misdiagnose RS for autism. According to Hagberg (1995) symptoms of classic RS include:

- initial normal development in infancy (prenatal and birth period as well as first six months or longer)
- decelerated growth in head circumference somewhere between three months and four years of age
- loss of purposeful use of the hands between nine months and two-and-a-half years of age
- psychomotor regression during the same time period, including loss of speech or babbling, social withdrawal, and signs of mental retardation
- somewhere between the ages of one and three, development of constant hand-wringing, clapping, or other abnormal hand movements
- gait and postural abnormalities, developing at two to four years of age.

Hagberg (1995) outlines a four-stage scheme of RS development:

1. a stagnation period, generally beginning before the age of two, at which physical and mental symptoms first appear
2. a stage of rapid regression, somewhere between the ages of one and four
3. a 'pseudostationary' period, which may last years or even decades, during which symptoms stabilize and some autistic behaviours disappear
4. a stage of late motor deterioration, during which even patients who were ambulatory generally lose their ability to walk.

Recently another distinctive feature of RS has been reported – individuals with RS undergo periods of near-total unresponsiveness to sensory and social stimuli (Smith, Klevstrand and Lovaas 1995).

RS, like autism, is a spectrum disorder. Girls with mild RS tend to have fewer motor problems, and a number have partially retained their ability to speak. At the other end of the spectrum are girls who are abnormal from birth, or experience rapid deterioration shortly afterward. About 5 to 10 per cent of girls with RS have infantile seizures (Hagberg 1995).

Disintegrative disorder

In disintegrative disorder apparently normal development for at least the first two years after birth is followed by regression and loss of previously required skills: expressive or receptive language, social skills or adaptive behaviour, bowel or bladder control, motor skills – all before age ten years. The cause is supposed to be some neurological diseases. The regression eventually stabilizes, and the child will then display symptoms of autism.

William's syndrome

People with William's syndrome seem to have very good language skills, but these skills are superficial. Their speech is empty of content, and their receptive language is very poor. Their social difficulties seem to come from their intellectual failures rather than a specific social impairment (Wang and Bellugi 1993).

Obsessive-compulsive disorder (OCD)

People with HFA may be often misdiagnosed with OCD. The main difference between autism and ACD is in the nature of compulsions: for autistic people rituals and obsessions are pleasurable and calming; for individuals with OCD, compulsions bring unhappiness and worry – they do not want to do it but cannot help it. However, OCD may co-occur with ASDs.

disorder from the child's psychiatrist; sensory integration disorder from the occupational therapist, etc. In fact, these are often manifestations of the same autistic spectrum disorder and the child would benefit immensely from an integrated therapeutic package delivered by an integrated multi-disciplinary team (Stanton 2001).

With the 'discovery' of *'new' disorders* such as semantic pragmatic disorder, non-verbal learning disability disorder, disorders of attention, motor co-ordination and perception, pathological demand avoidance syndrome and others of the same kind the diagnosis of ASDs has become more problematic (see Box 4.5). The focus on just one aspect of the condition brings more confusion rather than specifying the problem. It is quite possible (at least theoretically) to expect soon 'avoidance of eye contact syndrome', or 'rocking disorder', or 'tip-toeing disability' (the fact that not all autistic people avoid eye contact, or rock, or tip-toe could justify these separate 'syndromes').

Box 4.5 Some new disorders

Schizoid personality disorder

Wolff and Chess (1964) described a group of children whom they diagnosed to have 'schizoid personality disorder', who are oversensitive, emotionally detached, solitary, rigid/obsessive, lacking in empathy, and prone to bizarre thoughts. Some researchers (see, e.g., Wing 1996) believe that the 'schizoid personality disorder' diagnosis may be an alternative way of looking at ASDs, especially in adults, although there is not a complete overlap between 'schizoid disorder' and autism.

Semantic pragmatic disorder (SPD)

SPD was originally defined by Rapin and Allen (1983) and developed by Bishop (1989). It is used to describe children who are not autistic but who initially exhibit language delay and receptive language impairment, and who then learn to speak clearly and in complex sentences, with semantic and pragmatic abnormalities becoming more obvious as their verbal proficiency increases. The limitation of this concept is that the real underlying difficulties are often ignored, as only one aspect of the child's development is taken into account.

Nonverbal learning disability syndrome (NLD)

The neuropsychological characteristics of NLD (Rourke 1989) are very similar to those of AS. They include deficits in psychomotor coordination, visual–spatial organization, tactile perception, non-verbal problem-solving, mathematical computation, cognitive flexibility, speech pragmatics and prosody, appreciation of non-verbal forms of communication, social judgement and social interaction skills. It has been suggested that most individuals with AS meet criteria for NLD. However, some researchers argue that NLD may be a broader condition, and not all individuals with NLD meet criteria for AS.

Developmental learning disability of the right hemisphere
Developmental learning disability of the right hemisphere (Denckla 1983) is characterized by profound disturbances in interpretation and expression of affect and other basic interpersonal skills.

Disorders of attention, motor coordination and perception (DAMP)
Gillberg et al. (1982) identified a group of children with disorders of attention, motor coordination and perception (DAMP). However, these are symptoms many autistic children have, and the question arises of whether it is just a collection of symptoms shared by other disorders, or a separate syndrome.

Some diagnosticians are unwilling to 'give a label of autism' to the child either because they do not want to 'upset the parents' and prefer something vague like PDD, 'communication disorder with autism-like behaviours', sensory integration dysfunction, etc. These professionals often question the need to label the child and suggest that they might address the child's problems without 'giving names'. One may argue, however, that diagnosis is vital in many cases, as to know what the problem is and the ways to treat it is half the battle. Besides, the 'label' may explain a lot of behaviours which otherwise are interpreted as inappropriate. And lastly, the 'name' may give access to services and professional support that is so important not only for the child, but for the whole family. Another reason for the 'unwillingness' to diagnose ASDs is the lack of provision for autistic people in the area. What is the point of diagnosing the condition if you have no means to treat it? This accounts for regional variations in the incidence of autism by statisticians.

Many people with autism have other non-autism-related disorders. Some professionals concentrate on the autism-related problems while ignoring other (treatable) conditions. The result is that the person gets the diagnosis but is denied the help needed to improve the general functioning and, hence, shows very slow (if any) improvement of social interaction and communication, whatever treatment or educational programme is in place. Whereas, if these additional problems (for example, sensory hypersensitivities or metabolic problems) are addressed the therapy may be more successful. Paradoxically, sometimes autistic children benefit from being misdiagnosed as having visual and/or auditory impairments. It often happens with children at the LF end of the spectrum whose sensory perceptual problems are usually very severe. When their sensory difficulties are addressed these children might respond to social and communication intervention better than if they were diagnosed autistic and received only training in social/communicative behaviours. Mike Stanton (2001) sums up the problem of autism diagnosis as follows:

- A medical profession that is, with notable exceptions, ill-equipped to meet a growing need for diagnosis for a condition that is still widely misunderstood.

- An absence of agreed protocols for intervention that offers little incentive for physicians to enhance their knowledge and understanding of diagnostic procedures for autism.

- As a consequence there is continuing ignorance of autistic spectrum disorders among physicians who diagnose what they are trained to recognize and, crucially, who diagnose conditions for which there are proven treatments. (Stanton 2001).

Prevalence

The question is, 'do we know the real prevalence of autism? Do those who have been formally diagnosed represent the absolute number and the true nature of the condition?' Bearing in mind all the variables making the diagnosis difficult (the difficulty of 'seeing' autism if it is complicated by other disorders; the different diagnostic tools which can be used; disagreement about the validity of diagnostic criteria; different terms to describe the same phenomenon used by different disciplines – psychiatry, speech therapy, occupational therapy, psychology – with their own narrow perspective of interpretation;

the level of experience of the clinicians; the unwillingness to diagnose the condition because of lack of services), can we be sure that the numbers presented are real representations of the prevalence of autism? (Walker Undated.)

For 'horizontal reading':

1.2 – pp.29–38
2.2 – pp.97–103
3.2 – pp.187–190

Causes

Much research on the causes of autism is currently going on around the world. As yet, the dominant theory of autism aetiology is that it may have several causes, but it has a genetic predisposition (or vulnerability) within it. The genetic predisposition does not mean that a child will develop an ASD, but it does mean that the child is susceptible to it, and any external or internal factor may trigger the development of autism. The potential triggers include the following.

Pre-, peri- or postnatal difficulties

Research has shown that mothers of autistic children may have problems during pregnancy and/or delivery. However, it is not known yet whether these difficulties trigger autism, or autism causes pregnancy and delivery problems. The following 'risk' factors have been reported as most commonly associated with autism:

- *prenatal factors*: toxaemia, congenital rubella

- *perinatal factors*: trauma, anoxia, excessive uterine bleeding in the middle trimester between the fourth and eighth months of pregnancy, medication during pregnancy

- *postnatal factors*: asphyxy, reanimation of the child, postnatal encephalitis.

Structural and/or functional brain abnormalities

Structural brain abnormalities in different autistic people have been found in different parts of the brain. As yet, no abnormality specific only for autism and not for other conditions have been found. Many researchers report reduced Purkinje cell density in the cerebellum of autistic people (Arin, Bauman and Kemper 1991; Bauman 1991; Bauman and Kemper 1985). Although no gross structural abnormalities were reported, post-mortem measurements of the brains of four autistic children revealed that three were heavier than the mean for normal population (Bailey, Phillips and Rutter 1996). Several studies have shown that more than a third of autistic subjects had increased head circumferences. However, increased brain size alone cannot cause autism as many people with macrocephaly are not autistic. One of the possible explanations is that megalencephaly is the result of a pathological process that also underlies autistic symptomatology (Bailey *et al.* 1996).

Numerous MRI studies of autistic people have revealed that abnormalities of the cerebellum have been reported as being the most consistent neuroanatomical lesion in autism (Courchesne, Townsend and Saitoh 1994). Research (Courchesne 1995, 1996) shows that in autism the cerebellum is anatomically abnormal, beginning at an early stage during development, and a regression curve suggests a prenatal onset. Cerebellar damage apparently occurs before or shortly after birth. The cause is unknown, but may include genetic defects, oxygen deprivation in utero or during birth, infections, metabolic disorders and toxic exposure. Hashimoto *et al.* (1995) found that the size of the cerebellum and brainstem did increase in a developmentally appropriate manner in both autistic and control groups, suggesting that the changes in autistic subjects are not a progressive degenerative process but rather occur early in development. Courchesne (1995, 1996) considers that an early developmental loss of cerebellar neurons will alter intrinsic cerebellar circuitry and will result in abnormal neuron activity. The researcher hypothesizes that abnormal cerebellar activity creates an abnormal structure and function in many systems which are physioanatomically connected to the cerebellum, and that the pattern of anatomical findings in the cerebral cortex, limbic system and brainstem in autism may be understood in the context of abnormal cerebellar activity which alters brain development. The author concludes that autism is the result of a fundamental neurodevelopmental process in which abnormal activity from the cerebellum leads to misspecification and misorganization in neural form and function in diverse systems; moreover, there are likely to be genetic and/or nongenetic susceptibility factors that mute or increase the hypothesized abnormal cerebellar that affects brain development (Courchesne 1995, 1996).

Abnormal biochemistry of the brain

Many studies have been conducted to determine neurotransmitter abnormalities in autism. High levels of serotonin in the blood of about one third to one fourth of autistic children have been reported (Cook *et al.* 1994). However, it is not clear yet if high blood serotonin levels mean that serotonin levels in the brain are high as well. Studies of other neurotransmitters have not revealed any consistent abnormalities in autistic people.

Metabolic abnormalities

It has been suggested that autism may be the consequence of a metabolic disorder or of the combined effects of a number of metabolic abnormalities, the incomplete breakdown of certain proteins, particularly, but not necessarily exclusively, gluten from wheat and some other cereals and casein from milk and dairy products, which may result in the production of peptides which are potentially biologically active (Shattock and Savery 1996). This is known as the leaky gut syndrome. In many cases autism is strongly connected to digestive problems and a 'leaky gut'. Some children with late-onset autism are reported to have coeliac disease, characterized by an allergy to gluten. The antigens produced by casein and gluten cause damage to the intestinal wall that lead to permeability and malabsorption of nutrients. It means that bacteria, toxins and undigested food particles leak into the bloodstream. The most common symptoms are diarrhoea, weight loss, gas and bloating. When not fully digested these proteins turn into peptides which are morphine-like in nature and act almost like a drug. They affect neurological transmission and can lead to behaviours characterized by autism (for example, behavioural and language difficulties).

Other studies (see, for example, O'Reailly and Waring 1993) showing abnormalities in metabolism in autism report enzyme and sulphur deficiencies in autistic individuals.

A dysfunctional immune system

Growing evidence links autism to immune system abnormalities (Gupta *et al.* 1996; Comi *et al.* 1999). Recently there has arisen a tide of interest in MMR as a possible causal factor in autism. In 1998 Dr Andrew Wakefield published a scientific paper in the leading medical journal *The Lancet*, in which he described how he and his colleagues had discovered the pattern of inflamation of the bowel which they described as autistic enterocolitis in 12 children with late-onset autism. Dr Wakefield reported that parents of eight of the children said that their behaviour began to deteriorate after their MMR vaccination. He suggested that the MMR vaccine could cause autism and bowel disturbances in some children. Dr Wakefield was severely attacked by both health and governmental authorities for causing unnecessary worry in parents and the MMR vaccine was defended as being safe and effective.

There have been a number of studies that have produced controversial results; some conclude that there is no link between the MMR vaccine and autism, while others claim they have found evidence of this connection. All the studies so far were somehow flawed (for example, in some studies children were followed up for side-effects for only three weeks). Those who are against MMR cite the recent tremendous increase in autism that, they think, cannot be explained just by better diagnosis. There is a third point of view on this controversial issue: MMR may be safe for the majority of children; for some (who are genetically susceptible to autism) it may be the trigger of the development of autism. While the debate remains, it is beyond the scope of this book to comment either in favour or against MMR as a possible cause of autism. Obviously, this is a controversial issue and more long-term studies are needed to weigh the benefits of vaccinations versus the risks. But until we are certain about the safety, it is worth remembering the Hippocratic principle – 'first do not harm'. Doctors should not only listen to the parents' concerns but also inform them about the possible risks of the vaccine. Each case should be individual. And if there are any worries (because of genetic history, for example), separate vaccinations may be offered.

Some professionals (typically ill-informed ones) may still blame parents as the main cause of the child's problems.

For 'horizontal reading':

1.3 – pp.39–44
2.3 – pp.104–112
3.3 – pp.191–196

4.4

Development

The success of any treatment seems to depend on the knowledge, experience and personal qualities of those who implement this treatment. It is not enough to send those who (are going to) work with autistic children/adults on a one-day training course and consider them to be qualified to diagnose/teach/treat autistic individuals. Often very well-meaning specialists are failing people with autism, and most autistic people have not been helped at all, many have felt degraded and some have been harmed because of the misunderstanding and misinterpretation of the condition (Gerland 1998).

While researchers are generally up-to-date in their area of expertise those who work with autistic individuals on a day-to-day basis are not necessarily very knowledgeable about the condition. The ill-informed 'specialist' is not just useless, he or she is a danger to these people. The professional with 'my understanding of autism is...' can, in fact, hinder the development of the autistic individuals with whom they work. Consider the following scenario:

> *The scene:* The provision (three rooms, a kitchen, dining-room, a bathroom) for autistic teenagers where students do not know in which room or with whom they will work today, tomorrow...; where disruption of the classes is an 'everyday routine'.

> *The philosophy* expressed by the person in charge: 'Autistic students do not need structure. They have to learn to be flexible.' (When asked what programme is in place) – 'What the children need is to feel safe and happy [I cannot argue with that]. And it is more important than any regime, doctrine, structure and programme taken together! By the way, it is "an equal systemic approach" [?] which means that the environment must be modified to the child' [I have to confess, I've never heard about the approach and the explanation does not help much – they do not need any structure but the environment must be modified to the child?]

Characters: nine students with ASDs – we will name them A, B, C, D, E, F, G, H, I; eight staff (one teacher and seven support staff).

A Monday morning

9.00 a.m. The students arrive; A, B, C and D go straight away to the kitchen to look for lemonade and biscuits. D stays outside to play with a ball. E and F (both with AS) talk about their weekend. G sits at the sofa. H, I and J do not know what to do and walk from one room to another. The level of noise is so high that in a few minutes H covers his ears and starts screaming. E and F angrily shout 'Shut up!' One of the staff interferes and escorts H into the bathroom where he sits on the floor, covering his ears and rocking.

9.30 a.m. Three of the staff sit with six children copying the weekly text. G is still sitting on the sofa (the teacher is happy about this – G is not disturbing anyone, let him sit there). Some staff are at the computer (in the room where the six children are trying to concentrate on the task) preparing material for the next lesson. Two members of staff are talking (in the same room).

9.45 a.m. The teacher enters the classroom and asks the staff about the forms they were supposed to fill in the day before. The discussion is in progress when A throws a pencil on the floor and kicks his support assistant. C (using the opportunity) turns to the computer to see what is on the screen.

9.50 a.m. E enters the room and insists that he needs the computer to finish his project. D shouts at him because he was told it would be his turn next to play at the computer. Several cries of 'shut up' / 'you shut up' have been exchanged. C starts rocking and crying. Somebody remembers that H is still in the bathroom.

9.57 a.m. The telephone rings and the teacher plunges into a long conversation. A screams and runs out of the room knocking over the computer. He throws himself on the sofa in the next room where G has fallen asleep. G is startled and hits A. The staff try to restrain them both while the other students are running around – some are crying, the others are laughing.

10.00 a.m. The first lesson is over.

This scenario is not a fiction (though, fortunately, it is not typical). One of the students (who was considered very difficult because there was no single day when he did not display some aggressive behaviour) was transferred to a different school where his aggressive outbursts...disappeared. For his mother it seemed a miracle. But the new school happened to have structure in place and well-trained staff. His progress in all the areas of development was amazing. Unfortunately, there are schools as described above. In this case, for the staff it is just a place of employment, while for the students it is a baby-sitting service. So many autistic individuals have wasted so many years there. For some, it was a sensory hell, for others, the place where they could withdraw from the outside world and do nothing, a very few improved *despite* this treatment. One mother (whose son attended a school very similar to that described above) wrote to me after her son ended up in hospital – a caretaker unfamiliar with autism had knocked him out. She failed to get more information about what had happened – the school promised to investigate, but it was about the repu-tation of the school, wasn't it?

> You send your child to school every morning. You are happy about the arrangements. At last you have found a provision where they can cope with your child's challenging behaviour. No complaints from the school about his aggression, tantrums, etc. which were your main concerns in previous places. But are you aware of what is going on behind the closed doors from 9 a.m. till 3.15 p.m.? Can you be sure that your child's needs are being met and his problems are being addressed? How can we be sure that people who work with our children under-stand their deficits and strengths and use the appropriate methods and techniques to help them achieve their potential? I thought everything was fine till I received this dreadful telephone call from school – 'Sorry, Mrs A, your son is in hospital. Could you come as soon as possible?'...
>
> Why are these people allowed to work with autistic children?! Just because they can talk about autism and use a lot of 'academic' words (often disconnected – when you write down what they have said and then read it – it's a random string of words that are meaningless). In fact their *knowledge* is very limited. They just don't know much about autism, and its treatment. What beats me completely is they don't know that they don't know!
>
> If a child needs an operation on appendicitis, we do not take him to the dentist. It is not good enough that the dentist knows where appendicitis is located and can talk about scalpels and anaesthetics. Why do we allow our autistic children to be treated by non-specialists? (from a letter from Mrs A 2002)

Parents are often powerless to do anything about it. There are not many schools available to choose from. If the authorities are happy (it is not their child after all) and you are not, 'you are free to take him and educate him at home' (and many parents do just that).

Another problem between the specialists and parents is, 'if the staff are in danger (your child is violent, for example), the child may be expelled. However, if the professionals do not know what to do and cannot cope, why don't they change their profession? Provisions for autistic individuals are for *autistic individuals*. If all autistic people were compliant and easy to cope with, there would not be any need for these provisions (and no employment for the staff).

What is urgently needed is to *develop* (train) those who work with autistic individuals. They must be well-trained in autism *before* they start working with autistic people and have regular follow-ups to update their knowledge with the latest research data and new developments in the field. Unfortunately, at present, it is possible for professionals who are not trained in autism to start working with autistic people. In this way parents and children remain too vulnerable. Too much still depends upon the goodwill of professionals and decision-makers. A fully specialized training programme for those who choose to work with autism is a necessity. At present training is seen as something for periods of crisis only (Peeters and Gillberg 1999). What is more, training must be obligatory not only for those who directly work with autistic people, but also for those who have an indirect impact on their lives. Here I mean special educational needs (SEN), and education and social services administration workers – those who make decisions about the suitability of provisions and treatments, and financial support for families. Paradoxically, however, the higher the position of SEN or education officers, the less knowledge and empathy can be found.

Theo Peeters, Director of the Centre for Training in Autism, Antwerp, Belgium, defines the five axes of training necessary for *all* who work with autistic people as follows:

1. *A sound theoretical knowledge of autism.*
   One cannot work with people with autism without understanding what autism is. A teacher of the blind should know what blindness means, a professional for the deaf should know about the effect of deafness in development. This is why a 'pervasive understanding' of autism spectrum disorders is necessary for those who work in the field of autism.

2. *Training in assessment as a basis for an individualized programme of education.*

3. *Adaptation of the environment to the condition.*
   The world for an autistic individual is an unpredictable and confusing mass of events, people, places and sights (Jolliffe *et al.* 1992). Before we start teaching them we have to adjust the environment, make it predictable and safe, otherwise no learning is possible.

4. *The functional preparation for adulthood.*

5. *The way in which training and education should be adapted to autism.*
   (Peeters and Gillberg 1999)

It is important to remember that training is never finished: 'If learning in autism does not expand it contracts. Regular in-service training and other forms of "post-training" are not luxury but a necessity' (Peeters and Gillberg 1999, p.82).

Nobody argues that working with autistic individuals is a *very* difficult, demanding and challenging job. That is why people who work in the field should be given not only training but also support and help when necessary. Professionals should not be ashamed to ask for this help, or even ask other professionals to see what they are doing, to share their ideas and doubts and give them advice about how they can improve the situation or solve the particular problem. And last but not least, it is important to listen to the parents, and to engage them as partners. The parents often have new and useful information and ideas to share. It is time to look at parents as part of the solution, not as 'a necessary evil' (Sullivan 1984, p.245).

Persons with autism need professionals bitten by the bug of autism

> Extraordinary youngsters require extraordinary professionals… In order to help these different youngsters with autism, professionals must be a little bit 'qualitatively different' themselves… It is useless to 'force' someone to work with autistic children… It just does not work. Professionals must choose autism themselves… We know professionals who will never be bitten by the microbe, who are 'immune' from the bug. The problem is that bugs are invisible to the authorities. (Peeters 1999)

For 'horizontal reading':

1.4 – pp.45–46
2.4 – pp.113–125
3.4 – pp.197–201

4.5

Theories

Autism has inspired numerous (and growing) attempts to account for this puzzling condition. Many researchers have originated theoretical constructs, which are based on different (sometimes opposite) psychological assumptions (depending on the interests and fields of expertise of each particular researcher). As manifestations of autism are plentiful, literally any theory can explain at least some features of the condition. Rita Jordan (1999) identifies the following criteria necessary to consider a theory as useful:

- The theory should account for *all* the behavioural features that distinguish ASDs from other conditions and normal development.

- The theory should not only describe but also explain how the Triad of Impairments are related.

- The theory should account for several psychological mechanisms (that are likely to be involved in autism) and ways in which these mechanisms work together to produce autism.

So far, there is no universal single explanation of autism that satisfies these criteria. Below are both the 'old' and well-established (though criticized) theories, 'new old' theories (that have been originated in the past and been ignored until recently) and 'new and promising' theories in the field of autism.

Some of Bettelheim's views are still held by a small number of professionals. Sometimes Bettelheim's theory is modified, but the main basis is the same. For example, Nico and Elizabeth Tinbergen claimed that autism is caused by a breakdown in the bonding process between mother and child, and this theory provides the basis for a 'cure' – holding therapy that was supposed to 'restore' this bonding (Tinbergen and Tinbergen 1972/1984).

ToM

ToM theory has stimulated a great amount of further research in cognitive deficits of individuals with autism and…a lot of criticism. Numerous studies have shown that ToM cannot be a primary impairment in autism. The problem is that ToM does not develop in normal children before the age of four, while autism is clearly seen before that age (Jordan and Powell 1995). Second, although Baron-Cohen (1998) claims that a lack of ToM seems to be a core abnormality in autism because mind-blindness may be manifested in different degrees from severe, through to moderate, or even just very mild, some children with autism do pass the test (and some children without autism fail it). Happé (cited in Baron-Cohen 1998) backs up the claim that ToM difficulties are universal in ASDs and cannot be questioned just because a proportion of children with ASDs pass them. Happé insists that these children would not pass the test if the tasks were of the *right* mental age. However, what is the *right* mental age of autistic children for ToM tasks? They manifest a very different path of development and the results of different intelligence tests are often contradictory (and unreliable). To define the right mental age one should first work out the right criteria to measure it, which has not yet been done. Third, the lack of ToM is not specific for autism only and can be observed in people with other disabilities (Dahlgren *et al.* 1996; Muris, Steerneman and Merchelbach 1998). And last but not least, theory of lack of ToM fails to account for other cognitive strengths and weaknesses, and repetitive behaviours, specific to autism. All these confirm that deficit in ToM fall into secondary deficit in autism caused by some other fundamental impairment(s). Bowler and Thommen (2000) suggest that such high-level cognitive systems like ToM need further explanation in terms of lower-level processes such as perception. Interestingly, congenitally deaf children of hearing parents show similar ToM deficits to those with autism (Peterson and Siegel 1995). Similar difficulties have been reported in congenitally blind children (Hobson 1995).

Paradoxically, despite the growing evidence that ToM difficulties are secondary to some primary (and as yet unidentified) deficit(s) in autism, the theory of ToM has grown in popularity among professionals working with autistic individuals. Having failed to explain the development of autism, this theory has proved to be very useful when applied to practical work with people with ASDs. It gives professionals and parents explanations of what would otherwise have been seen as idiosyncratic behaviours, and provides ideas on how to address these problems. So-called lack of ToM in autistic children implies a different interpretation of 'rudeness' and 'deliberate stubbornness', as well as suggesting the necessity to explain explicitly our intentions and emotions.

Lack of ToM can help identify 'misunderstandings' not only between autistic and non-autistic individuals, but also between those who have different backgrounds and experiences (for example, professionals dealing with autistic children and their families, and parents of children with ASDs; or parents and HF autistic individuals). In Box 4.6 there is an example of a ToM exercise for professionals to develop theory of parents' minds.

Box 4.6 ToM test for professionals

You are an Education Officer in SEN Administration Service. Your workload is tremendous while time and resources are limited. You have all these files of SEN children who need special provision, but you have never met them nor their families in person. You try to keep your anger at bay when parents phone you to find out about the progress of their child's case. You feel they do not understand you. Do the following test and tick the answer you want to give. (Be honest with yourself. It is not what you would say, but what you *want* to say.)

The mother phones you and urges you to transfer her autistic son from the provision she thinks is inadequate to a specialist one where his needs can be better met, by the start of a new school year. You *want* to say to her:

A   I have hundreds of SEN children in my files. Your child is not the only one who needs a specialist provision. Why do you think your son should be given priority?

B   I have neither time nor resources now. Please come again in three to four months and I'll see what I can do.

C   I don't care.

(Whichever answer you give, the mother will be angry with you.)

Now move onto the second part, and consider a fictional scenario, but try to imagine that it concerns your own personal situation.

Your child is very ill. He needs urgent help, and you rush him to hospital. There you are told:

A   Sorry, we have a lot of patients to attend to now. Your child is not the only one who needs help, you know.

B   The doctor has no time now. Please come again in three to four months and we'll see what we can do.

C   We don't care.

Will you be happy with any of these answers? It is unlikely. You will be angry and your anger will be directed to the doctor who has let you and your child down. This feeling is an approximate feeling the mother from the first scenario experiences. It is comparable because if autistic children are not helped and educated, their chances of developing their potential decrease. They cannot afford to waste time: a day, a week without proper treatment will turn into a year's delay in their development.

Weak central coherence theory

One of the most influential cognitive theories of autism attempting to account for not only deficits but also strengths of autistic individuals – weak central coherence theory – was formulated on the basis of intriguing experiments which showed that:

- in memorization tasks children with autism were not helped by semantic meaning of words and memorized equally well strings of random words (Frith 1970)
- children with autism were superior in performance of an embedded figures test and the block design tests (Shah and Frith 1983). (These experiments are described by Uta Frith in her book *Autism: Explaining the Enigma* (1989/2003).)

The hypothesis that individuals with autism display weak central coherence seems to explain both the strengths and weaknesses of autism as resulting from a single characteristic of an abnormal information processing. However, a growing number of research studies reveal that it is not always the case, and weak central coherence attributed to autism does not, in fact, characterize autistic information processing. On the contrary, autistic individuals seem to show a global bias to a local one (Mottron, Burack and Robaey 1999); that is, displaying a strong central coherence. Studies (Jordan and Riding 1995; Mottron *et al.* 1999; Ozonoff *et al.* 1994a) indicate the tendency in autism to process information 'wholistically' rather than 'analytically'.

The attempt to present weak central coherence as a cognitive style in autism (Happé 1994a) has not been convincing, either. Happé (1996) demonstrated that effects of weak central coherence can be seen not just in higher-level tasks but also in low-level visual tasks and found that autistic individuals are less susceptible to visual illusions. The author interpreted her findings as another proof of weak central coherence processing style in autism. However, other studies (Garner and Hamilton 2001; Ropar and Mitchell 1999) have challenged the proposition of universal weak central coherence in autism. Contrary to Happé's findings, individuals with autism and AS participating in these studies were just as likely as comparison participants to be susceptible to illusions (i.e. implement strong central coherence) (Ropar and Mitchell 1999). Some autistic individuals experienced visual illusions even before the non-autistic persons (Garner and Hamilton 2001). The results of the study of Ozonoff *et al.* (1994) have also questioned the weak central coherence in autism. They show that the autistic group demonstrated no particular difficulty processing global features of a stimulus, nor did they exhibit superiority in processing local features, relative to the two matched groups, one with Tourette's syndrome and the other with normal development. In contrast to 'universal weak central coherence' in autism, Ozonoff *et al.* (1994) hypothesize that autistic individuals do indeed focus on details at the expense of seeing the big picture, but do it at a *conceptual*, rather than a *perceptual*, level. That is, they may have no problem visually processing the whole picture; difficulty may only be apparent when the individual elements are meaningful pieces of information that must be integrated to form a general idea or understanding at a higher-order conceptual level.

There is much evidence that on a perceptual level many autistic individuals experience the difficulty of distinguishing between foreground and background sensory stimuli. They perceive everything without filtration and selection. This results in a paradoxical phenomenon: sensory information is received in infinite detail and *holistically* at the same time. It can be described as 'gestalt perception' – perception of the whole scene as a single entity with all the details perceived (but not processed!) simultaneously. This indicates strong coherence at a perceptual level. It is often difficult for the autistic person to break down the whole picture into meaningful entities, to group them together and to 'draw the boundaries' around plenty of tiny sensory pieces to make them meaningful units (Bogdashina 2003). The examples of autistic savants are often used to illustrate weak central coherence as a cognitive style of focusing on separate elements, especially in relation to drawing skills (Frith 2003). Such autistic artists are shown to draw their pictures piece by piece. However, it is the ability of autistic savants to start the picture from any (often insignificant) detail and complete it with ease which is the best illustration of gestalt perception, or strong coherence, in autism. They do give all the tiny details in their drawings, but not as separate pieces, but without these bits there is no 'whole' picture. All these tiny elements are perceived *as* a whole. Kanner's comments on a universal feature of autism as the 'inability to experience wholes without full attention to the constituent parts' are interpreted as a characteristic that would follow from a deficit in central coherence (Happé 1994b). Whereas these very comments may be interpreted as an indicator of strong central coherence at the perceptual level, as 'a situation, a performance, a sentence is not regarded as complete if it is not made up of exactly the same elements that were present at the time the child was confronted with it' (Kanner 1943, p.246). If the slightest detail is changed, the whole scene (gestalt) is different; that is, unfamiliar. For autistic children to recognize things, things must be exactly the same as they have already experienced. Only then will they know what to do with them (Williams 1996). The same is true about routines: if something goes differently, they do not know what to do. The gestalt of the situation is different. All this results in fear, stress and frustration. This may explain their dislike of changes and preference for routines (Bogdashina 2003). On the conceptual level, gestalt perception leads to rigidity of thinking and lack of generalization. Autistic children can perform in exactly the same situation with exactly the same prompts but fail to apply the skill if anything in the environment, routine or prompt has been even slightly changed. For individuals with gestalt perception, each and every situation is unique. They can learn what to do in one situation but be lost if the slightest detail is different. Autistic children might be baffled when things change or go differently. Even the slightest changes may confuse and upset them. Another confusing (and frightening) thing for autistic children may be when something emerges in the situation that does not belong to it, as it destroys 'gestalt' of the situation. To feel safe they create gestalt behaviours – rituals and routines. These behaviours bring reassurance and order in daily life which is otherwise unpredictable and threatening. These rituals may seem long and complicated for outsiders. However, for an autistic person it is *one* act of meaningful experience, and if any part of it is missing (for example, a person is prevented from completing a seemingly meaningless ritual) the whole experience becomes incomplete, unfamiliar and frightening (Bogdashina 2004).

Autistic people may experience gestalt perception (a 'strong coherence on the perceptual level') in any sensory modality. A person who experiences visual gestalt has great difficulty in separating a single detail of the scene from the whole picture (without this detail, the whole picture would be different). People with auditory gestalt perception seem to pick up all the sounds with equal intensity. They often feel 'drowned' in the 'sea of background noise' and cannot isolate, for example, the words of the person they are talking to from other noises in the room: fans working, doors opening, somebody coughing, etc. As there is too much information coming in, it is hard to know which stimuli to attend to. Because of gestalt perception (strong perceptual coherence), when too much information needs to be processed simultaneously, very often people with autism are not able to break down the whole picture into *meaningful* units and interpret objects, people, surroundings as constituents of a whole situation. Instead they process the 'bits' that happen to get their attention. Bearing this in mind, one may hypothesize that in contrast to the weak central coherence hypothesis in autism, autistic people possess a very strong drive for coherence (i.e. a holistic perception of the world) with the main difficulty being to break the gestalt into meaningful units in order to analyse them separately. Without perceiving separate units as integrated parts of a whole, it is impossible to interpret the situation (Bogdashina 2003).

Gestalt perception often results in fragmented processing (that is when weak central coherence may fit in). When too much information needs to be processed simultaneously, autistic people may end up with processing 'bits' that happen to get their attention. For example, where non-autistic individuals see a room, an autistic person sees a door handle, a leg of the table, or a ball under the chair. As autistic children perceive their surroundings and people they encounter in 'bits and pieces', they 'store' their individual (and idiosyncratic – from the non-autistic point of view) impressions of their experiences, which they use later to recognize and define places, things and people.

Contrary to the weak central coherence explanation of language peculiarities in autism (for example, echolalia), Prizant (1982) suggests that autistic children use a gestalt strategy in language acquisition; that is, they imitate unanalysed chunks of speech (echolalia) and only at later stages of development do they learn how to break down these units into meaningful segments. This can account for the pattern of language acquisition manifested by many autistic children: from echolalia with no or little evidence of comprehension or communicative intent, through mitigated echolalia used for a variety of communicative functions, to spontaneous speech. A gestalt strategy is also reflected in other peculiarities of the use of language by autistic children, such as, for instance, the insistence on certain verbal routines (Prizant and Wetherby 1989). In a gestalt mode (strong coherence again), language is relatively inflexible in the early stages with limited generative use (Prizant 1983). Despite seemingly complex grammatical structures, gestalt 'words' are very limited – they 'mean' specific situational 'notions'. For example, 'Say hello, Paul' may mean 'hello' to a child with autism, because he has learnt this phrase while being taught to greet people. While Uta Frith (2003) accounts for this phenomenon as weak central coherence: an autistic child attends only to small bits of information, he cannot comprehend the context and does not understand the deeper intentional aspects of communication because he lacks central coherence drive. However, it may be explained 'via strong coherence', as the gestalt perception of speech blocks, where the meaning of the whole block is understood by the child producing echolalia which has nothing in common with our intended meaning (Bogdashina 2004). The same applies to other areas of cognitive functioning (for example, memory). One of the characteristics of 'autistic perceptual memory' is gestalt (inability to 'break' memory units and conceptualize them in accordance with conventional meaning). In gestalt memory the 'items' (whole episodes of the situation) are not 'condensed'; that is, are not filtered, not categorized, not summarized for a gist. In a way, each unit of the memory is a 'gist'! These memory units ('gists') are remembered as whole chunks of events and situations, including all the irrelevant (from the non-autistic perspective) stimuli. That is why, while retrieving information (whether to answer a question or prepare a response), people with this type of memory have to 'play' the whole piece in their memory to 'find' the right 'word' (image, situation, etc.); for instance:

> By having a key point…triggered, I can 'let the scene run' and I might
> find a string of things said in a certain order in relation to the order of

> other things done. I may even be able to repeat these strings, even if I hadn't processed them for meaning. (Williams 1996, p.148)

Is it a surprise that they are often unable to give the gist of a story, if they have the whole chunks ('gestalts') stored in their memory as single entities (Bogdashina 2004)?

As Happé (1994a) notes, the weak central coherence account of autism suffers from a certain degree of over-extension as it tries to take on the whole problem of 'meaning'. It is clear there should be identified and drawn the limits of this theory. Otherwise, the theory of weak central coherence would give an incorrect interpretation of many autistic features. This theory has been very useful in stimulating a great deal of research. Even if the data of this research do not always support the theory, at least our understanding is richer following the quest to find out (Mitchell and Ropar 2004). At present, more research indicates the need to go beyond the weak central coherence model to look for explanations of the condition.

An elegant theoretical construct of cognitive differences in autism as key factors of the condition has been put forward by Professor Allan Snyder and colleagues – autism is the state of retarded acquisition of concepts (Snyder, Bossomaier and Mitchell 2004). The arguments are as follows: we are not conscious of the details of percepts. Such details are inhibited from our conscious awareness. Instead, we often see what we expect to see or what is closer to our mental representations (Snyder 1998; Snyder and Barlow 1986). We force fit every image into a known percept and become concept driven (Snyder *et al.* 2004)! That is why we are easily fooled by visual illusions. It is the object labels (concepts) that are of ultimate importance, as they give us the idea of what is there without any need to be aware of all the details. We are blinded by our 'mental paradigms' or 'mindsets'. On the other hand, certain brain-damaged people, like autistic savants, would appear to have the opposite strategy. They have privileged access (Snyder and Mitchell 1999) to non-conscious information but are not concept driven (Snyder 1998). This model suggests that autism appears like failure (or retarded acquisition) of concept formation. This hypothesis builds on research that newborns, unlike adults, are probably aware of the raw sensory data available at lower levels of neural processing and that they quite possibly have excellent recall of this information. But, with maturation, there is a strategy to suppress such awareness. Instead, the maturing mind becomes increasingly aware only of concepts to the exclusion of the details that comprise the concepts. Snyder *et al.* (2004) believe that this strategy of suppression is continued with the formation of metaconcepts (groupings of concepts) resulting in the awareness of metaconcepts, to the exclusion of the concepts comprising them.

There is growing evidence that infants see the world much more literally than adults. For example, the infants are said to have eidetic imagery and that this becomes less pronounced with development (Giray *et al.* 1976; Harber and Harber 2000). Concerning auditory modality, at four to six months, infants can discriminate between phonetic differences in foreign languages, but by ten to twelve months this ability becomes restricted to their native tongue only (Kuhl *et al.* 1992). With maturation, children learn to conceptualize the world, creating mental paradigms and mindsets. Once a concept is formed, there is a loss of awareness of the sensory details which comprise the concept. Such details are inhibited from executive awareness. Once the metaconcepts are in place, the concepts that comprise them are suppressed from conscious awareness (Snyder *et al.* 2004). On the other hand, as Snyder (1996) puts it, an autistic mind – a mind without paradigms – is more conscious and hence potentially aware of alternative interpretations. However, there are disadvantages to this 'superability':

- Such a mind would have difficulty in coping with the flood of information and would need routines and structure to make sense of the world, because every detail has to be examined anew each time it is perceived and with equal importance to every other detail.

- There would be lack of (or delay in) development of symbolic systems, such as communication, language and verbal thought (Snyder 1996).

Snyder hypothesizes that autism may be considered as a 'retarded acquisition of mental paradigms'. At the low-functioning end of the autism spectrum we may find a lack of paradigms across various domains; and at the other end (HFA and AS) individuals can be deficient in only the most elaborate mindsets, such as those necessary for subtle social interaction (Snyder 1996). Interestingly, because autistic individuals have fewer mental models (concepts) of the world, they can be more aware of novelty (Hermelin 2001; Pring and Hermelin 2002; Snyder *et al.* 2004). This explains creativity and unusual solutions to problems by individuals whose autism is not complicated by co-morbid conditions.

Deficient executive functioning

Executive function as a cognitive construct to describe behaviours mediated by the frontal lobes was introduced by Ozonoff (1995). These behaviours include impulse control, inhibition of responses, planning, set maintenance and flexibility of thought and action. Deficits in executive function in autism may account for many autistic symptoms. For example, deficiency in word fluency seems to be related to an inability to self-cue by categories; that is, the inability to execute (Turner 1999). Jarrod, Boucher and Smith (1993) reviewed studies of symbolic play in autism, and concluded that deficit in symbolic play of autistic children might be due to a performance rather than a competence problem. However, executive function deficits are not specific to autism only, and have been found in other groups (Tourette's syndrome, frontal lobe damage, attention deficit disorder and others) (Bishop 1993). More research is needed to find out how executive functioning is disrupted in autism in contrast to other related disorders.

Sensory perceptual theory

In his book *The Ultimate Stranger: The Autistic Child* (1974) Carl Delacato proposed his neurological and sensory theory of autism, which can be summarized as the following:

- autistic children are not psychotic; they are brain injured

- brain injury causes sensory perceptual dysfunction in which sensory channels (sight, hearing, taste, touch, or smell) are made abnormal in one of the following ways:

  o *hyper:* the channel is too open and, as a result, too much stimulation gets in for the brain to handle comfortably

  o *hypo:* the channel is not open enough and, as a result, too little stimulation gets in and the brain is deprived

  o *white noise:* the channel creates its own stimulus because of its faulty operation and, as a result, the message from the outside world is overcome by the noise in the system

- the repetitive behaviours of the autistic child ('sensorisms') are the child's attempts to normalize the affected sensory channels.

Unfortunately, at the time, these ideas were (unjustifiably) ignored by the researchers. However, the research continued and in the 1960s and 1970s it was suggested (Ornitz 1969, 1974) that autism may be identified in young children if we look at very specific and easily described behaviours caused by sensory perceptual differences – unusual responses to sensory stimuli. It was noticed that before the age of six, these behaviours were observed with almost the same frequencies as behaviours related to social and communication impairments (Ornitz, Guthrie and Farley 1977, 1978; Volkmar, Cohen and Paul 1986).

The indirect evidence of the role of sensory perceptual problems in the disruption of social, communicative and cognitive development comes from the research in the fields of sensory deprivation, and visual and auditory impairments. Sensory deprivation studies (Doman 1984) reveal that sudden and nearly complete deprivation of stimulation through the sensory channels can lead to autistic-like behaviours. The symptoms of sensory deprivation in animals and many autistic symptoms are similar as well: animals confined to a barren environment are excitable and engaged in stereotyped behaviours and self-injury (Grandin 1996b). The research in the field of visual impairments (Cass 1996; Gense and Gense 1994) has shown that some similar patterns of behaviour occur in children with visual impairments and in those with autism: impairments in social interaction, communication, and stereotyped move-ments (for example, rocking, rhythmic head banging, spinning objects or perimeter hugging). Common features have also been observed in the language development of children with autism and those with visual impair-ments, for example echolalia and pronoun reversal (Fay and Schuler 1980), and in children with hearing impairments.

Another strand of research has been carried out in the field of occupa-tional therapy (OT). It was started by A. Jane Ayres (1979) who formulated the theory of sensory integration dysfunction (SID) to describe a variety of neurological disorders. This theory attempted to account for the relationship between sensory processing and behavioural deficits in different develop-mental disorders including autism. Having defined SI as 'the neurological process that organizes sensation from one's own body effectively within the environment and makes it possible to use the body effectively within the environment' (Ayres 1989, p.11), Ayres originally limited her investigation to three senses – tactile, vestibular and proprioceptive. She identified (and limited) the problems in these three 'basic' senses to tactile defensiveness (for tactile sense), gravitational insecurity (vestibular system) and postural insecurity (proprioception).

One of the main drawbacks of this theory is that it was developed in 'isolation' from other research and failed to accumulate research findings from related fields of interest. The fact that SI theory is limited to occupational therapy means that a lot of useful data from the research of sensory perceptual impairments and sensory dysfunction have been overlooked. As a result, after several decades of development, the SI theory still remains a theory and, has unfortunately, little recognition and support from the fields outside occupational therapy. Unlike Delacato's concepts of 'hyper-/hypo-sensitivities', describing the inner experiences (and problems), Ayres defined SI deficits mostly via behavioural reactions; for example, tactile defensiveness is defined as avoiding or negative reactions to non-noxious tactile stimuli (Ayres 1964) and is manifested in 'fright, flight or fight' response or reaction. With development, the shift from using 'behavioural terminology' to describing the phenomena (experiences) was made. This turn of attention from behaviours to experiences probably prevented such terms as, for example, 'visual/auditory defensiveness' from being spread in the OT literature and now the OT researchers prefer to use 'hyper-/hyposensitivities', or 'modulation problems'; that is, the concepts of sensory dysfunction and sensory modulation disturbances introduced by the researchers in the field of sensory and information processing (see, for example, Delacato 1974; Ornitz 1969, 1974, 1983, 1985).

Recently, the OT researchers have proposed to update terminology used in SI (to facilitate communication between occupational therapists and other professionals) and proposed 'sensory processing disorder' as a global umbrella term which includes three primary diagnostic groups (sensory modulation disorder, sensory discrimination disorder, and sensory-based motor disorder) and the subtypes found within each (Miller *et al.* 2004). The aim of this change is to advocate the inclusion of this new nosology in future editions of DSM and formal recognition of these disorders. So far, there is more confusion and different interpretations of one and the same 'disorder' by different OT researchers (for example, on one and the same website, sensory modulation disorder is defined as 'difficulty adjusting their responses to match the needs of the situation' and patterns of over-responsivity, under-responsivity and sensory-seeking are given as examples; and then Dr Koomar explains that 'Sensory Modulation Disorder refers to the ability to filter and screen incoming information so we can respond appropriately to the situation' –

The SPD Network 2004). Besides, all these descriptions are, once again, 'behaviourally biased'. If the sensory processing disorders are seen as a separate diagnostic category, there is little hope that they will help in identification of 'autism-specific' sensory processing problems. It contradicts the findings that there are distinct sensory processing characteristics in people with different conditions (for instance, developmental disorders, genetic and brain disorders) (Dunn 2001).

Another model of sensory processing was introduced by Dunn (1997). It aims to account for the nervous system's thresholds for acting and the person's propensity for responding to those thresholds. In this model, thresholds and responding strategies represent a continuum of possible conditions and are characterized as reflecting both a particular threshold *and* a responding strategy: high thresholds with passive responding strategies are called low registration; high thresholds with active responding strategies are called sensory seeking; low thresholds with passive responding strategies are called sensory sensitivity; and low thresholds with active responding strategies are called sensory avoiding (Dunn 2001). This model simplifies sensory perceptual problems and, in the case of autism (and possibly, other developmental disorders), does not provide insights into the nature and qualitative differences of sensory processing. So far, the OT research has not given a conceptual model that could be a framework for studying autism and other developmental disorders. That is why most research of sensory perceptual differences in autism has been deeply rooted in Delacato's theory, which has inspired a lot of studies.

While recognizing the revolutionary contribution to the understanding of autism made by Delacato, it seems necessary to argue one point in his theory. Delacato considered that a channel could be either hyper- or hypo- or 'white noise'. However, it turns out that often one and the same person can experience sensory inputs of one and the same channel at different times from all three of Delacato's categories – hyper-, hypo- and 'white noise' – because the intensity (the volume) with which the channels work often fluctuates (Bogdashina 2003).

Thanks to the work of Delacato, Ornitz, Rimland and some others, who pioneered and laid the theoretical foundation of the research of sensory processing problems in autism, the 'sensory theory' of autism is 'taking shape', incorporating findings from other related fields and producing a framework for studying sensory perceptual differences in autism and their impact not only on behaviours, but also language and social impairments of individuals with ASDs. What hinders this development, however, is over-simplification of sensory problems in autism by some researchers, reducing them to hypersensitivities. If it were as simple as that, does it mean that if we identify the hypersensitivities of each individual and adjust the environment, we would solve all the problems? A short answer is 'no'. Hypersensitivities may merely be the consequences of other sensory perceptual differences which may include the inability to filter sensory information, fragmentation of perception, sensory agnosia, delayed processing, monotropism, peripheral perception, systems shutdowns and others. What is more, the differences of sensory processing lead to different routes of cognitive and language develop-ment which are eventually reflected in different systems of communication and social interaction (Bogdashina 2003, 2004).

As 'sensory perceptual' behaviours ('sensorisms') are not included in diagnostic classification, few empirical studies of sensory difficulties in young autistic children have yet been conducted. There is some evidence from recent research, though, that does indicate that sensory perceptual differences may be among the first signs of autism in young children. Thus, based on retrospective home video studies, the research has revealed that, overall, the autistic children showed problems in sensory attention and arousal; they oriented less to visual information in their environments; they put objects in their mouths more often; they needed more cues before they looked when someone called their names; and they pulled away from social touch more than other groups of children – normally-developing children and children with developmental disabilities other than autism (Baranek 1999). Other 'sensory symptoms' that are more commonly seen in infants with autism than in normally-developing infants or infants with other developmental disorders include lack of responsiveness to certain sounds, hypersensitivity to certain foods, and insensitivities to pain (Hoshino *et al.* 1982); atypical interest in visual stimuli, overexcitement when tickled, unusual visual behaviours, play limited to hard objects (Dahlgren and Gillberg 1989; Gillberg *et al.* 1990); unusual reactions to vestibular tasks (Gepner *et al.* 1995; Kohen-Raz, Volkmar and Cohen 1992); hand–finger mannerisms, whole body mannerisms other than rocking, and unusual sensory interests (Le Couteur *et al.* 1989; Lord, Rutter and Le Couteur 1994); watching hands and fingers, and arm flapping (Volkmar *et al.* 1986); stereotypic behaviours, under- and overreactions to auditory stimuli, unusual postures, and unstable visual attention. These autistic 'sensory' symptoms observed during the first years seem to persist into the second year of life (Adrien *et al.* 1992, 1993). Autistic toddlers and pre-school children display atypical sensorimotor behaviours (including both heightened sensitivities or reduced responsiveness across sensory modalities, and motility disturbances such as stereotypies) at some point in their development (Ermer and Dunn 1998; Kientz and Dunn 1997; Rapin 1996). Numerous individual differences, indicating possible subtypes based on different patterns of sensory perceptual problems, have been reported (Greenspan and Wielder 1997; Stone and Hogan 1993; Wing and Gould 1979).

Other theories

Autism as a disorder of affective and social relations

This theory developed by Hobson (1989, 1995) is founded on the views of Kanner (1943) and Bosch (1970). Like Kanner (1943) who suggests that these children's primary deficit is their *inability to relate themselves* in the ordinary way to people and situations from the beginning of life' (p.242), Hobson (1995) sees the primary impairment as an inability to engage emotionally with others, which leads to an inability to receive the necessary social experiences to develop cognitive structures for understanding.

However, there is some evidence contradicting these views. For example, Knobloch and Pasamanick (1975) reported that children who were referred to them for displaying abnormal social responsiveness in the first year of life did not develop autism, whereas those who showed disturbance of social interaction at the age of two were found to have autism on follow-up. On the other hand, there is much evidence for real personal attachment in autistic children and adults (Frith 1989), though it may be expressed unconventionally. Having studied developmental records, Frith, Soares and Wing (1993) found that two thirds of mothers of autistic children were not disturbed by their child's social interaction in the first year.

An affect diathesis hypothesis

In *Growth of Mind* (1997) Stanley Greenspan presented a theory suggesting that affective interactions emerge earlier than the sensorimotor schemes postulated by Piaget (1962) and that they are the most primary probes we use to understand, conceptualize and 'double code' our experiences of the world. Greenspan also suggested that most types of abstract thinking are based on reflections of these personal affective experiences. According to the author, 'the core psychological deficit in autism may, therefore, involve an inability to connect affect (i.e., intent) to motor planning and sequencing capacities and symbol formation' (Greenspan 2001, p.3). Greenspan (2001) developed this theory further and put forward the affect diathesis hypothesis. This examines the critical role of affective interactions in self-regulation, communication, language, creative meanings, and constructing a sense of reality. It also attempts to show how various types of deficits of affects during early development contribute to our understanding of autism. This hypothesis explores the connection between affect and different processing capacities (the core deficit). In this hypothesis, a child uses his affect to provide intent for his actions and meaning for words. If it were not the name of the theory, it would perfectly fit into the sensory perceptual category of theories. For example, although Greenspan (2001) suggests that 'affect invests not simply the capacity for complex interactions to give meaning to sounds, words, and behaviours, but also invests processing capacities, such as motor planning and visual spatial processing' (p.11), he admits that many children with autistic spectrum disorders:

> ...are capable of relatively quickly forming, patterns of engagement... They are capable of engaging with pleasure, warmth, and joy. They're, therefore, capable of the earlier levels of affect transformation, involving basic engagement, even though they have difficulty with forming reciprocal affective interchanges. (Greenspan 2001, p.15)

Clinical observation has shown that:

> ...often these children can be helped to enjoy fundamental relating in a deep and satisfying manner, once we figure out *their sensory processing and motor profiles* [emphasized by O.B.]. For example, some of the children are very sensory over-reactive and, therefore, uncomfortable with closeness involving touch or high- or low-pitched sounds. When the sensory environment is tailored to their unique profiles, these children begin evidencing enormous pleasure in relating. (Greenspan 2001, pp.15–16)

Greenspan further concludes that many children with autistic spectrum disorder:

> ...have biological differences that express themselves in the way the child processes sensations and organizes and plans responses. These biologically based processing differences can make the expectable milestones of learning to relate and communicate very challenging... Due to their unique sensory processing profiles, the negotiation of a

deep sense of intimacy is a complex and subtle process. The capacity appears to be there, but needs to be met with caregiving overtures that are sensitive to the child's unique processing patterns. (Greenspan 2001, p.18)

Greenspan defines the caregiving environment as vital in helping children with ASDs. While children without processing difficulties might easily have a flexible capacity to engage with others, children with complex processing profiles are very vulnerable to the subtleties in their environment, and can easily regress or develop patterns of avoidance and self-absorption (Greenspan 2001).

Autism as an extreme version of the male brain

Based on the findings of higher levels of fetal testosterone (typical for males) in autistic individuals, and cognitive characteristics of males ('systemizing type') vs. females ('emphasizing type'), Baron-Cohen (2003a) proposed both an ambitious and provocative theory – that autism may be seen as an extreme version of the male brain. Though it does not account for some of the many neurological features of ASDs (for example, stereotyped movements), Baron-Cohen argues that his theory aims to pick out the universal or core features that would be found in *any* individual with an ASD. Some symptoms of autism (for example, language delay, self-injury, sleep disturbance and others) are not universal and do not need to be accounted for by this theory, while impairments in emphasizing and superior 'systemizing' may be seen in *all* autistic individuals including people with AS. However, some argue that some people with ASDs do emphasize (and have a very strong sense of 'fairness'), and, on the other hand, it is difficult to see repetitive behaviours as 'systemizing exercise'. The example of a child spinning the wheel of a toy car as if he were learning small details of how the wheel turns with varying force, or how different diameter wheels turn at different speeds, is not very convincing. Personal accounts reveal that these repetitive activities are to do with the fascination of patterns and other sensory stimuli, rather than 'educational exercises'.

There are (and will be) many more theories attempting to account for autism. Some of them are mostly speculative and theorizing. They tend to draw together 'bits and pieces' of research from wide sources and create a conceptual framework in which their particular theory fits. The authors of these 'new theories of autism' claim that their theoretical construct can account for *all* autistic symptoms, and often conclude their speculations with a sensational claim – 'autism explained'. Other theories contain very promising hypotheses and good potential to develop further, but, so far, they still remain in the margin of the autism research as their approach is unconventional and contradicts well-established 'mainstream views of autism'.

For 'horizontal reading':

1.5 – pp.47–53
2.5 – pp.126–137
3.5 – pp.202–207

4.6

Treatments

Biomedical approaches

Vitamin B₆, magnesium and DMG (dimethylglycine)

Vitamin B_6, magnesium and DMG (dimethylglycine)

High dosages of Vitamin B_6 and magnesium have been reported to be beneficial in controlling self-injurious and aggressive behaviours, and increasing eye contact and speech in autistic children (Rimland 1987). Like with any other treatment it works for some individuals but not for others. People vary enormously in their need for B_6. If autism is aggravated by the lack of it (what Rimland calls a vitamin B_6 dependency syndrome) the children will show improvement of the B_6 therapy (Rimland 1987).

Secretin

Secretin

Secretin is a natural hormone which stimulates the pancreas to aid digestion. A synthetic version of it is used in diagnosing pancreatic disorders. It was discovered accidentally that secretin may help to treat autism. In 1996, Victoria Beck took her autistic son to check for gastrointestinal problems. The boy was given secretin, and his mother soon noticed a rapid improvement in his development. Secretin seemed to become that 'miraculous remedy' for which so many desperate parents had been waiting. The news was reported on the television and in newspapers, and a lot of clinical trials have been carried out. So far, no study has shown any benefit beyond that from the placebo.

Diets

Diets

Removing gluten and casein from the child's diet can bring improvements in the behaviour. However, the researchers warn that the diet has to be 100 per cent strict. Younger children show faster results, while for older children it can take up to a year to manifest themselves, as their bodies have stored up greater amounts of these substances.

Neurosensory approaches

Delacato's method

Delacato's method is based on the assumptions that:

- the repetitive behaviours ('sensorisms') are the child's messages which should be observed and interpreted. These behaviours show which channels are affected and whether the channel is hyper, hypo, or white noise

- when we have learned which channels are affected and how they are affected, we can help the child to normalize the channels by giving him the proper experience and stimulation through the affected channels

- as the channel is normalized, the behaviour ceases

- when the behaviour ceases, the child's attention is shifted and he becomes able to learn to deal with the real world and to learn to interact with things and people around him

- at that point we treat the child as we would treat any other mildly to moderately brain-injured child.

Delacato's programmes to work on the senses in order to normalize them are devised for parents to carry out at home. They are designed to programme the stimulation coming through the senses in accordance with the deficiencies of each particular child and may include massage for tactility, tasks for smell and taste, auditory and visual exercises, movement development as well as education, communication and speech. Since the publication of Delacato's book (1974) his ideas have been found in many similar models of his original concepts (for example, SIT – Ayres 1979; Brain Gym – Dennison 2004). Many therapies use the same methods but under different titles.

Sensory integration therapy (SIT)

The same principles are used in SIT. In the past, the therapy was aimed at the 'three major senses' (tactility, proprioception and vestibular system) (Ayres 1979). Now it is recognized that all the senses should be evaluated and worked at. There are several types of SIT; for example, multi-sensory integration and desensitization. They involve sensory activities aimed at raising the children's threshold for arousal. A widely used concept of SIT at present is that of sensory diet. It is a planned and scheduled programme of 'sensory exercises', designed to meet the needs of each particular child's nervous system. An occupational therapist teaches the parents to use different techniques with the child at home, and monitors the child's responsiveness to the strategies. The supporters of SIT hypothesize that SI treatment can influence brain organization and brain change. As it is difficult to observe any changes in the brain, the only means to evaluate the effectiveness of the therapy is limited to observable behaviours. To complicate matters, there is still no agreement about what to consider 'truly SI' treatments. Until there is a sound theoretical foundation for the theory of SI and SIT, proper evaluation of this treatment is unlikely.

Irlen method

The Irlen method consists of two steps:

Screening. Irlen has designed a special questionnaire, which serves as a screening tool. The questionnaire has to be completed by either the individuals themselves or a family member. Each questionnaire is evaluated to determine whether the individual is a candidate for the Irlen method.

Testing. There is a standardized set of procedures to determine the correct colour for the overlay and the tinted lenses.

A large number of studies have reported positive results in using coloured filters (Robinson 1996). The Irlen method seems to work for those whose visual problems are overwhelming and helps slow down visual processing, helping to filter visual information. However, these filters do not solve the problem of autism. They improve perception and make learning more effective, and must be accompanied by appropriate educational methods.

Auditory integration training

AIT is based on two theories:

- Behaviour is a direct result of how well a person hears.

- The hearing mechanism can be retrained. As a result, improved hearing leads to improved behaviour.

The principle of AIT originated from the concept of the possibility of a cure by mechanical needs. For example, if the movement of a limb is restricted, it can be cured (trained) by special physical exercises to increase its mobility. This 'mechanical' treatment influences not only the related muscles but also the related area of the brain.

Numerous pilot studies of the AIT method demonstrated significant results: a reduction in self-stimulatory behaviours, hyperactivity, anxiety, social withdrawal, distractibility and echolalia, and an increase in attention, comprehension, articulation and auditory memory. AIT administered to the person whose main difficulties are caused by auditory problems may produce a significant improvement of functioning. If AIT is administered to the person whose primary difficulties lie in other sensory modalities, little or no improvement is seen.

Psychodynamic approaches

The options ('Son-Rise') approach

The 'options' philosophy is total acceptance of the child, with the main motto being that the children show us the way in, and then we show them the way out. The main techniques and principles derived from this are:

- joining a child in a repetitious behaviour in order to create a deeper relationship with the child
- using the child's own motivations to teach them critical skills.

To carry out the programme, a specially designed room (playroom) is created – with minimum distractions – where the child feels safe and relaxed.

The 'options' approach applied to working with adults with autism and severe intellectual disabilities is referred to as 'intensive interaction' (see, for example, Caldwell 2004; Nind and Hewett 1994).

Floor time

Greenspan *et al.* (1998) describe six emotional milestones of development that form a developmental ladder:

- self-regulation and interest in the world (the ability to take an interest in sensations and calm oneself down)

- intimacy (the ability to engage in relationships with other people)

- two-way communication (the ability to engage in two-way communication)

- complex communication (the ability to make and understand gestures, to string together a series of actions into a problem-solving sequence)

- emotional ideas (the ability to create ideas)

- emotional thinking (the ability to make logical reality-based ideas).

Children with special needs (including autism) are seen to have a variety of biological challenges such as:

- difficulty with sensory reactivity

- processing difficulty

- difficulty creating and planning responses.

These challenges make it difficult for these children to relate to and communicate with others. Therefore special programmes are designed to eliminate these challenges. The 'floor time' approach is aimed to help the child master the six developmental skills and learn how to relate to other people. It is an intensive one-on-one treatment consisting of six to ten play sessions a day, each lasting for 20 to 30 minutes (usually on the floor, hence the name).

Behavioural/educational approaches

Applied Behaviour Analysis (ABA)

The best outcome of ABA that has not been replicated yet is 47 per cent success in Dr Lovaas's original 1987 study. After two or more years of intensive 40 hours per week ABA programme, 9 out of 19 pre-school autistic children were reported to have 'recovered' and became indistinguishable from their peers. Other studies have produced far more modest results (for example, Smith 1999). Many agree that the 1987 study's spectacular results might be attributed to the use of aversives (used in the original but not the following studies). The ABA (like any other approach) does work with some autistic children, but not with others. The widely spread myth that ABA is the only approach that is 'scientifically proven and medically necessary', however, attracts a lot of (justifiable) criticism. For example, a strong supporter and advocate of ABA, Bernard Rimland, is appalled at the ludicrous position taken by many other supporters of ABA, who claim that ABA is the only scientifically validated treatment for autism. Dr Rimland considers that position not only false but absurd, and provides evidence of several treatments that clearly meet the criterion of scientific validation and, of those, some surpass ABA in terms of scientific supportability (for example, gluten- and casein-free diets, anti-fungal treatment, vitamin B_6 and magnesium therapy) (Rimland 1999). No one disagrees with the fact that it is extremely difficult, if not impossible, to develop a double-blind evaluation (necessary for rigorous scientific validity) of intensive ABA treatment, but that does not change the fact that a double blind was not used, thereby making the results to some extent contaminated by participant bias and expectancy (Rimland 1999).

In general, behavioural principles in teaching skills and an intensive interaction are beneficial for *all*, not only autistic children. What is often criticized in the Lovaas approach is using different techniques to eliminate certain behaviours, irrespective of the causes of these behaviours (which can be treated effectively via diets, addressing hypersensitivities, etc.).

TEACCH

There are seven key principles:

1. Improved adaptation – through developing skills and modifying the environment to accommodate deficits.

2. Parent collaboration – parents work with professionals as co-therapists for their children, thus providing consistency and continuity of the approach.

3. Assessment for individualized treatment – on the basis of a regular assessment of abilities, special individualized educational programmes are designed for each individual.

4. Structured teaching.

5. Skill enhancement – work focuses on the development of 'emerging' skills.

6. Cognitive behaviour therapy – educational strategies are guided by the cognitive and behavioural theories suggesting that challenging behaviour results from underlying problems in perception and understanding.

7. Generalist training – professionals are trained as generalists who understand the whole child and do not specialize as speech therapists, psychologists, etc.

The TEACCH approach is said to lead to greater independence and adaptability because it focuses on meaningful routines and visual clarity to teach autistic people how to function without constant adult assistance (Mesibov 1993). TEACCH addresses difficulties in organization, auditory processing, memory and making transitions. It introduces structure which helps the individual to feel safe and relaxed and emphasizes positive strategies of behaviour management. Another important feature of the TEACCH programme is visual teaching (for example, visual timetables).

Cognitive approaches
Cognitive behaviour therapy
Cognitive behaviour therapy has been successfully used with people with mood disorders. As children and adults with AS are likely to develop secondary mood disorders (Tonge *et al.* 1999), cognitive behaviour therapy modified to the unusual cognitive profile of individuals with AS may be beneficial for them.

The therapy consists of two stages:

- an assessment of the nature and degree of mood disorder using self-reported scales and interviews

- affective education (discussions and exercises: cognitive restructuring, stress management, self-reflection, etc.).

Modifications are made to accommodate specific cognitive profiles in AS. For instance, at the assessment stage, a pictorial representation of the gradation in experience and expression of mood ('thermometer', a 'volume scale', etc.) is used. During the affective education stage, individuals are taught to detect the degree of emotion within themselves and others (for example, identification of the salient cues in the person's facial expression, body language, tone of voice). They are tutored in Theory of Mind, social reasoning, conflict resolution and friendship skills. Cognitive restructuring is aimed to enable the person to correct distorted conceptualizations and dysfunctional beliefs. The process involves challenging their current thinking with logical evidence and ensuring the rationalization of their emotions (Attwood 1999). It is achieved with the help of Social Stories and Comic Strip Conversations, techniques developed by Carol Gray (1998). Stress management strategies (for example, cue-controlled relaxation) are taught as a counter-conditioning procedure (Attwood 1999).

Communication/language approaches

Picture Exchange Communication System (PECS)

The research (Bondy and Frost 1994) has shown that of 66 previously non-verbal children under the age of five who were using PECS for more than one year, 44 learned to speak spontaneously and 14 developed some speech. Some children who did not develop speech continued using PECS success-fully.

Sign language

Sign language is not successful with all autistic individuals. Research (Bonvillian and Nelson 1978) has shown that, in a study sample, although none of nearly 70 autistic children failed to acquire at least one sign, the final outcome, in terms of each individual's linguistic performance, appeared to vary significantly. Some of the children, after acquiring facility in sign language, learned to use spoken English. For those who progress in speech as well as sign, the progress in sign language appeared crucial as a basis for the changes in speech skills. On the other hand, a number of children never learned to use more than a few signs and remained mute (Bonvillian and Nelson 1978).

Facilitated communication (FC)

The theoretical foundation of FC is based on the following assumptions:

- There are people who cannot communicate because of their apraxia or developmental dyspraxia: they experience problems with imitating and stopping action, modulating the pace of action, impulsiveness, an inability to speak or automatic echolalic speech, articulation and prosody problems (Biklen 1990; Crossley and Remington-Gurney 1992).

- Many people with autism and other developmental disabilities have literacy skills without other people knowing that they can read or spell. They just have no way of demonstrating them.

According to the proponents of FC, FC overcomes dyspraxic difficulties through physical and emotional support where a facilitator helps a person to point at pictures, symbols or letters. The physical support may include:

- assistance in isolating the index finger

- stabilizing the arm to overcome tremor

- backward resistance on the arm and pulling it back to overcome impulsiveness and prevent the person from striking the same key repetitively

- a touch of the arm or shoulder to help the person to initiate pointing/typing.

The FC proponents emphasize that FC is not a cure from a disability but a means of communicating, and its long-term goal is independent typing. Although successful stories of people who have learned to communicate through FC have been documented, and some of them have achieved complete independence in typing, there has been and still is a lot of controversy about FC.

Eclectic approaches

Some therapies use different elements from different approaches in order to accommodate the unique needs of each autistic individual. It works well if there are not too many 'bits and pieces'. For example, some approaches (usually referred to as 'holistic') claim to be beneficial not only for autistic people but for other disabilities – 'ADD/ADHD, PDD, brain injury, cerebral palsy, Down syndrome, Tourette syndrome, stroke, bipolar disorder, depression, obsessive-compulsive disorder, behavioural difficulties, dyslexia, dyspraxia, language delay, and more' – because they use techniques from many disciplines, including medicine, rehabilitation, psychology, education and nutrition. Theoretically, specialists providing such treatments have to have numerous qualifications in several disciplines.

In their report on efficiency of treatments in autism, Jordan *et al.* (1998) conclude that there is no strong evidence to suggest that one approach for a child with ASD is better than another, although research findings show that:

- early intervention may result in greatly enhanced positive outcomes

- individuals with autism benefit from a highly structured educational programme, tailored to their particular individual needs

- there are rare cases of 'recovery' claimed by every approach but there needs to be further research to determine the validity and reliability of this finding

- there are always some children who do well and others who do not

- what works best is usually a combination of more than one approach (eclectic approach), even though one approach is likely to dominate

- it is possible that certain improvements are the result of normal development and not the treatment provided

- parents should be seen as critical partners of any intervention

- the choice of the treatment should be based not only on the effectiveness of the treatment but also on the evaluation of possible side-effects for the child and the whole family

- some approaches have been reported by parents as producing negative results.

Because of the spectrum nature of autism and many possible causes of the condition, no one approach is effective for all individuals with autism: what works for one child will not work for the other; treatment should be chosen individually, depending on the particular child's strengths and weaknesses.

Is autism curable?

There is general agreement that autism is treatable, but is it curable? Some researchers (see, for example, Rimland 1994) believe that recovery from autism (conventionally considered as a lifelong disability) is possible. Rimland

(1994) distinguishes between recovery and partial recovery, or near-recovery, and supports his view with statements from personal accounts of 'recovered autistic people' and mother–child accounts (chronicles of recoveries written by mothers, with chapters or afterwords written by the children themselves). According to Rimland (1994), the cases of 'partial recovery' are those of HF autistic people who have achieved independent living, successful professional careers, and accomplished more with their lives than most 'non-disabled' people can hope to achieve; for example, Temple Grandin, Donna Williams and Sean Barron. However, here we have different interpretations of the concept of recovery. For Rimland,

> if they *look* recovered, if they *act* recovered, and if they [are] thought *to be* recovered, they *are* recovered. Perhaps some of these 'recovered' individuals may have some quirks and odd behaviors. If so, so what? Who doesn't? (Rimland 1994, p.3)

This interpretation does not include the concept of 'an intelligent HF autistic person' who can live a successful and productive life. It excludes the possibility of being autistic but successful. It is more about how the person *looks* ('indistinguishable from their peers'), and how the person is perceived by the majority, than about how the individual *feels*. If a person who has developed from a LF autistic child to HF autistic adult is called 'recovered', then yes, 'recovery' from autism *is* possible. There are many (undiagnosed) people with ASDs who may be considered to 'have recovered spontaneously', but why, then, do many of them seek diagnosis later in life?

Based on the philosophy that recovery is possible and inspired by an urgency of research in the field of causes and treatments, the projects such as Defeat Autism Now! and Cure Autism Now! have been launched. The main goal of these movements is to bring together pioneers and advocates in the field of autism, to share their knowledge and expertise, and promote the research aimed at the cure of this condition.

For 'horizontal reading':

1.6 – pp.54–66
2.6 – pp.138–161
3.6 – pp.208–219

Miscellany

Thoughts to Share

Autism: disability or difference?

There has been an interesting suggestion put forward as to whether AS or high-functioning autism necessarily leads to disability or whether they simply represent a 'difference'. There is a view that the term 'difference' in relation to AS/HFA is a more neutral and fairer description than such terms as 'impairment', 'disability' or 'deficiency' (Baron-Cohen 2000). Hans Asperger (1944), fascinated with the unusual abilities of his patients, argued that these individuals had much to offer to society and should be nurtured to develop their talents. Simon Baron-Cohen (2000) supports this view and proposes an important shift of emphasis in the description of autism – from autism as a deficiency to a different cognitive style. While recognizing that low-functioning autism may well be considered as a disability, Baron-Cohen builds his case to show that AS/HFA may be better explained as a difference. The author argues that:

- certain characteristics (for example, strong, persistent interests, fascination by systems and not people) do not 'disable' the person, but rather indicate the difference in thinking

- the neurobiology of AS/HFA is neither better nor worse than in typical development: a range of neural abnormalities (for example, increased cell density in some regions of the brain) show differences between brains of people with and without AS/HFA and cannot be taken as evidence that one type of brain is better or worse than the other

- many features of AS/HFA may be presented in terms of a different 'cognitive style' without any implication that it is better or worse than a non-autistic cognitive style

- the difference view is more compatible with the 'continuum' concept. (Baron-Cohen 2000)

Further, Baron-Cohen considers two different models that attempt to show the dimensions of differences between AS/HFA and so-called normality:

- the folk psychology–folk physics model: autistic people seem to be very poor at mindreading (folk psychology) but are very good (even superior) at understanding systems (folk physics)

- the central coherence model (Frith 2003).

In his article, Simon Baron-Cohen (2000) enumerates arguments (with contra-arguments) for viewing AS/HFA as a disability rather than a difference:

- Differences are caused by cognitive deficits (lack of theory of mind; weak central coherence; 'executive disorder'). However, we cannot yet prove that differences are due to disability and not the other way round.

- Lack of social interest reflects disability. However, to highlight the lack of normal sociability or communication while ignoring the strength is an unfair description of a person.

- AS/HFA is a disability when viewed from the family or peer perspective. However, a clash of interests and styles is not necessarily a disability, and individuals need to accommodate to each other.

- AS/HFA is associated with medical conditions such as epilepsy or mental retardation. However, such associated medical conditions are not specific to AS/HFA and may be found in the non-autistic population as well.

- AS/HFA is a disability because it involves special needs and extra support. However, this is an issue relating to social, health and education policy and economics, and the legal system.

Autism in different cultures

Autism can vary in its 'disability' part depending on the culture. It is a disorder because it deviates from what is considered to be the norm (cultural norms and values vary considerably and change with time). Paradoxically, within contemporary society in highly developed countries where social and communicative skills are at the top of cultural values, autism may be seen as a severe disability. On the other hand, computerization may improve the prospects of HF autistic and AS individuals whose 'disability' (with computer skills as 'byproducts') can enable many of them to live productive lives.

Treating symptoms

It is extremely difficult to find an appropriate provision or service for an autistic individual not only because of lack of available provisions but also because of the incompetence and inadequacy of some (easily available) institutions. While looking for a suitable school for my autistic son, I was shocked to my core when two out of the three I visited proudly emphasized their goals (printed in red in their leaflets) as:

- 'to reduce autistic behaviours'
- 'to reduce the symptoms of an ASD in a child'.

The problem is, I do not want them to work to reduce my son's 'autistic behaviours' or the 'symptoms of an ASD', but rather to work with his abilities while addressing his weaknesses. If his needs are addressed and a structured educational programme is in place, his 'autistic behaviours' will decrease.

I wanted to ask the staff how they were going to work to reduce his flapping his hands – would they tie them up? But seeing that the headteacher was disappointed that I was not impressed by their 'goals', I left without saying a word, never to return.

Some hints to professionals

From parents

> Take the autistic child. Restore his self-esteem and teach him to take pride in himself. Educate his parents in the best ways to raise him and teach them coping strategies for the challenges he will present. Counsel the brothers and sisters and teach them how to draw strength rather than weakness from their autistic sibling. You may not have a cure. But

there are ample opportunities for you to heal. There is an important lesson here. When parents walk into the consultant's office we are usually at the end of our tether after a long and exhausting run-around. You are healers. Your natural inclination is to offer reassurance and ease our pain. But everyone else has tried that already and it has not worked. We want answers but, more than that, we need and welcome honesty, as when our child psychiatrist had the courage to say, 'I could be wrong,' and referred us on for diagnosis. (Stanton 2001)

From autistic people

The role of professionals should be to help people use their natural processes to learn and grow. This might mean helping people develop strategies for dealing with sensory oversensitivities: using earplugs or colored lenses, adapting clothing to accommodate tactile sensitivities, providing opportunities for deep pressure or vestibular stimulation, etc. It might mean teaching self-monitoring and self-management of behaviour and emotions. Probably it always means learning and teaching translation skills to enable people with different communication systems to communicate with each other. There is no inherent conflict between accepting and working with autism on one hand, and promoting increased skill development on the other. It is the role of all teachers, counsellors, and therapists to promote growth and learning. For professionals working with autistic people, the important issue is that autistic people should be assisted in growing and developing into more capable autistic people, not pushed to become like non-autistic people. (Sinclair 1998)

What's in a name?

There are both very many and very few treatments for autism. It is not a contradiction. If you search for all the treatment approaches available you will find hundreds (!) of them. However, in fact, there are very few original approaches; most have been modified and...given a new name. None of them offers anything new. Basically they present old ideas in a different format. As one of the parents puts it, 'these "new" and "revolutionary" ideas are all someone else's work re-worded' (Mrs C, a mother of two autistic children). Sometimes it happens because those who 'originate' a new idea do not know that something like this has been in existence long before they began their work (rather like inventing the wheel, without knowing that people have been driving cars for many years). This is often the case when the 'originators' are practitioners who have not done any research in the field. The drawback of this is twofold: first, as a rule the 'unknown (somebody else's) ideas' are much better researched and developed than 'new' ones; second, for the general public and for those new in the field, it may be confusing – different 'names' for one and the same approach. An example of these synonymous terms is the 'intensive interaction' approach, meaning the application of 'options' principles to working with adults with autism and severe intellectual disabilities. Similar things have happened in the field of sensory integration which has not incorporated research and findings from outside occupational therapy. So sometimes the 'name' may make the whole difference and either promote or hinder the development in the field of autism. The right thing to do seems to acknowledge the research done in the past and develop it further (with reference to the original ideas). It will give continuity, an opportunity to see the outcomes of previous research and trials and possible pitfalls to be avoided. Isn't it better, instead of reinventing the wheel, to improve the existing car? *Just a thought.*

Theories of autism: is the enigma explained?

There are more theories on autism than any other developmental disorder. As autism is so complicated, *any* theoretical construct may explain a 'bit' of it. All of these theories are useful in a way – each brings some new insight and new approach to the same problem. With accumulation of research findings, old ideas may be either rejected or modified. It is a sound approach to theorizing – accommodating the existing theory to new data or, if it is impossible, creating a new theory to explain new evidence. The problem begins when new data are being accommodated to the theory. And if these data (oh, horror!) cannot be 'bent' to fit the theory, then it is usually thrown out as insignificant. For example, it is not difficult to manipulate the definitions to fit the condition to each particular theory – if some symptoms cannot be explained, it is easy to move them from the definition of 'pure autism'. Very few researchers are humble enough to say, 'Sorry, I was wrong. New evidence contradicts my conclusions. I'll have to reconsider my approach.'

Another problem is the attitude to some (new and old) theories which are unconventional, go against the tide and challenge 'well-established' beliefs. In the past, some brilliant ideas were ignored by the mainstream researchers for decades, or were ridiculed and then dismissed as ridiculous, thus having hindered their development. We often see what we want to see. We are limited in our perception of the problem by our 'mindsets' – anything new that does not fit them is rejected or forced to fit into the existing concepts. If Einstein had been afraid to imagine the impossible, we wouldn't have been where we are now.

Despite claims that the enigma of autism is explained, there is still a long way to go to find the solution to this puzzle. Only when we learn how to 'break' our mindsets which prevent us from seeing the same problem from different perspectives can we be able to see the 'whole elephant'. *Just a thought.*

For 'horizontal reading':

1.7 – pp.67–71
2.7 – pp.162–173
3.7 – pp.220–226

Further Reading

Bauman, M.L. and Kemper, T.L. (1994) *The Neurobiology of Autism*. Baltimore: Johns Hopkins University Press.

Schopler, E. and Mesibov, G.B. (eds) (1995) *Diagnosis and Assessment in Autism*. New York: Plenum Press.

Schopler, E. and Mesibov, G.B. (eds) (1995) *Learning and Cognition in Autism*. New York: Plenum Press.

Jordan, R. and Powell, S. (1995) *Understanding and Teaching Children with Autism*. Chichester: John Wiley and Sons.

Howlin, P. (1997) *Autism: Preparing for Adulthood*. London: Routledge.

Diet

Le Breton, M. (2004) *Diet Intervention and Autism: Implementing the Gluten Free and Casein Free Diet for Autistic Children and Adults: A Practical Guide for Parents*. London: Jessica Kingsley Publishers.

Sensory dysfunction in autism

Delacato, C. (1974) *The Ultimate Stranger: The Autistic Child*. Noveto, CA: Academic Therapy Publications.

Bogdashina, O. (2003) *Sensory Perceptual Issues in Autism and Asperger Syndrome: Different Sensory Experiences – Different Perceptual Worlds*. London: Jessica Kingsley Publishers.

Son-Rise

Kaufman, B.N. and Kaufman, S.L. (1986) *Son-Rise*. New York: Warner Books.

Floor time

Greenspan, S.I., Wieder, S. and Simons, R. (1998) *The Child with Special Needs: Encouraging Intellectual and Emotional Growth.* Cambridge, MA: Da Capo Press.

TEACCH

Mesibov, G.B. (2004) *The TEACCH Approach to Autism Spectrum Disorders.* New York: Plenum Press.

Communication in autism

Bondy, A. and Frost, L. (2002) *Picture's Worth: PECS and Other Visual Communication Strategies in Autism.* Bethesda, MD: Woodbine House.

Bogdashina, O. (2004) *Communication Issues in Autism and Asperger Syndrome: Do We Speak the Same Language?* London: Jessica Kingsley Publishers.

Epilogue
The APP Triad and Theory of Mind

At the beginning of the book we compared autism with an iceberg; here I would like to introduce another metaphor to describe the condition. As autism has multiple aetiology but a 'common pathway' at the psychological level, I'd compare it to a fruit tree, with the roots spread very deep in the soil (different biological causes, unknown yet), a trunk (the same pattern of psychological development resulting in the similar symptoms), and branches and twigs (the uniqueness of each individual's features). It is in our power to let the tree blossom. And here we will need a triad again. But this time, not a Triad of Impairments, but the Triad of Perspectives – an APP (Autistic individuals, Parents and Professionals) Triad: the triad of united efforts of autistic people, parents and professionals (see Figure 5.1).

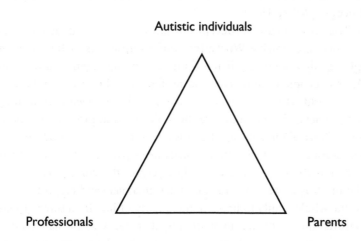

Figure 5.1 The APP Triad

Before we can educate the outside world about ASDs and create environmental conditions that make both autistic and non-autistic individuals comfortable, we should stop fighting amongst ourselves and learn to understand Theory of Different Minds. The first step is to remove one-sidedness from whatever theory or interpretation of the condition we use. Then, accept that we all lack (or have very little) empathy towards each other and work out how we can address this deficit in each of us. Lack of empathy is often caused by misunderstanding. Misunderstanding results from a lack of shared experiences, beliefs and attitudes. Let's follow the example of autistic people – they have to learn theoretically what non-autistic individuals pick up intuitively. Let us 'try each other's shoes on' and share the experiences (even if it is only in our imagination – theoretically). Only then we can achieve mutual understanding and learn to 'mind-read'. For all the parties involved the main goal should be to develop Theories of Mind. It can be done in two steps:

- to accept that people do have alternative viewpoints
- to accept that other people's viewpoints have equal validity.

Another obstacle to the development of Theories of Mind is fear. Many fear what is different and fear creates rigidity. The avoidance of experience is the avoidance of growth. It is stagnation. It is death within life (Williams 1996). To overcome this fear, we all have to break the boundaries of 'normal', the boundaries so many cannot see and so many cannot find. And then, maybe then, the world really will welcome all people (Willey 1999).

The APP Triad is a very useful concept as it shows that we need each other to make the world (a triangle) stable. What affects one group affects all. If we want to achieve a higher quality of life for all, it is through working together rather than separately. Autistic people need parents and professionals because they have to learn about the world which is 'foreign' to them, and they need help to treat autism-related problems that often disable them. Parents and professionals need autistic people to learn about autism, what it is like to live with an ASD, and the ways to communicate with them. Professionals need parents who know their child better than anybody else and can help interpret the child's behaviours. Parents need professionals who can provide advice, treatment and support to help the child and the whole family to improve the quality of life. If all three groups unite their efforts and really try to work together, we will be half-way to 'mind-sightedness'. We have to learn from each other. However, sometimes parents and professionals see themselves as 'teachers' and people with ASDs as 'students'. This rigid 'mindset' is another obstacle in the Triad of APP. The cause of it is in the Triad of Impairments that describes autistic individuals as having impairments of communication (how can they possibly communicate to us properly?) and imagination (how can they understand their own condition?).

The three groups have the same goal to achieve – a brighter future for all. However, they may use different strategies and approaches to 'get there'. The most common are: autistic individuals may seek understanding of themselves and then share this understanding with parents and professionals in order to teach them the ToAM. They may also learn from parents and professionals the ways of the world and the ways they can function successfully in this world. Parents may seek understanding of their children through the ToAM and sharing the acquired knowledge with other parents and professionals. It is time to learn from each other (see Figure 5.2).

Figure 5.2 Swap the roles. A teacher and a student: let us teach and learn from each other

All the groups should accept that they are not perfect and that they do not know everything. We all may make mistakes and it is OK to err if we are prepared to learn from our mistakes. Only open discussion of different views, cooperation and empathy will replace misunderstanding and prevent hurt and frustration. If we all are willing to learn and understand, we will succeed in bringing harmony to the APP Triad of Perspectives, and uncomfortable coexistence will be replaced by comfortable cooperation. Then everybody will win.

References

Aarons, M. and Gittens, T. (1993) *The Handbook of Autism: A Guide for Parents and Professionals.* London and New York: Routledge.

Adrien, J. L., Lenoir, P., Martineau, J., Perrot, A., Hameury, L., Larmande, C. and Sauvage, D. (1993) 'Blind ratings of early symptoms of autism based upon family home movies.' *Journal of American Academy of Child and Adolescent Psychiatry*, 32, 617–626.

Adrien, J. L., Ornitz, E., Barthelemy, C., Sauvage, D. and Lelord, G. (1987) 'The presence or absence of certain behaviors associated with infantile autism in severely retarded autistic and nonautistic retarded children and very young normal children.' *Journal of Autism and Developmental Disorders*, 17, 407–416.

Adrien, J. L., Perrot, A., Sauvage, D., Leddet, I., Larmande, C., Hameury, L. and Barthelemy, C. (1992) 'Early symptoms in autism from family home movies: evaluation and comparison between 1st and 2nd year of life using I.B.S.E. scale.' *Acta Paedopsychiatrica*, 55, 71–75.

American Psychiatric Association (1994) *Diagnostic and Statistical Manual of Mental Disorders* (4th edition) (DSM-IV). Washington, DC: American Psychiatric Association.

Arin, D. M., Bauman, M. L. and Kemper, T. L. (1991) 'The distribution of Purkinje cell loss in the cerebellum in autism.' *Neurology*, 47 (Suppl. 1), 307.

Arnold, L. (2002) 'A piece for action: bringing the NAS into the twenty-first century, thoughts on the governance review.' *Communication*, 36 (1), Spring, 27–28.

Arnold, L. (2004) *Autism, its relationship to science and to people with the condition* (adapted from an academic essay for Birmingham University). www.geocities.com/CapitolHill/7138/lobby/Essay.htm

Asarnow, R. F., Tanguay, P. E., Bott, L. and Freeman, B. J. (1987) 'Patterns of intellectual functioning in nonretarded autistic and schizophrenic children.' *Journal of Child Psychology and Psychiatry*, 28, 273–280.

Asperger, H. (1944) 'Die "autistischen Psychopathen" im Kindesalter.' *Nervenkrankheiten*, 117, 76–136. (English translation in Frith 1991.)

Aston, G. (2000) 'Through the eyes of autism.' *Good Autism Practice*, 1 (2), 57–61.

Attfield, R. (1998) 'My half of the tide.' *Facilitated Communication Digest*, 6 (2), 11.

Attwood, T. (1998) *Asperger's Syndrome: A Guide for Parents and Professionals.* London: Jessica Kingsley Publishers.

Attwood, T. (1999) 'Modifications to Cognitive Behaviour Therapy to accommodate the unusual cognitive profile of people with Asperger's Syndrome.' *Autism99 Conference Papers.* www.autism99.org

Attwood, T. (2000) 'The Autism epidemic: Real or imagined?' *Autism and Asperger's Digest*, November/December, London: NAS.

Aylott, J. (2004) 'The social model and autism.' www.is2d.org.uk/socialmodel.html

Ayres, A. J. (1964) 'Tactile functions: their relation to hyperactive and perceptual motor behavior.' *American Journal of Occupational Therapy*, 18, 6–11.

Ayres, A. J. (1979) *Sensory Integration and the Child.* Los Angeles: Western Psychological Services.

Ayres, A. J. (1989) *Sensory Integration and Praxis Tests.* Los Angeles: Western Psychological Services.

Baggs, A. M. (1999) 'Being a spatial thinker.' www.autistics.org/library/spatial.html

Baggs, A. M. (Undated) 'Rewriting history for their own ends: cure autism now and The Mind Tree.' www.autistics.org/library/tito-can.html

Bailey, A., Phillips, W. and Rutter, M. (1996) 'Autism: towards an integration of clinical, genetic, neuropsychological and neurobiological perspectives.' *The Journal of Child Psychology and Psychiatry and Allied Disciplines*, 37 (1), 89–126.

Baranek, G. T. (1999) 'Autism during infancy: a retrospective video analysis of sensory-motor and social behaviours at 9–12 months of age.' *Journal of Autism and Developmental Disorders*, 29, 213–224.

Baron-Cohen, S. (1995) *Mindblindness: An Essay on Autism and Theory of Mind.* Boston: MIT Press.

Baron-Cohen, S. (1998) 'Autism and "theory of mind": an introduction and review.' *Communication*, Summer, 9–12.

Baron-Cohen, S. (2000) 'Is Asperger's syndrome/High-Functioning Autism necessarily a disability?' *Invited submission for Special Millennium Issue of Development and Psychopathology Draft: 5th January 2000.* www.geocities.com/CapitolHill/7138/lobby/disability.htm

Baron-Cohen, S. (2003a) *The Essential Difference.* London: Penguin Books.

Baron-Cohen, S. (2003b) *Mind Reading: An Interactive Guide to Emotions.* London: Jessica Kingsley Publishers.

Baron-Cohen, S. and Bolton, P. (1993) *Autism: The Facts.* Oxford: Oxford University Press.

Baron-Cohen, S., Allen, J. and Gillberg, C. (1992) 'Can autism be detected at 18 months? The needle, the haystack and the CHAT.' *British Journal of Psychiatry*, 161, 839–843.

Baron-Cohen, S., Leslie, A. M. and Frith, U. (1985) 'Does the child with autism have a theory of mind: a case specific developmental delay?' *Cognition*, 21, 37–46.

Barron, J. and Barron, S. (1993) *There's a Boy in Here.* London: Chapmans.

Bartak, I. and Rutter, M. (1976) 'Differences between mentally retarded and normally intelligent autistic children.' *Journal of Autism and Childhood Schizophrenia*, 6, 109–120.

Bashina, V. M. (1980) *Early Childhood Schizophrenia: Statics and Dynamics* (in Russian). Moscow: Medicine.

Bauman, M. (1991) 'Microscopic neuroanatomic abnormalities in autism.' *Pediatrics*, 87, 791–796.

Bauman, M. L. and Kemper, T. L. (1985) 'Histoanatomic observations of the brain in early infantile autism.' *Neurology*, 35, 866–874.

Bauman, M. and Kemper, T. L. (1994) *The Neurobiology of Autism.* Baltimore: Johns Hopkins University Press.

Belmonte, M. (1997) 'Behavioural consequences of cerebellar damage in the developing brain.' *Link*, 22 (15), 18.

Bemporad, M. L. (1979) 'Adult recollection of a formerly autistic child.' *Journal of Autism and Developmental Disorders*, 9, 179–197.

Bender, L. (1947) 'Childhood schizophrenia: clinical study of one hundred schizophrenic children.' *American Journal of Orthopsychology*, 17, 40–56.

Bettelheim, B. (1967) *The Empty Fortress: Infantile Autism and the Birth of Self.* New York: Free Press.

Biklen, D. (1990) 'Communication unbound: autism and praxis.' *Harvard Educational Review*, 60, 291–314.

Bishop, D. V. M. (1989) 'Autism, Asperger's syndrome and semantic-pragmatic disorder: where are the boundaries?' *British Journal of Disorders of Communication*, 24, 107–121.

Bishop, D. V. M. (1993) 'Autism, executive functions and theory of mind: a neuro-psychological perspective.' *Journal of Child Psychology and Psychiatry*, 34, 79–293.

Blackburn, J. (1999) *My Inside View of Autism.* www.planetc.com/urers/blackjar/aisub (site no longer active).

Blackburn, R. (2000) 'Within and without autism.' *Good Autism Practice*, 1 (1), 2–8.

Blackman, L. (2001) *Lucy's Story: Autism and Other Adventures.* London: Jessica Kingsley Publishers.

Bogdashina, O. (2003) *Sensory Perceptual Issues in Autism and Asperger Syndrome: Different Sensory Experiences – Different Perceptual Worlds.* London: Jessica Kingsley Publishers.

Bogdashina, O. (2004) *Communication Issues in Autism and Asperger Syndrome: Do We Speak the Same Language?* London: Jessica Kingsley Publishers.

Bolton, P., Macdonald, H., Pickles, A., Rios, P., Goode, S., Crowson, M., Bailey, A. and Rutter, M. (1994) 'A case-control family history study of autism.' *Journal of Child Psychology and Psychiatry*, 35, 877–900.

Bondy, A. S. and Frost, L. A. (1994) 'The Delaware Autistic Program.' In S. L. Harris and J. S. Handleman (eds.) *Pre-school Education Programs for Children with Autism.* Austin, TX: Pro-Ed.

Bono, E. de (1971) *Lateral Thinking for Management.* London: Penguin Books.

Bonvillian, J. D. and Nelson, K. E. (1978) 'Development of sign language in autistic children and other language-handicapped individuals.' In P. Siple (ed.) *Understanding Language Through Sign Language Research.* New York: Academic Press.

Bosch, G. (1970) *Infantile Autism* (translation D. Jordan and I. Jordan). New York: Springer-Verlag.

Bovee, J. P. (Undated) 'My experiences with autism and how it relates to Theory of Mind.' *Geneva Centre for Autism publication.* www.autism.net/infoparent

Bowler, D. M. and Thommen, E. (2000) 'Attribution of mechanical and social causality to animated displays by children with autism.' *Autism*, 4, 147–171.

Caldwell, P. (2004) *Crossing the Minefield.* Brighton: Pavilion Publishing.

Callahan, M. (1987) *Fighting for Tony.* New York: Fireside.

Carpenter, A. (1992) 'Autistic adulthood: A challenging journey.' In E. Schopler and G. B. Mesibov (eds) *High-Functioning Individuals with Autism.* New York: Plenum Press, 289–294.

Cass, H. (1996) 'Visual impairments and autism – What we know about causation and early identification.' Autism and Visual Impairment Conference. *Sensory Series,* 5, 2–24.

CIBRA (2004) *Open Letter to Families Considering Intensive Behavioural Therapy for Their Child with Autism.* http://users.1st.net/cibra/about.htm

Cohen, D. J., Paul, R. and Volkmar, F. R. (1986) 'Issues in the classification of pervasive and other development disorders: Towards DSM-IV.' *Journal of the American Academy of Child Psychiatry,* 25 (2), 213–220.

Comi, A. M., Zimmerman, A. W., Frye, V. H., Law, P. A. and Peden, N. J. (1999) 'Familial clustering of autoimmune disorders and evaluation of medical risk factors.' *Journal of Child Neurology,* 14 (6), 388–394.

Cook, E. H. Jr., Charak, D. A., Arida, J., Spohn, J. A., Roizen, N. J. M. and Leventhal, B. L. (1994) 'Depressive and obsessive-compulsive symptoms in hyperserotonemic parents of children with autistic disorder.' *Psychiatry Research,* 52, 25–33.

Courchesne, E. (1995) 'New evidence of cerebellar and brainstem hyposlasia in autistic infants, children and adolescents: the MRI imaging study by Hashimoto and colleagues.' *Journal of Autism and Developmental Disorders,* 25, 19–22.

Courchesne, E. (1996) 'Biological aspects of autism: abnormal cerebellar activity in autism alters cortical and subcortical systems.' *International Pediatrics,* 10 (2), 155–165.

Courchesne, E., Carper, R. and Akshoomoff, N. (2003) 'Evidence of brain overgrowth in the first year of life in autism.' *Journal of the American Medical Association,* 290 (3), 337–344.

Courchesne, E., Townsend, J. and Saitoh, O. (1994) 'The brain in infantile autism: posterior fossa structures are abnormal.' *Neurology,* 44, 214–223.

Creak, M. (1961) 'Schizophrenia syndrome in childhood: progress report of a working party.' *Cerebral Palsy Bulletin,* 3, 501–504.

Crossley, R. and Remington-Gurney, J. (1992) 'Getting the words out: facilitated communication training.' *Topics in Language Disorders,* 12 (4), 29–45.

Dahlgren, S. O. and Gillberg, C. (1989) 'Symptoms in the first two years of life: a preliminary population study of infantile autism.' *European Archives of Psychiatry and Neurological Sciences,* 238, 169–174.

Dahlgren, S. and Trillingsgaard, A. (1996) 'Theory of mind in nonretarded children with autism and Asperger syndrome and nonspeaking children with cerebral palsy: a non handicap specific deficit?' Paper presented at Autism-Europe Congress, Barcelona.

Dawson, G. and Osterling, J. (1997) 'Early intervention in Autism.' In M. Guralnick (ed.) *The Effectiveness of Early Intervention.* Baltimore: Brookes.

Delacato, C. (1974) *The Ultimate Stranger: The Autistic Child.* Noveto, CA: Academic Therapy Publications.

DeMyer, M. K., Barton, S. and Norton, J. A. (1972) 'A comparison of adaptive, verbal, and motor profiles of psychotic and non-psychotic subnormal children.' *Journal of Autism and Childhood Schizophrenia,* 2, 359–377.

Denckla, M. B. (1983) 'The neuropsychology of social-emotional learning disabilities.' *Archives of Neurology*, 40, 461–462.

Dennison, P. (2004) *Brain Gym International.* www.braingym.org/faq.html

Doman, R. Jr. (1984) 'Sensory deprivation.' *Journal of the National Academy of Child Development*, 4, 6.

Dunn, W. (1997) 'The impact of sensory processing abilities on the daily lives of young children and families: a conceptual model.' *Infants and Young Children*, 9 (4), 23–25.

Dunn, W. (2001) 'The sensations of everyday life: Empirical, theoretical, and pragmatic considerations.' *The American Journal of Occupational Therapy*, 55 (6), 608–620.

Eaves, R. (1996) 'Autistic disorders.' In P. Wehman and P. McLaughlin (eds.) *Mental Retardation and Developmental Disabilities* (2nd edition). Boston: Andover Medical Publishers, pp.201–216.

Ehlers, S. and Gillberg, C. (1993) 'The epidemiology of Asperger syndrome: a total population study.' *Journal of Child Psychology and Psychiatry*, 34 (8), 1327–1350.

Eisenmajer, R., Prior, M. and Leekam, S. (1996) 'Comparison of clinical symptoms in autism and Asperger's disorder.' *Journal of the American Academy of Child and Adolescent Psychiatry*, 35, 1523–1531.

Ermer, J. and Dunn, W. (1998) 'The sensory profile: a discriminant analysis of children with and without disabilities.' *American Journal of Occupational Therapy*, 52, 283–290.

Evans, L. (1999) 'Other people's children.' *Special Children*, November/December, 11–12.

Fay, W. and Schuler, A. (1980) *Emerging Language in Children with Autism.* Baltimore, MD: University Park Press.

Flanagan, P. (2001) 'What is autism?' *Autism Today.* www.autismtoday.com/creative/What_is_Autism.htm

Fleisher, M. (2003) *Making Sense of the Unfeasible: My Life Journey with Asperger Syndrome.* London: Jessica Kingsley Publishers.

Flynn, J. (1987) 'Massive IQ gains in 14 nations: What IQ tests really measure.' *Psychological Bulletin*, 101 (2), 171–191.

Frith, U. (1970) 'Studies in pattern detection in normal and autistic children: 1. Immediate recall of auditory sequences.' *Journal of Abnormal Psychology*, 76, 413–420.

Frith, U. (1989) *Autism: Explaining the Enigma*, first edition. Oxford: Basil Blackwell.

Frith, U. (ed.) (1991) *Autism and Asperger Syndrome.* Cambridge: Cambridge University Press.

Frith, U. (2003) *Autism: Explaining the Enigma*, second edition. Oxford: Basil Blackwell.

Frith, U., Soares, I. and Wing, L. (1993) 'Research into the earliest detectable signs of autism: What parents say.' *Communication*, 27 (3), 17–18.

Gaffney, G. R. and Tsai, L. Y. (1987) 'Brief report: magnetic resonance imaging of high level autism.' *Journal of Autism and Developmental Disorders*, 17, 433–438.

Garner, I. and Hamilton, D. (2001) 'Evidence for central coherence: Children with autism do experience visual illusions.' In J. Richer and S. Coates (eds.) *Autism: The Search for Coherence.* London: Jessica Kingsley Publishers.

Gense, M. H. and Gense, D. J. (1994) 'Identifying autism in children with blindness and visual impairment.' *Review*, 26, 56–62.

Gepner, B., Mestre, D., Masson, G. and de Schonen, S. (1995) 'Postural effects of motion vision in young autistic children.' *Neuroreport*, 6, 1211–1214.

Gerland, G. (1997) *A Real Person – Life on the Outside.* (Translated from the Swedish by J. Tate.) London: Souvenir Press.

Gerland, G. (1998) 'Now is the time! Autism and psychoanalysis.' *Code of Good Practice on Prevention of Violence against Persons with Autism.* The DAPHNE Initiative of the European Commission: Autism-Europe Publication.

Gerland, G. and Sainsbury, S. (1999) 'Right to reply: an autistic perspective on "Live Company".' *British Journal of Child Psychotherapy*, 25 (1), 153–157.

Gernsbacher, M. A. (2004) 'Autistics need acceptance, not cure.' www.autistics.org/library /acceptance.html

Ghaziuddin, M., Butler, E., Tsai, L. and Ghaziuddin, N. (1994) 'Is clumsiness a marker for Asperger syndrome?' *Journal of Intellectual Disability Research*, 38, 519–527.

Ghaziuddin, M., Tsai, L. and Ghaziuudin, N. (1992) 'A brief report: A comparison of the diagnostic criteris for Asperger Syndrome. *Journal of Autism and Developmental Disorders*, 22, 643–649.

Gilchrist, A., Green, J., Cox, A., Burton, D., Rutter, M. and LeCouteur, A. (2001) 'Development and current functioning in adolescents with Asperger's syndrome.' *Journal of Child Psychology and Psychiatry*, 42, 227–240.

Gillberg, C. (1991) 'Clinical and neurological aspect of Asperger syndrome in six family studies.' In U. Frith (ed.) *Autism and Asperger Syndrome.* Cambridge: Cambridge University Press.

Gillberg, C. (1998) 'Asperger syndrome and high-functioning autism.' *British Journal of Psychiatry*, 172, 200–209.

Gillberg, C., Ehlers, S., Schaumann, H., Jacobson, G., Dahlgren, S. O., Lindbolm, R., Bagenhold, A., Tjus, T. and Blidner, E. (1990) 'Autism under age 3 years: a clinical study of 28 cases referred for autistic symptoms in infancy.' *Journal of Child Psychology and Psychiatry*, 31, 921–934.

Gillberg, C., Rusmussen, P., Carlstrom, G., Svenson, B. and Waldensrom, E. (1982) 'Perceptual, motor and attentional deficits in six-year-old children: epidemiological aspects.' *Journal of Child Psychology and Psychiatry*, 23, 131–144.

Gillberg, C., Steffenburg, S. and Jakobson, G. (1987) 'Neurobiological findings in 20 relatively gifted children with Kanner-type autism or Asperger syndrome.' *Developmental Medicine and Child Neurology*, 29, 641–649.

Gillberg, I. and Gillberg, C. (1989) 'Asperger syndrome: some epidemiological considerations.' *Journal of Child Psychology and Psychiatry*, 33, 813–842.

Gilliam, J. (1995) *Gilliam Autistic Rating Scale.* Austin, TX: Pro-Ed.

Giray, E. F., Altkin, W. M., Vaught, G. M. and Roodin, P. A. (1976) 'The incidence of eidetic imagery as a function of age.' *Child Development*, 4 (47), 1207–1210.

Grandin, T. (1992) 'An inside view of autism.' In E. Schopler and G. B. Mesibov (eds.) *High-Functioning Individuals with Autism.* New York: Plenum Press, pp.105–126.

Grandin, T. (1996a) *Thinking in Pictures: And Other Reports from My Life with Autism.* New York: Vintage Books.

Grandin, T. (1996b) *My Experiences with Visual Thinking, Sensory Problems and Communication Difficulties.* Centre for the Study of Autism. www.autism.org/temple/visual.html

Grandin, T. (1996c) 'Making the transition from the world of school into the world of work.' *Autism Today.* www.autismtoday.com/articles

Grandin, T. (1999) Feb. 'Social problems: understanding emotions and developing talents.' www.autism.org/temple/social.html

Grandin, T. (2000) 'My mind is a web browser: how people with autism think.' *Cerebrum*, 2 (1), 14–22.

Grandin, T. (2002) *An Inside View of Autism.* www.autismtoday.com/articles/An_ Inside_ View_of_Autism.htm

Grandin, T. and Scariano, M. (1986) *Emergence: Labeled Autistic.* Novato, CA: Arena Press.

Gray, C. A. (1998) 'Social Stories and Comic Strip Conversations with students with Asperger syndrome and high-functioning autism.' In E. Schopler, G. Mesibov and L. J. Kunce (eds.) *Asperger's Syndrome and High-functioning Autism.* New York: Plenum Press.

Greenspan, S. (1997) *Growth of Mind.* Cambridge, MA: Da Capo Press.

Greenspan, S. I. (2001) 'The Affect Diathesis Hypothesis: the role of emotions in the core deficit in autism and in the development of intelligence and social skills.' *The Journal of Developmental and Learning Disorders, Special Edition,* 5 (1), 1–46.

Greenspan, S. I. and Wieder, S. (1997) 'Developmental patterns and outcomes in infants and children with disorders in relating and communicating: a chart review of 200 cases of children with autistic spectrum diagnoses.' *Journal of Developmental and Learning Disorders,* 1, 87–141.

Greenspan, S., Wieder, S. and Simons, R. (1998) *The Child with Special Needs: Encouraging Intellectual and Emotional Growth.* Cambridge, MA: Da Capo Press.

Gupta, S., Aggarwal, S. and Heads, C. (1996) 'Brief report: dysregulated immune system in children with autism: beneficial effects of intravenous immune globulin on autistic characteristics.' *Journal of Autism and Developmental Disorders,* 26 (4), 439–452.

Hadcroft, W. (2004) *The Feeling's Unmutual: Growing up with Asperger Syndrome (Undiagnosed).* London: Jessica Kingsley Publishers.

Hagberg, B. (1995) 'Rett syndrome: clinical peculiarities and biological mysteries.' *Acta Pediatrica,* 84, 971–976.

Hale, A. (1998) *My World Is Not Your World.* Tadcaster, N. Yorkshire: Archimedes Press.

Hall, K. (2000) *Asperger Syndrome, the Universe and Everything: Kenneth's Book.* London: Jessica Kingsley Publishers.

Handley, G. (2003) 'The gift.' http://within.autistics.org/gift.html

Happé, F. (1994a) *Autism: An Introduction to Psychological Theory.* London: UCL Press.

Happé, F. (1994b) 'Wechsler IQ profile and theory of mind in autism: a research note.' *Journal of Child Psychology and Psychiatry,* 35, 1461–1471.

Happé, F. (1995) 'The role of age and verbal ability in the theory of mind task performance of subjects with autism.' *Child Development,* 66, 843–855.

Happé, F. (1996) 'Studying weak central coherence at low levels: children with autism do not succumb to visual illusions. A research note.' *Journal of Child Psychology and Psychiatry*, 37, 873–877.

Happé, F. (1999a) 'Autism: cognitive deficit or cognitive style?' *Trends in Cognitive Sciences*, 3, 216–222.

Happé, F. (1999b) 'Why success is more interesting than failure: understanding assets and deficits in autism.' *Autism Conference Papers* (Unpublished), Oxford, 17–19 Sept.

Harber, R. N. and Harber, L. R. (2000) 'Eidetic imagery as a cognitive skill.' In A. H. Forman (ed.) *Encyclopedia of Psychology*. Washington, DC: The American Psychological Association.

Hashimoto, T., Tayamata, M., Murakawa, K., Yoshimoto, T., Miyazaki, M., Harada, M. and Kuroda, Y. (1995) 'Development of the brainstem and cerebellum in autistic patients.' *Journal of Autism and Developmental Disorders*, 25 (1), 1–18.

Hawthorne, D. (2002) 'My common sense approach to autism.' *Autism Today*. www.autismtoday.com/articles/commonsense.htm

Hermelin, B. (2001) *Bright Splinters of the Mind: A Personal Story of Research with Autistic Savants*. London: Jessica Kingsley Publishers.

Hobson, R. P. (1989) 'Beyond cognition: a theory of autism.' In G. Dawson (ed.) *Autism: Nature, Diagnosis, and Treatment*. New York: Guilford, pp.22–48.

Hobson, R. P. (1995) 'Blindness and psychological development 0–10 years.' *Paper to Mary Kitzinger Trust Symposium*, September 1995, University of Warwick.

Holland, O. (2002) *The Dragons of Autism: Autism as a Source of Wisdom*. London: Jessica Kingsley Publishers.

Hoshino, Y., Kumashiro, H., Yashima, Y., Tachibana, R., Watanabe, M. and Furukawa, H. (1982) 'Early symptoms of autistic children and its diagnostic significance.' *Folia Psychiatrica et Neurologica Japanica*, 36, 367–374.

Howlin, P. (1997) *Autism: Preparing for Adulthood*. London: Routledge.

Howlin, P. (1998) *Children with Autism and Asperger Syndrome: A Guide for Practitioners and Carers*. London: John Wiley and Sons.

Howlin, P. and Moore, A. (1997) 'Diagnosis in autism: a survey of over 1200 parents in the UK.' *Autism: The International Journal of Research and Practice*, 1, 135–162.

Howlin, P., Baron-Cohen, S. and Hadwin, J. (1999) *Teaching Children with Autism to Mind-Read: A Practical Guide for Teachers and Parents*. New York: Wiley.

Hughes, C. and Russel, J. (1993) 'Autistic children's difficulty with mental disengagement from an object: its implications for theories of autism.' *Developmental Psychology*, 29, 498–510.

Irlen, H. (1989) 'Improving reading problems due to symptoms of Scotopic Sensitivity Syndrome using Irlen lenses and overlays.' *Education*, 109, 413–417.

Irlen, H. (1991) *Reading by the Colors: Overcoming Dyslexia and Other Reading Disabilities through the Irlen Method*. New York: Avery.

Irlen, H. (1997) 'Reading problems and Irlen coloured lenses.' *Dyslexia Review*, 8 (5), 4–7.

Jackson, L. (2002) *Freaks, Geeks and Asperger Syndrome: A User Guide to Adolescence.* London: Jessica Kingsley Publishers.

Jarrod, C., Boucher, J. and Smith, P. (1993) 'Symbolic play in autism: a review.' *Journal of Autism and Developmental Disorders,* 23, 281–307.

Jennings Linehan, S. (2004) 'Commentary for Aspar: Asperger's Syndrome as a parenting-disability.' www.aspires-relationships.com/articles_commentary_for_ aspires.htm

Joan and Rich (1999) *What is Autism?* www.ani.autistics.org/joan_rich.html

Jolliffe, T., Lakesdown, R. and Robinson, C. (1992) 'Autism, a personal account.' *Communication,* 26 (3), 12–19.

Jones, V. and Prior, M. (1985) 'Motor imitation abilities and neurological signs in autistic children.' *Journal of Autism and Developmental Disorders,* 15, 37–46.

Jordan, R. (1999) *Autistic Spectrum Disorders: An Introductory Handbook for Practitioners.* London: David Fulton Publishers.

Jordan, R. (2001) *Autism with Severe Learning Difficulties.* London: Souvenir Press.

Jordan, R. R. and Powell, S. D. (1992) *Investigating Memory Processing in Children with Autism.* British Psychological Society Conference, 15–16 December, London.

Jordan, R. and Powell, S. (1995) *Understanding and Teaching Children with Autism.* Chichester: John Wiley and Sons.

Jordan, R. and Riding, R. (1995) 'Autism and cognitive style.' In P. Shattock (ed.) *Proceedings of the International Conference: Psychological Perspectives in Autism.* Durham, Sunderland: Autism Research Unit/NAS.

Jordan, R., Jones, G. and Murray, D. (1998) *An evaluative and comparative study of current educational interventions for children with autism: a literature review and current research.* DfEE Research Report, 77. London: DfES.

Kadesjo, B., Gillberg, C. and Hagberg, B. (1999) 'Brief report: autism and Asperger syndrome: a total population study.' *Journal of Autism and Developmental Disorders,* 29 (4), 327–331.

Kanner, L. (1943) 'Autistic disturbances of affective contact.' *Nervous Child,* 2, 217–250.

Kanner, L. (1971) 'Follow-up study of eleven autistic children, originally reported in 1943.' *Journal of Autism and Childhood Schizophrenia,* 2, 119–145.

Kaufman, B. N. (1995) 'The awakening: one family's struggle to reclaim an autistic child.' *UTNE Reader,* November–December, 97–103.

Kaufman, B. N. and Kaufman, S. L. (1986) *Son-Rise.* New York: Warner Books.

Kientz, M. A. and Dunn, W. (1997) 'A comparison of the performance of children with and without autism on the Sensory Profile.' *American Journal of Occupational Therapy,* 51, 530–537.

Kim (1999) *What is Autism?* http://ani.autistics.org/kim.html

Klein, F. (2002) 'The truth of the myth of the lack of recovery from autism.' http://home.att.net/~ascaris1/recovery.html

Klein, F. (Undated, a) *Introduction for Parents of Autistic/AS Kids.* http://home.att.net/~ascaris1/intro.html

Klein, F. (Undated, b) *But My Kid is Low-Functioning... You're Not... What You Wrote Does Not Apply!* http://home.att.net/~ascaris1/lfa.html

Klein, F. (Undated, c) 'Autism, Genius, and Greatness.' http://home.att.net/~ascaris1/genius.html

Klein, F. (Undated, d) 'What's the difference?' http://home.att.net/~ascaris1/whats-diff.html

Klin, A. (1994) 'Asperger syndrome.' *Child and Adolescent Psychiatry Clinic of North America*, 3, 131–148.

Klin, A. and Volkmar, F. R. (1996) *Asperger Syndrome: Some Guidelines for Assessment, Diagnosis and Intervention.* Yale/LDA Social Learning Disability Study. Yale: Learning Disabilities Association of America.

Kiln, A., Sparrow, S. S., Volkmar, F. R., Cicchetti, D. V. and Rourke, B. P. (1995) 'Asperger syndrome.' In B. P. Rourke (ed) *Syndrome of Nonverbal Learning Disabilities: Neurodevelopmental Manifestations.* New York Guildford Press, pp.93–118.

Klin, A., Volkmar, F. R. and Sparrow, S. S. (1992) 'Autistic social dysfunction: some limitations of the theory of mind hypothesis.' *Journal of Child Psychology and Psychiatry*, 3 (3), 861–876.

Knobloch, H. and Pasamanick, B. (1975) 'Some etiological and prognostic factors in early infantile autism and psychosis.' *Pediatrics*, 55, 182–191.

Kochmeister, S. (1995) 'Excerpts from "Shattering Walls".' *Facilitated Communication Digest*, 5 (3), 9–11.

Kohen-Raz, R., Volkmar, F. R. and Cohen, D. J. (1992) 'Postural control in children with autism.' *Journal of Autism and Developmental Disorders*, 22, 419–432.

Krug, D., Arlick, J. and Almond, P. (1980) 'Behaviour checklist for identifying severely handicapped individuals with high levels of autistic behaviour.' *Journal of Child Psychology and Psychiatry*, 21, 221–229.

Kuhl, P., Williams, K. A., Lacerda, F., Stevens, K. N. and Lindblom, B. (1992) 'Linguistic experience alters phonetic perception in infants by six months of age.' *Science*, 255, 606–608.

Lane, H. (1977) *The Wild Boy of Avayron* (translations into English of J. M. G. Itard's reports). London: Allen and Unwin.

Lawson, W. (1998) *Life Behind Glass: A Personal Account of Autism Spectrum Disorder.* London: Jessica Kingsley Publishers.

Lawson, W. (2001) *Understanding and Working with the Spectrum of Autism: An Insider's View.* London: Jessica Kingsley Publishers.

Lawson, W. (2003) 'Asperger's Syndrome: A matter of attention.' www.emr.vic.edu.au/disabwel/docs/Wendy%20Lawson.doc (no longer active)

Le Couteur, A., Rutter, M., Lord, C., Rios, P., Robertson, S., Holdgrafer, M. and McLennan, J. (1989) 'Autism diagnostic interview: a standardized investigator-based instrument.' *Journal of Autism and Developmental Disorders*, 19, 363–387.

Lord, C. (1984) 'The development of peer relations in children with autism.' In F. Morrison, C. Lord and D. P. Keating (eds.) *Applied Developmental Psychology.* New York: Academic Press, (Vol. 1, pp.165–229).

Lord, C., Rutter, M. and Le Couteur, A. (1994) 'Autism diagnostic interview – revised: a revised version of a diagnostic interview for caregivers of individuals with possible pervasive developmental disorders.' *Journal of Autism and Developmental Disorders*, 24, 659–685.

Lord, C., Rutter, M., Goode, S., Heemsbergen, J., Jordan, H., Mawhood, L. and Schopler, E. (1989) 'Autism diagnostic observation schedule.' *Journal of Autism and Other Developmental Disorders*, 19 (2), 185–212.

Lovaas, O. I. (1987) 'Behavioral treatment and normal intellectual and educational functioning in autistic children.' *Journal of Consulting and Clinical Psychology*, 55, 3–9.

McDonnell, J. (1993) *News from the Border.* Boston, MA: Ticknor and Fields.

McKean, T. (1994) *Soon Will Come the Light.* Arlington, TX: Future Horizons, Inc.

McKean, T. (1999) 'Sensory anomalies.' www.geocities.com/~soonlight/SWCTL/ARTICLES/sensanom.htm

Manjiviona, J. and Prior, M. (1995) 'Comparison of Asperger syndrome and high-functioning autistic children on a test of motor impairment.' *Journal of Autism and Developmental Disorders*, 25 (1), 23–39.

Maurice, C. (1994) *Let Me Hear Your Voice: A Family Triumph over Autism.* New York: Fawcett Columbine.

Mesibov, G. B. (1993) 'Treatment outcome is encouraging.' *American Journal of Mental Retardation*, 97, 379–390.

Meyerding, J. (Undated) *Thoughts on Finding Myself Differently Brained.* www.invl.demon.n1/subm-brain.jane.eng.html

Miller, J. L., Cermak, S., Lane, S. and Anzalone, M. (2004) 'Defining SPD and its subtypes: position statement on terminology related to sensory integration dysfunction.' www.spdnetwork.org/aboutspd/defining.html

Mitchell, P. and Ropar, D. (2004) 'Visuo-spatial abilities in autism: A review.' *Infant and Child Development*, 13, (3), 185–198.

Morrell, F., Whisler, W. and Smith, M. (1995) 'Landau-Kleffner syndrome: Treatment with subpial intracortical transection.' *Brain*, 118, 1529–1546.

Morris, B. (1999) 'New light and insight, on an old matter.' *Autism99 Internet Conference Papers.* www.autism99.org

Mottron, L. and Burack, J. A. (2001) 'Enhanced perceptual functioning in the development of autism.' In J. A. Burack, T. Charman, N. Yirmiya and P. R. Zelazo (eds.) *The Development of Autism: Perspectives from Theory and Research.* Mahwah, NJ: Erlbaum, pp.131–148.

Mottron, L., Burack, J. and Robaey, P. (1999) 'Perceptual processing among high-functioning persons with autism.' *Journal of Child Psychology and Psychiatry*, 40 (2), 203–211.

Moynahan, M. (1999) 'Thank you for saving my son from autism.' *You*, August, 35–36.

Mukhopadhyay, R. (Tito) (1999) 'When silence speaks: the way my mother taught me.' *Autism99 Internet Conference Papers.* www.autism99.org

Mukhopadhyay, R. (2000) 'My memory.' www.cureautismnow.org/tito/memories/my_memory.pdf

Muris, P., Steerneman, P. and Merchelbach, H. (1998) 'Difficulties in understanding of false belief: specific to autism and other developmental disorders?' *Psychological Reports*, 82, 51–57.

Muskie (1999) 'Institute for the study of the neurologically typical.' http://isnt.autistics.org/isnt_text.html

Myers, P., Baron-Cohen, S. and Wheelwright, S. (2004) *An Exact Mind: An Artist with Asperger Syndrome*. London: Jessica Kingsley Publishers.

Naseef, R. (2001) *Special Children, Challenged Parents*. Baltimore: Paul H. Brookes.

Newson, R. (2001) 'A lifetime of living with Asperger's syndrome.' Unpublished paper for Thorne House Services for Autism Regional Conference, 7 October 2001, Doncaster, UK.

Nind, M. and Hewett, D. (1994) *Access to Communication: Developing the Basics of Communication with People with Severe Learning Difficulties through Intensive Interaction*. London: David Fulton.

O'Neill, J. L. (1999) *Through the Eyes of Aliens: A Book about Autistic People*. London: Jessica Kingsley Publishers.

O'Neill, J. L. (2000) *I Live in a Home Within Myself*. The NAS publication. http://w02-0211.web.dircon.net/peoplew/personal/jasmine.html

O'Reilly, B. A. and Waring, R. H. (1993) 'Enzyme and sulphur oxidation deficiencies in autistic children with known food/chemical intolerances.' *Journal of Orthomolecular Medicine*, 8 (4), 198–200.

Ornitz, E. M. (1969) 'Disorders of perception common to early infantile autism and schizophrenia.' *Comprehensive Psychiatry*, 10, 259–274.

Ornitz, E. M. (1974) 'The modulation of sensory input and motor output in autistic children.' *Journal of Autism and Childhood Schizophrenia*, 4, 197–215.

Ornitz, E. M. (1983) 'The functional neuroanatomy of infantile autism.' *International Journal of Neuroscience*, 19, 85–124.

Ornitz, E. M. (1985) 'Neurophysiology of infantile autism.' *Journal of the American Academy of Child Psychiatry*, 24, 251–262.

Ornitz, E. M. (1989) 'Autism at the interface between sensory and information processing.' In G. Dawson (ed.) *Autism: Nature, Diagnosis and Treatment*. New York: Guilford.

Ornitz, E. M., Guthrie, D. and Farley, A. J. (1977) 'The early development of autistic children.' *Journal of Autism and Childhood Schizophrenia*, 7, 207–229.

Ornitz, E. M., Guthrie, D. and Farley, A. J. (1978) 'The early symptoms of childhood autism.' In G. Serban (ed.) *Cognitive Deficits in the Development of Mental Illness*. New York: Brunner/Mazel.

Ozonoff, S. (1995) 'Executive function in autism.' In E. Schopler and G. B. Mesibov (eds.) *Learning and Cognition in Autism*. New York: Plenum Press.

Ozonoff, S., Rogers, S. J. C. and Pennington, B. F. (1991) 'Asperger's syndrome: evidence of empirical distinction from high-functioning autism.' *Journal of Child Psychology and Psychiatry*, 32, 1107–1122.

Ozonoff, S., Strayer, D. L., McMahon, W. M. and Filloux, F. (1994) 'Executive function abilities in autism and Tourette syndrome: an information processing approach.' *Journal of Child Psychology and Psychiatry*, 35 (6), 1015–1032.

Peeters, T. (1997) *Autism: From theoretical understanding to educational intervention*. London: Whurr Publishers.

Peeters, T. (1999) 'The training of professionals and parents in autism: key-code in the development of services.' *Autism99 Internet Conference Papers*. www.autism99.org

Peeters, T. and Gillberg, C. (1999) *Autism: Medical and Educational Aspects*. London: Whurr Publishers.

Perner, L. (2002) 'If I'd known then what I know now: what I have learned about life with Asperger's syndrome – and what still eludes me.' *A paper presented at the annual meeting of the Autism Society of America* (Unpublished), Indianapolis, Indiana, July 17–21.

Perner, L. (Undated, a) 'The "big picture" of autism: science and theory in *reasonably* plain English.' http://as.larsperner.com/Big%20Picture.htm

Perner, L. (Undated, b) 'Perspectives on autism.' http://www.larsperner.com/autism/perspectives_on_autism.htm

Peterson, C. C. and Siegel, M. (1995) 'Deafness, conversation and theory of mind.' *Journal of Child Psychology and Psychiatry*, 36, 459–474.

Phillips, K. (Undated) *KJP's Asperger's Syndrome site and many other things*. www.angelfire.com/amiga/aut

Piaget, J. (1962) 'The stages of intellectual development of the child.' In S. Harrison and J. McDermott (eds.) *Childhood Psychopathology*. New York: International Universities Press, pp.157–166.

Piven, J., Amdt, S., Bailey, J., Havercamp, S. and Andreasen, N. (1995) 'An MRI study of brain size in autism.' *American Journal of Psychiatry*, 1145–1149.

Plaisted, K. (2001) 'Reduced generalization in autism: an alternative to weak central coherence.' In J. A. Burack, T. Charman, N. Yirmiya and P. R. Zelazo (eds.) *The Development of Autism: Perspectives from Theory and Research*. Mahwah, NJ: Erlbaum, pp.149–169.

Plaisted, K., O'Riordan, M. and Baron-Cohen, S. (1998) 'Enhanced visual search for a conjunctive target in autism: a research note.' *Journal of Child Psychology and Psychiatry*, 39, 777–783.

Pomeroy, J. C., Friedman, C. and Stephens, L. (1991) 'Autism and Asperger's: same or different?' *Journal of the American Academy of Child and Adolescent Psychiatry*, 30 (1), 152–153.

Powell, S. D. and Jordan, R. R. (1993) 'Being subjective about autistic thinking and learning to learn.' *Educational Psychology*, 13, 359–370.

Powers, M. D. (1989) *Children with Autism: A Parent's Guide*. Rockville, MD: Woodbine House.

Pring, L. and Hermelin, B. (2002) 'Numbers and letters: exploring an autistic savant's unpractised ability.' *Neurocase*, 8, 330–337.

Prior, M., Leekam, S., Ong, B., Eisenmajer, R., Wing, L., Gould, J. and Dowe, D. (1998) 'Are there subgroups within the autistic spectrum? A cluster analysis of autism group of children with autistic spectrum disorders.' *Journal of Child Psychology and Psychiatry*, 39 (6), 893–902.

Prizant, B. M. (1982) 'Gestalt processing and gestalt language acquisition in autism.' *Topics in Language Disorders*, 3, 16–23.

Prizant, B. M. (1983) 'Echolalia in autism: assessment and intervention.' *Seminar in Speech and Language*, 4, 63–78.

Prizant, B. M. and Wetherby, A. M. (1989) 'Enhancing language and communication in autism: from theory to practice.' In G. Dawson (ed.) *Autism: Nature, Diagnosis, and Treatment.* New York: Guilford Press.

Rapin, L. (1996) 'Neurological examination.' In L. Rapin (ed.) *Preschool Children with Inadequate Communication: Developmental Language Disorder, Autism, Low IQ.* London: MacKeith Press, pp.98–122.

Rapin, L. and Allen, D. (1983) 'Developmental language disorders: nosologic consideration.' In U. Kirk (ed.) *Neuropsychology of Language, Reading and Spelling.* New York: Academic Press.

Rimland, B. (1964) *Infantile Autism: The Syndrome and Its Implications for a Neural Therapy of Behavior.* New York: Appleton Century Crofts.

Rimland, B. (1987) 'Megavitamin B_6 and magnesium in the treatment of autistic children and adults.' In E. Schopler and G. Mesibov (eds.) *Neurobiological Issues in Autism.* New York: Plenum Press.

Rimland, B. (1994) 'Recovery from autism is possible.' *ARRI*, 8 (2), p.3.

Rimland, B. (1995) 'Landau-Kleffner: More cases seen.' *ARRI*, 9 (2), pp.1, 2.

Rimland, B. (1999) 'The ABA controversy.' *ARRI*, 13 (3), p.3.

Riva, G. (1999) 'The life of Brian…and me.' *Autism99 Internet Conference Papers.* www.autism99.org

Robinson, G. L. (1996) 'Irlen lenses and adults: Preliminary results of a controlled study of reading, speed, accuracy and comprehension.' *The Fourth International Irelen Conference Papers*, 1–3 July, Cambridge, UK. San Diego, CA: Irlen Institute Press.

Ropar, D. and Mitchell, P. (1999) 'Are individuals with autism and Asperger's Syndrome susceptible to visual illusions?' *Journal of Child Psychiatry and Psychology*, 40, 1283–1292.

Ropar, D. and Mitchell, P. (2001) 'Susceptibility to illusions and performance on visuospatial tasks in individuals with autism.' *Journal of Child Psychology and Psychiatry and Allied Disciplines*, 42, 539–549.

Ropar, D., Mitchell, P. and Ackroyd, K. (2003) 'Do children with autism find it difficult to offer alternative interpretations to ambiguous figures?' *British Journal of Developmental Psychology*, 21, 387–396.

Rourke, B. (1989) *Nonverbal Learning Disabilities: The Syndrome and the Model.* New York: Guilford Press.

Rumsey, J. M., Rapoport, J. L. and Sceery, W. R. (1985) 'Autistic children as adults: psychiatric, social and behavioral outcomes.' *Journal of the American Academy of Child Psychiatry*, 24, 465–473.

Rutter, M., Andersen-Wood, L., Beckett, C., Bredenkamp, D., Castle, J., Groothues, C., Kreppner, J., Keaveney, L., Lord, C. and O'Connor, T. (1999) 'Quasi-autistic patterns following global privation.' *Journal of Child Psychology and Psychiatry*, 40, 537–549.

Sainsbury, C. (2000a) *The Martian in the Playground: Understanding the Schoolchild with Asperger's Syndrome.* Bristol: Lucky Duck Publishing.

Sainsbury, C. (2000b) 'Holding Therapy: An Autistic Perspective.' www.nas.org.uk/pubs/archive/hold.html

Schafer Report (2004) http://home.sprynet.com/~schafer

Schneider, E. (1999) *Discovering My Autism: Apologia Pro Vita Sua (with Apologies to Cardinal Newman).* London: Jessica Kingsley Publishers.

Schopler, E. and Mesibov, G. B. (eds) (1995) *Learning and Cognition in Autism.* New York: Plenum Press.

Schopler, E. and Reichler, R. (1979) *PEP.* Austin, TX: Pro-Ed.

Schopler, E., Reichler, R. and Lansing, M. (1980) *PEP-R.* Austin, TX: Pro-Ed.

Schopler, E., Reichler, R. and Renner, B. (1980) *Childhood Autism Rating Scale.* Austin, TX: Pro-Ed.

Schulman, E. (1999) 'Jake's puzzle.' http://trainland.tripod.com/elayne.htm

Scragg, P. and Shah, A. (1994) 'Prevalence of Asperger's Syndrome in a secure hospital.' *British Journal of Psychiatry,* 165, 769–782.

Segar, M. (Undated) 'The battles of the autistic thinker.' *A Survival Guide for People with Asperger's Syndrome.* www.shifth.mistral.co.uk/autism/marc1.htm

Shah, A. and Frith, U. (1983) 'An islet of ability in autistic children: a research note.' *Journal of Child Psychology and Psychiatry,* 24, 613–620.

Shattock, P. and Savery, D. (1996) 'Urinary profiles of people with autism: Possible implications and relevance to other research.' *Therapeutic Intervention in Autism: Perspectives from Research and Practice.* Durham: University of Durham Press.

Shore, S. (2001) *Beyond the Wall: Personal Experiences with Autism and Asperger Syndrome.* Shawnee Mission, KS: Autism Asperger Publishing Company.

Shore, S. (2003) 'Life on and slightly to the right of the Autism Spectrum.' *EP Magazine* [Exceptional Parent], October, 85–90.

Shore, S. (Undated) *My Life with Autism: Implications for Educators.* www.behaviorstore.com/behavior/default.asp?pgC=article2

Shull, R. (2003) *Autism: Pre Rain Man.* Lighting Source UK Ltd.

Sinclair, J. (1989) 'A letter to the MAAP editor.' *The MAAP Newsletter,* Spring 1989, p.1.

Sinclair, J. (1992a) 'Bridging the gap: an inside view of autism.' In E. Schopler and G. B. Mesibov (eds.) *High-functioning Individuals with Autism.* New York: Plenum Press, pp.294–302.

Sinclair, J. (1992b) 'What does being different mean?' *Our Voice,* 1.

Sinclair, J. (1992c) Untitled. http://groups.google.com/group/bit.listserv.autism/msg/de557de57f3efaf4

Sinclair, J. (1993) 'Don't mourn for us.' *Our Voice,* 1 (3), 3–6.

Sinclair, J. (1998) 'Is cure a goal?' www.members.xoom.com/JimSinclair

Sinclair, J. (1999) 'Why I dislike "person first" language.' http://web.syr.edu/~jisincla/person_first.htm

Skinner, B. F. (1971) *Beyond Freedom and Dignity.* New York: Bantam/Vintage Books.

Smith, I. and Bryson, S. (1998) 'Gesture imitation in autism I: Nonsymbolic postures and sequences.' *Cognitive Neuropsychology,* 15, 747–770.

Smith, J. (2005) 'Why I don't want to be an autistic advocate anymore.' www.autistics.org/library/noautadvocate.html

Smith, M. D. (1990) *Autism and Life in the Community: Successful Interventions for Behavioral Challenges.* Baltimore, MD: Paul H. Brookes.

Smith, T. (1999) 'Outcome of early intervention for children with autism.' *Clinical Psychology: Science and Practice,* 6, 33–49.

Smith, T., Klevstrand, M. and Lovaas, O. I. (1995) 'Behavioral treatment of Rett's disorder: ineffectiveness in three cases.' *American Journal of Mental Retardation,* 100, 317–322.

Snyder, A. W. (1996) Breaking mindset. *Keynote address 'The Mind's New Science'.* Cognitive Science Miniconference, Macquarie University, 14 November. www.centreforthemind.com/publications/Breaking_Mindset.htm

Snyder, A. W. (1998) 'Breaking mindsets.' *Mind Language,* 13, 1–10.

Snyder, A. W. and Barlow, H. B. (1986) 'Revealing the artist's touch.' *Nature,* 331, 117–118.

Snyder, A. W. and Mitchell, J. D. (1999) 'Is integer arithmetic fundamental to mental proceeding? The mind's secret arithmetic.' *Proceedings of the Royal Society of London,* 266, 587–592.

Snyder, A., Bossomaier, T. and Mitchell, D. J. (2004) 'Concept formation: "Object" attributes dynamically inhibited from conscious awareness.' *Journal of Integrative Neuroscience,* 3 (1), 31–46.

SPD Network, The (2004) www.spdnetwork.org/

Sperry, V. W. (2001) *Fragile Success: Ten Autistic Children, Childhood to Adulthood,* 2nd edition. London: Jessica Kingsley Publishers.

Spicer, D. (1998a) 'Self-awareness in living with Asperger syndrome.' *Asperger Syndrome Conference Papers,* Vasteras, Sweden, 12–13 March.

Spicer, D. (1998b) 'Autistic and undiagnosed: my cautionary tale.' *Asperger Syndrome Conference Papers,* Vasteras, Sweden, 12–13 March.

Stacey, P. (2004a) *The Boy Who Loved Windows: Opening the Heart and Mind of a Child Threatened with Autism.* London: John Wiley and Sons.

Stacey, P. (2004b) 'The boy who loved windows: my autistic son lived in his own world. I would try anything to bring him back into mine.' *Readers' Digest,* January, 94–99.

Stanton, M. (2000) *Learning to Love with High-Functioning Autism: A Parent's Guide for Professionals.* London: Jessica Kingsley Publishers.

Stanton, M. (2001) 'Educating the Health Professionals: The Challenge for Parents.' Talk delivered at AUTISM: Challenging Issues; Continuing Ignorance conference, 14 June 2001. www.mikestanton.dsl.pipex.com/speech1.html

Stefanatos, G. A., Grover, W. and Geller, E. (1995) 'Corticosteriod treatment of language regression n in pervasive developmental disorder.' *Journal of the Academy of Child and Adolescent Psychiatry,* 34, (8), 1107–1111.

Stehli, A. (1991) *Sound of a Miracle: A Child's Triumph Over Autism.* New York: Avon Books.

Stone, W. L. and Hogan, K. L. (1993) 'A structured parent interview for identifying young children with autism.' *Journal of Autism and Developmental Disorders,* 23, 639–652.

Stone, W. L., Ousley, O. Y., Hepburn, S. L., Hogan, K. L. and Brown, C. S. (1999) 'Patterns of adaptive behavior in very young children with autism.' *American Journal of Mental Retardation,* 104, 187–199.

Sullivan, R. C. (1984) 'Parents as trainers of legislators, other parents, and researchers.' In E. Schopler and G. Mesibov (eds) *The Effects of Autism on the Family: Current Issues in Autism.* New York: Plenum Press, pp.233–246.

Szatmari, P. (2000) 'The classification of autism, Asperger's syndrome and pervasive developmental disorder.' *Canadian Journal of Psychiatry,* 45, 731–738.

Szatmari, P., Archer, L., Fisman, S., Streiner, D. L., Wilson, F. (1995) 'Asperger's syndrome and autism: differences in behavior, cognition, and adaptive functioning.' *Journal of American Academy of Child and Adolescence Psychiatry,* 34, 1662–1671.

Tanguay, P. E. and Edwards, R. (1982) 'Electrophysiological studies of autism: the whisper of the bang.' *Journal of Autism and Developmental Disorders,* 12 (2), 177–184.

Thompson, D. (2003) 'Restoration.' www.Aspergia.com

Tinbergen, N. and Tinbergen, E. (1972/1984) *Autism: New Hope for a Cure.* Hemel Hempstead: Allen Unwin.

Tonge, B. J., Brereton, A. V., Gray, K. M. and Einfeld, S. L. (1999) 'Behavioural and emotional disturbance in high-functioning autism and Asperger Syndrome.' *Autism,* 3, 117–130.

Turner, M. (1999) 'Generating novel ideas: fluency performance in high-functioning and learning disabled individuals with autism.' *Journal of Child Psychology and Psychiatry,* 40, 189–202.

VanDalen, J. G. T. (1995) 'Autism from within: looking through the eyes of a mildly afflicted autistic person.' *Link,* 17, 11–16.

Volkmar, F. R., Cohen, D. J. and Paul, R. (1986) 'An evaluation of DSM-III criteria for infantile autism.' *Journal of American Academy of Child Psychiatry,* 25, 190–197.

Wakefield, A. (1998) 'Ileal-lymphoid-nodular hyperplasia, non-specific colitis, and pervasive developmental disorder in children.' *Lancet,* 351 (9103, 28 February), 637–641.

Walker, A. (Undated) *How Many?* http://isn.net/~jypsy/owpsawalker2.htm

Walters, A. S., Barrett, R. P. and Feinstein, C. (1990) 'Social relatedness and autism: current research, issues, and directions.' *Research in Developmental Disabilities,* 11, 303–326.

Wang, P. P. and Bellugi, U. (1993) 'William's syndrome, Down syndrome and cognitive neuroscience.' *American Journal of Diseases of Children,* 147, 1246–1251.

Waterhouse, S. (1999) *A Positive Approach to Autism.* London: Jessica Kingsley Publishers.

Welch, M. G. (1983) 'Retrieval from autism through mother–child holding.' In N. Tinbergen and E. Tinbergen (eds) *Autistic Children – New Hope for a Cure.* London and Boston: George, Allen and Unwin.

Willey, L. H. (1999) *Pretending to be Normal: Living with Asperger's Syndrome.* London: Jessica Kingsley Publishers.

Willey, L. H. (Undated) 'It's good to be happy with who you are.' www.aspie.com/articlea8.html

Williams, D. (1996) *Autism: An Inside-Out Approach: An Innovative Look at the 'Mechanics' of 'Autism' and its Developmental 'Cousins'.* London: Jessica Kingsley Publishers.

Williams, D. (1998) *Autism and Sensing. The Unlost Instinct.* London: Jessica Kingsley Publishers.

Williams, D. (1999a) *Like Colour to the Blind: Soul Searching and Soul Finding.* London: Jessica Kingsley Publishers.

Williams, D. (1999b) *Nobody Nowhere: The Remarkable Autobiography of an Autistic Girl.* London: Jessica Kingsley Publishers.

Williams, D. (1999c) *Somebody Somewhere: Breaking Free from the World of Autism.* London: Jessica Kingsley Publishers.

Williams, D. (2003) *Exposure Anxiety – The Invisible Cage: An Exploration of Self-Protection Responses in the Autism Spectrum and Beyond.* London: Jessica Kingsley Publishers.

Williams, D. (Undated, a) *Not Thinking In Pictures.* www.donnawilliams.net/new2/page5.html

Williams, D. (Undated, b) *Fleas and Autism.* www.donnawilliams.net

Williams, D. (Undated, c) *'Waking Up' Stories.* www.donnawilliams.net/new2/page14.html

Wing, L. (1979) 'Mentally retarded children in Camberwell (London).' In H. Hafner (ed.) *Estimating Needs for Mental Health Care.* Berlin: Springer-Verlag, pp.107–112.

Wing, L. (1981) 'Asperger's syndrome: a clinical account.' *Psychological Medicine,* 11, 115–129.

Wing, L. (1991) 'The relationship between Asperger syndrome and Kanner's autism.' In U. Frith (ed.) *Autism and Asperger Syndrome.* Cambridge, UK: Cambridge University Press, pp.93–121.

Wing, L. (1992) *The Triad of Impairments of Social Interaction: An Aid to Diagnosis.* London: NAS.

Wing, L. (1993) *Autistic Continuum Disorders: An Aid to Diagnosis.* London: The National Autistic Society.

Wing, L. (1996) *The Autistic Spectrum: A Guide for Parents and Professionals.* London: Constable and Company.

Wing, L. (1998) 'Classification and diagnosis – looking at the complexities involved.' *Communication,* 15–18.

Wing, L. (2000) 'Past and future of research on Asperger Syndrome.' In A. Klin, F. K. Volkmar and S. S. Sparrow (eds.) *Asperger Syndrome.* New York: The Guildford Press, pp.418–432.

Wing, L. and Attwood, A. (1987) 'Syndromes of autism and atypical development.' In D. Cohen and A. Donnellan (eds.) *Handbook of Autism and Pervasive Developmental Disorders.* New York: John Wiley and Sons.

Wing, L. and Gould, J. (1979) 'Severe impairments of social interaction and associated abnormalities in children: epidemiology and classification.' *Journal of Autism and Developmental Disorders,* 9 (1), 11–29.

Wing, L. and Gould, J. (1991) *Diagnostic Interview Schedule and Childhood Operation (DISCO).* Bromley: Elliot House.

Wolff, S. and Chess, S. (1964) 'A behavioural study of schizophrenic children.' *Acta Psychiatrica Scandinavica,* 40, 438–466.

World Health Organization (1992) *International Statistical Classification of Diseases and Related Health Problems,* 10th edition (ICD-10). Geneva: WHO.

A contents list for 'horizontal reading'

		Part 1	Part 2	Part 3	Part 4
1.	Definitions and Classifications	21–28	77–96	179–186	233–240
2.	Diagnosis	29–38	97–103	187–190	241–255
3.	Causes	39–44	104–112	191–196	256–259
4.	Development	45–46	113–125	197–201	260–264
5.	Theories	47–53	126–137	202–207	265–283
6.	Treatments	54–66	138–161	208–219	284–294
7.	Miscellany	67–71	162–173	220–226	295–300
	Further Reading	72–74	174–176	227–229	301–302

A contents list for horizontal reading

Subject Index

Author Index